COMPARATIVE POLITICS

Divided Government in Comparative Perspective

# COMPARATIVE POLITICS

Comparative politics is a series for students and teachers of political science that deals with contemporary issues in comparative government and politics. As Comparative European Politics it has produced a series of high quality books since its foundation in 1990, but now takes on a new form and new title for the the millennium—Comparative Politics. As the process of globalization proceeds, and as Europe becomes ever more enmeshed in world trends and events, so it is necessary to broaden the scope of the series. The General Editors are Max Kasse, Professor of Political Science, University of Mannheim and Research Professor Wissenschaftzentrum Berlin, and Kenneth Newton, Professor of Government, University of Southampton. The series is published in association with the European Consortium for Political Research.

## OTHER TITLES IN THIS SERIES

Coalition Governments in Western Europe
*Edited by Wolfgang C. Müller and Kaare Strøm*

Parties without Partisans: Political Change in Advanced Industrial Democracies
*Edited by Russell J. Dalton and Martin P. Wattenberg*

Political Institutions: Democracy and Social Change
*Josep H. Colomer*

Mixed-Member Electoral Systems
*Edited by Matthew Soberg Shugart and Martin P. Wattenberg*

# Divided Government in Comparative Perspective

*edited by*

## ROBERT ELGIE

**OXFORD**
UNIVERSITY PRESS

# OXFORD

UNIVERSITY PRESS

Great Clarendon Street, Oxford ox2 6DP

Oxford University Press is a department of the University of Oxford.
It furthers the University's objective of excellence in research, scholarship,
and education by publishing worldwide in

Oxford  New York

Athens  Auckland  Bangkok  Bogotá  Buenos Aires  Cape Town
Chennai  Dar es Salaam  Delhi  Florence  Hong Kong  Istanbul  Karachi
Kolkata  Kuala Lumpur  Madrid  Melbourne  Mexico City  Mumbai  Nairobi
Paris  São Paulo  Shanghai  Singapore  Taipei  Tokyo  Toronto  Warsaw
with associated companies in  Berlin  Ibadan

Published in the United States
by Oxford University Press Inc., New York

British Library Cataloguing in Publication Data
Data available
ISBN 0–19–829565–0

1 3 5 7 9 10 8 6 4 2

Typeset in Times
by  Hope Services (Abingdon) Ltd.
Printed in Great Britain
on acid-free paper by
T.J. International Ltd.,
Padstow, Cornwall

# Preface

Divided government may be defined as the situation where the executive fails to enjoy majority support in at least one working house of the legislature. To date, the study of divided government has been confined mainly to the United States. However, divided government is not confined either to the US or to presidential regimes more widely. Instead, as Laver and Shepsle (1991) have pointed out, divided government can occur in other types of political system as well. Accordingly, this book asserts that divided government in presidential regimes is functionally equivalent to minority government in parliamentary regimes and to both 'cohabitation' and minority government in semi-presidential regimes. This book examines the experience of divided government from a comparative perspective and identifies the similarities and differences between the various experiences of this undoubtedly common form of government.

The book consists of a comparative introduction and conclusion and a series of country studies. In the introduction, the concept of divided government is introduced and the themes of the book are established. The country studies then examine the politics of divided government within this framework. There are three studies of divided government in presidential systems (the US, Ecuador, and Mexico), three studies of 'cohabitation' and/or minority government in semi-presidential systems (Finland, France, and Poland) and three studies of minority government in parliamentary systems (Denmark, Germany, and Ireland).[1] In the conclusion, the similarities and differences between the experiences of the various countries are assessed.

In order to ensure that the case-study chapters follow common themes, the introduction identifies three particular issues which will be addressed throughout the book as a whole. These are the frequency and form of divided government, the causes of divided government, and the management of divided government. The section on the frequency and form of divided government aims to identify how often divided government has occurred in each country and the form that it has taken. Is divided government a regular or an exceptional feature of the political system? Does it take the form of an opposition majority in the both houses of the legislature (where applicable) or just

---

[1] Ireland has been classified as semi-presidential regime (Elgie, 1999). However, Ireland clearly operates like a parliamentary system. For the purposes of this book, therefore, it is categorized alongside Denmark and Germany.

one? Is there a coherent opposition majority or are the political forces in the legislature highly fragmented? The section on the causes of divided government examines the relevance of behavioural and institutional causes of divided government. In terms of behavioural reasons, are partisan preferences fragmented? Is there split-ticket voting? Do voters vote strategically to balance party control? In terms of institutional reasons, what is the role of the electoral system? How do mid-term elections affect the frequency of divided government? What is the effect of party organization on electoral outcomes? Finally, the section on the management of divided government assumes that political leaders are presented with an ongoing problem. How do leaders manage this problem? Can they avoid gridlock and maintain the flow of legislation? If so, do they try to pass legislation on a case-by-case basis, or do they try to win the support of one or more parties on a consistent basis? Are there institutional mechanisms to help the executive pass legislation, or is there a culture of compromise? These questions are at the heart of this book. They provide a set of conherent themes and produce a genuinely comparative study.

This is the first study of divided government from a comparative perspective. It is intended to provide a coherent framework for the cross-national study of divided government and it includes a wide-ranging set of case-studies. However, it is also intended as a point of departure. By setting out a coherent framework and by identifying similarities and differences between various experiences of divided government, it is hoped that this book will provide a spring-board for future work in this area.

The editor would like to thank everyone involved in this project for their patience. He is extremely grateful for all the comments from the contributors on the opening and closing chapters. Needless to say, the usual disclaimer applies. In addition, he would particularly like to thank Dominic Byatt and Amanda Watkins for their invaluable help during the course of this project.

R. E.

# Contents

# List of Figures

# List of Tables

# Contributors

**Monica Barczak** is Research Associate in the Department of Political Science at the University of Tulsa. Her research interests include issues in representation and democracy in Latin America. She has published articles in journals such as *Latin American Politics and Society* and *Electoral Studies*.

**Robert Elgie** is Professor of Government and International Studies at Dublin City University, Ireland. He has published widely in the field of French politics and comparative politics. His most recent publications include *French Politics: Debates and Controversies* with Steven Griggs (Routledge, 2000), *The Changing French Political System* as editor (Frank Cass, 2000) and *Semi-Presidentialism in Europe* as editor (Oxford University Press, 1999). He is also the author of *Political Leadership in Liberal Democracies* (Macmillan, 1995).

**John Fitzmaurice** is of British and Danish origin. He is Head of Unit in the Secretariat General of the European Commission, Professor at the Institute of European Studies of the Université Libre de Bruxelles. He is the author of *Politics in Denmark* (Hurst, 1981). His research interests cover small democracies, party systems, and elections in western and central Europe.

**Joseph L. Klesner** is Professor of Political Science at Kenyon College in Gambier, Ohio, USA. His research has focused on electoral reform, party system development and electoral politics in Mexico. He has published in *Comparative Politics*, *Electoral Studies* and *Mexican Studies/Estudios Mexicanos*.

**Paul Mitchell** is Lecturer at the London School of Economics and Political Science. He has published widely on the politics of coalitions in Ireland. He has published in journals such as the *European Journal of Political Research* and he was the co-editor of *How Ireland Voted 1997* (Westview, 1999).

**Heikki Paloheimo** is Professor of Political Science at the University of Turku, Finland. He is the author of *Politiikka, talous ja yhteiskunnan muutos* (*Politics, Economics and Social Change*, Annales Universitatis Turkuensis, 1981), *Governments in Democratic Capitalist States* (University of Turku, 1984), *Tasavallan presidentit: Koivisto* (a biography of President Koivisto, Weilin & Göös, 1994), and is the editor of both *Politics in the Era of Corporatism and Planning* (Finnish Political Science Association, 1984) and *Coping with the Economic Crisis* (Sage, 1987) with Hans Keman and Paul Whiteley.

**Roland Sturm** is Professor of Political Science and Head of Department at the University of Erlangen-Nürnberg, Germany. Most of his published work has been concerned with comparative politics, policy studies, political economy, and European, British and German politics. Amongst his most recent books are *Föderalismus in Deutschland* (Leske und Budrich, 2000) and *Die Strategie des 'dritten Weges'* (Olzog, 2001).

**Ania Krok-Paszkowska** is affiliated to the Robert Schuman Centre, European University Institute, Florence. She is currently working on a project on diversity and unity in the enlarged European Union. Recently she has written on the candidates' perceptions of EU enlargement (EUI Working Paper) as well as on the Polish Self-Defence Movement for a book entitled *Uncivil Society? Contentious Politics in Eastern Europe* (Routledge, forthcoming).

**Alan Ware** is Professor of Politics at Worcester College, University of Oxford. He has published widely on American and comparative politics and has a particular interest in party politics. He is the author of *The Breakdown of Democratic Party Organization, 1940–1980,* (Clarendon Press, 1985) and *Political Parties and Party Systems* (Oxford, 1997).

# 1

# What is Divided Government?

## *Robert Elgie*

Divided government is a very widespread political phenomenon, but one which from a comparative perspective remains remarkably understudied. In academic terms, most analyses of divided government have focused on the United States (US). Indeed, since the call was made to study the so-called 'new era of coalition government' (Sundquist, 1988) in the US, academics have 'responded enthusiastically' (Fiorina, 1996: p. vii) to the challenge. As a result, there is now a considerable body of top-quality work on the subject (for example, Fiorina, 1996; Jacobson, 1990; Mayhew, 1991). By contrast, little attention has been paid to the concept in other arenas. Shugart notes that 'there seems to be no literature specifically devoted to divided government in other presidential systems' (1995: 327). In a similar vein, von Mettenheim asserts that 'debate about divided government in American politics has yet to gain widespread influence among comparative political analysts' (1997: 9). Equally, the aim of Laver and Shepsle's path-breaking article is merely to 'start a conversation aimed at promoting a unified rather than a divided discussion' (1991: 252) of the concept in both presidential and non-presidential regimes. This book adds another voice to this, still somewhat stilted, dialogue. It shows that the concept of divided government is understood differently by different people, but also that the applicability of the concept is not confined to the US and that its counterpart can be found both in other presidential regimes and in parliamentary and semi-presidential regimes as well. Put simply, it provides the first systematic study of divided government from a comparative point of view.

This chapter serves as an introduction to the comparative study of divided government. Its first part examines the concept of divided government and identifies two ways in which the concept is commonly understood. The second part of the chapter introduces the study of divided government in practice. It focuses, first, on the debate about the causes of divided government and, second, on the political management of divided government. As such, it provides a framework for the case-study chapters which follow.

## THE CONCEPT OF DIVIDED GOVERNMENT

The concept of divided government is inextricably bound up with studies of the political system of the United States. As a result, work on the US case must provide the starting-point for any comparative analysis of the phenomenon. That said, many of those who write about the US experience of divided government fail to provide a precise definition of the term. This is presumably because they consider it to be so straightforward that it does not need to be explicitly specified. Everyone is thought to know what is meant by the term. However, when the work of these and other writers is examined more closely it becomes clear that different people understand the concept in different ways. In other words, the concept of US-style divided government is not quite as self-explanatory as it might at first appear. Consequently, the various nuances of the term need to be teased out, especially in the present context, a broad-ranging comparative analysis of the concept. It is useful to distinguish between two separate uses of the term 'divided government'. The first rests on an arithmetical definition of the concept. The second is derived from a behavioural interpretation of the term. Both ways of understanding divided government can be found in the academic literature on the US political system and both have slightly different counterparts in the context of political systems elsewhere.

### *Divided Government: An Arithmetical Definition*

The first way in which the concept of divided government is understood is in a purely arithmetical sense. Here, divided government refers to the absence of simultaneous same-party majorities in the executive and legislative branches of government. In other words, the presence or absence of divided government is simply a function of a particular legislative arithmetic. This meaning of the term has its foundation in the study of the US system of government, but it can also be applied to other presidential regimes and to non-presidential regimes as well.

In the US case, the arithmetical definition of divided government constitutes the standard understanding of the term. For example, Bingham Powell contends that divided government refers to the situation where 'different political parties [control] different branches of government' (1991: 231). Somewhat more precisely, Pfiffner states that divided government 'occurs when one political party does not control both houses of Congress along with the presidency' (1994: 167). In the same vein, Peterson and Greene define divided government as '[p]ower-sharing by two separately elected branches of government, each often controlled by a different party' (1993: 33). Perhaps most unambiguously, Laver and Shepsle assert that in US-style systems 'the meaning of divided government is straightforward' (1991: 252). Here, they say, it refers to the occasions when 'the presidency is controlled by one party and at least one chamber of the legislature is controlled by another party'. In the US, therefore, divided government is commonly understood as the situation where no single party controls both the executive and legislative branches of government simultaneously, or, alternatively, where the president's party fails to control a majority in at least one house of the legislature. In this sense, the concept concerns nothing more than a simple description of a certain arithmetic reality and is quite uncontroversial. Does the president's party hold a majority of seats in both houses of Congress? If so, there is unified government. If not, there is divided government. On the basis of this definition, therefore, it is possible to identify the various periods of unified and divided government that have occurred since the founding of the US system.[1]

To the extent that the US is the paradigm case of a presidential regime, it is not surprising that divided government, understood in this arithmetical sense, finds its equivalent in other presidential regimes as well. That said, care should be taken when examining the concept in these cases, since US-centred definitions of divided government tend to assume, either implicitly or explicitly, a two-party system, or at least a majoritarian system. For example, Pfiffner, who provides a more neutral view of the term in one piece of work (1994), proposes a more US-specific interpretation in another. In the latter, he suggests that divided government should be understood as 'the control of the presidency by one party accompanied by the control of one or both houses of Congress by *the other party*'[2] (1992: 226). Almost the same definition is provided by Foley and Owens: 'Divided government refers to a condition where the presidency is controlled by one party, and one or both elements of Congress are controlled by the other party' (1996: 412). Quirk defines unified government, quite uncontroversially, as the situation where 'the president and majorities of the House and Senate belong to the same party' (1991: 70). More problematically, he then defines divided government as being the situation where 'the president and the majority in one or both chambers are of different parties' (1991: 70). Other examples abound. Indeed, the previously cited definitions by Bingham Powell, Laver and Shepsle, and Peterson and Greene all adopt a similar majoritarian assumption.

It should be stressed that these arithmetical definitions of divided government are not false when applied to the US case. On the contrary, they provide a perfectly accurate description of US-style divided government. They are, however, somewhat misleading in the context of a comparative study of divided government. This is because they are simply an artefact of the two-party system in the US. In a two-party system the situation where one political party fails simultaneously to control the presidency and both houses of Congress is logically equivalent to the situation where one party controls the

---

[1] See e.g. the table in Jones (1997: 28).			[2] My emphasis.

presidency and where the other party controls at least one of those houses. By contrast, outside the US in presidential regimes where there are more than two parties in the system, this equivalence does not necessarily apply. In these cases, one party must control the presidency. The presidency is, after all, a winner-takes-all institution. It can only be occupied by the representative of one party.[3] However, if the president's party fails to control, say, one house of the legislature, then this does not mean that this house must automatically be controlled by another party. Instead, the majority opposed to the president may be composed of more than one party. Alternatively, there may be no majority at all. In a comparative context, therefore, an arithmetical definition of divided government in presidential regimes can be understood to comprise not simply the situations where a party opposed to the president actually controls at least one house of the legislature, but also the more general cases where the majority comprises more than one party and where a coherent legislative majority is absent altogether.

There is, however, at least one dissenting voice to this line of argument. In a comparative study Shugart (1995) distinguished between three types of government in presidential regimes: unified, divided, and no-majority government. He understands unified government in the same way as the traditional arithmetic definition of the term—the situation where one party simultaneously controls the presidency and has a majority in both houses of the legislature. However, he then makes a careful distinction between divided government and no-majority government. He uses the term 'divided government' in an arithmetic sense to 'refer only to those situations in which a legislative majority is held by a party or preelection coalition which is different from that of the president' (1995: 327). By contrast, he suggests that the term 'no-majority government' should be used to refer to the 'situation in which no party holds a majority' in one or both houses of the legislature. In this way, Shugart distinguishes between the situations where a party opposed to the president controls the legislature (or one part of it)—as happens in the two-party US presidential regime but does not necessarily happen in other multi-party presidential regimes—and the situations where the president's party fails to control both parts of the legislature—as may happen in all presidential regimes whatever the party system.

It is a moot point as to whether it is better to make the distinction, *à la* Shugart, between divided government and no-majority government, or whether the latter can simply be treated as a particular manifestation of the former. For the purposes of this book no-majority government is deemed simply to be a form of divided government that can occur in certain presidential regimes. It is certainly true that there are interesting differences

---

[3] As the case-study of Ecuador shows (Ch. 3), it may nevertheless be the case that in such a system the vice-presidency is occupied by a representative of another party.

between the politics of divided government in two-party presidential regimes and the politics of divided government in multi-party presidential regimes. Indeed, some of these differences will be explored in the chapters which follow.[4] However, it is also true that in arithmetic terms both situations are logically distinct from unified government. As a result, both can usefully be examined in the context of a comparative study of divided government which encompasses a broad range of constitutional and political situations. Here, then, the arithmetic definition of divided government is formulated so as to include examples of both opposing-majorities and no-majority forms of the concept in presidential regimes.

It is clear, therefore, that the concept of divided government can be applied, albeit with some care, not just to the US but to other presidential regimes as well. At first sight, however, it is not so clear that the concept can be applied outside this realm. After all, there are fundamental constitutional differences between presidential regimes (where the head of state is directly elected and where the executive and the legislature serve for fixed terms) and both parliamentary regimes (where the head of state is not directly elected and where the government can be dismissed by the legislature) and semi-presidential regimes (where the head of state is directly elected and serves for a fixed term, but where the government can be dismissed by the legislature and, in some cases, by the president as well).[5] And yet, despite these constitutional differences, the arithmetical definition of divided government does have its logical equivalent in non-presidential regimes. In the case of parliamentary regimes it corresponds to minority governments. In the case of semi-presidential regimes it corresponds to periods of 'cohabitation', or split-executive government, as well.

On the basis of an arithmetical definition of the term, majority and minority governments in parliamentary regimes are the equivalents of unified and divided governments respectively in presidential regimes. A majority government is one where the party (or parties) represented in the executive is (are) supported by more than 50 per cent of the deputies in parliament, whereas a minority government is where the governing party (or parties) is (are) supported by less than 50 per cent of the same.[6] The logic behind this reasoning

---

[4] The case-study of Ecuador which follows was chosen specifically because it was an instance of no-majority presidential government.

[5] Semi-presidential regimes remain a much misunderstood type of constitutional arrangement. For a full and recent treatment of the subject, see Elgie (1999).

[6] In parliamentary regimes where there are two working houses of parliament, the government is invariably only responsible to one house but still needs the support of both in order to pass legislation. In these cases, divided government occurs not just when the government is supported by less than 50% of the deputies in the house to which it is responsible (this is the usual meaning of the term minority government), but also when it has a majority in that house and yet lacks a majority in the other working house. In the chapters which follow, the German case was chosen to illustrate the dynamics of this situation in more detail.

is straightforward. If we take the basic arithmetical definition of unified government in a presidential context (both the US and elsewhere) to be the situation where the president's party has a majority in all the working houses of the legislature, then majority government clearly corresponds to this situation in the parliamentary context. Here, the executive—in this case the head of government and the cabinet—is composed of representatives from the party (or parties) which enjoys (or enjoy) majority support in the legislature. The executive and the legislature are, thus, linked by the arithmetic of parliament. There may, of course, still be differences of a political nature between the two branches of government. On such occasions, though, these differences, as Laver and Shepsle put it, 'must derive from divided parties, not divided government' (1991: 266). In other words, they are a consequence of the political rather than the arithmetical context in which the two branches of government find themselves. By contrast, minority governments are the unambiguous parliamentary equivalents of divided governments in presidential regimes. In both instances the party (or parties) which constitutes (constitute) the executive fails (fail) to enjoy majority support in the legislature. As Laver and Shepsle put it, 'just as in the analogous case in the US, the executive needs to add to its partisan support in the legislature in order to implement decisions requiring legislative approval' (1991: 253). In parliamentary regimes, therefore, as with the situation in presidential regimes, unified and divided government comes about simply by virtue of an arithmetical situation. Does the government enjoy a parliamentary majority? If so, there is unified government. If not, there is divided government. Again, therefore, on the basis of this definition it is possible to identify the various periods of unified and divided (majority and minority) governments in parliamentary regimes simply by looking at the levels of governmental party support in the legislature.[7]

Just as the arithmetical definition of presidential-style divided government can be applied to parliamentary regimes, so it can also be applied to semi-presidential regimes. Here, divided government can take not just one but two forms. In the first place, the parliamentary element of semi-presidentialism means that divided government occurs when there is a minority government. So, the situation where the president, prime minister, and the cabinet are all from the same party, but where that party fails to command a majority in the legislature, is the equivalent of a minority government in the parliamentary context and, therefore, is the equivalent of presidential-style divided government. In addition, though, the constitutional organization of semi-presidential regimes means that divided government can also manifest itself quite differently in this context. The parliamentary component of semi-presidentialism means that the prime minister must be acceptable to the legislature. If not, then the legislature can vote the prime minister and the

---

[7] See e.g. the appendix in Strøm (1990).

cabinet out of office. By contrast, the presidential component of semi-presidentialism means that the president can serve in office independently of the legislature's support. The combination of these two constitutional features means that the president may be faced with the situation where a party (or parties) opposed to the president enjoys (enjoy) a majority in the legislature and insists (insist) on a prime minister who is also opposed to the president, but where the president can choose to remain in office until his/her term expires. Thus, the executive will be split between two senior office-holders, only one of whom, the prime minister, is supported by a legislative majority. In this case, the effect of the parliamentary arithmetic is not to divide the executive *in toto* from the majority in the legislature, as in the case of presidential-style divided government or minority government in parliamentary regimes, but to divide one part of the executive from the majority in the legislature and, also, one part of the executive from the other. This is the situation that the French call 'cohabitation', but which, alternatively, might equally be termed split-executive government.[8]

On the basis of an arithmetical definition, therefore, divided government can be identified in various contexts. In presidential regimes it is characterized by both opposing executive–legislative majorities and no-majority situations. In parliamentary regimes, it manifests itself in minority governments (single-party and coalition). In semi-presidential regimes it can be found when there is either minority government or split-executive government. Whatever the constitutional configuration, what links all of these cases is the basic arithmetical fact that the executive fails to be supported by a legislative majority. It is in this sense that there is divided government.

## Divided Government: A Behavioural Interpretation

The concept of divided government can also be understood in a behavioural way. In this case, divided government is equated with 'divisiveness'. In other words, divided government is not so much a function of a particular legislative arithmetic but of a certain type of political behaviour. More specifically, divided government corresponds to the situation where there is conflict between the executive and legislative branches of government whatever the support for the executive in the legislature. As with the arithmetical definition of divided government, this meaning of the term has its roots in the study of the political system of the US, but it also finds a clear counterpart in studies of parliamentary and semi-presidential regimes as well.

---

[8] In some semi-presidential regimes, at least as defined in Elgie (1999), the president has no powers to speak of. This is true for countries such as Austria and Iceland. Here, split-executive government has no bearing on the functioning of the political system. In the chapters which follow, this is true for the case-study of the Republic of Ireland.

In the US many people associate divided government with divided politics. That is to say, they assume that the consequence of divided government is a particular type of political behaviour. More specifically, they assume that divided government is synonymous with gridlock, legislative paralysis, and conflict between the president and Congress. Mark P. Jones (1995: 18) shows that this assumption has a long history and can be traced back to the work of Wilson, Bryce, and Laski amongst others. More recently, this line of argument is particularly prevalent in the work of Sundquist (1988, 1992). He argues that politicians, journalists, and the public all tend to judge divided government negatively (Sundquist, 1992: 93–9). So, for example, referring to the occasions when the president lacks a congressional majority, he states: 'At worst, the executive and legislative branches become intent on discrediting and defeating each other's initiatives, and the government is immobilized' (1992: 94). Sundquist also argues that many academics make the same assumption. Indeed, he quotes one writer who asserts: 'When control is divided, it is difficult for the public to hold anyone accountable. Voters are left angry, disgusted, and wondering why the people they elect always seem to be incompetent, inept and ineffectual' (Sinclair, 1991: 183). There are, needless to say, dissenting voices to this line of reasoning within the academic community. For example, Mayhew's (1991) research showed that significant pieces of legislation were just as likely to be passed whether the president enjoyed a majority in Congress or not. It remains, though, that for many people divided government is associated with inter-branch confrontation. Indeed, the consequence of this position is that for these people the opposite of divided government is not so much unified government understood in the arithmetical sense, but party government, implying presidential leadership, the enactment of party programmes, and the executive and legislature operating *in tandem* (Sundquist, 1992: 90–2).

This association between divided government and divisiveness leads to the seemingly paradoxical argument that divided government in a behavioural sense can occur even when there is unified government in an arithmetical sense. This line of reasoning has been adopted quite explicitly by Galderisi. He argues that many 'academics, journalists, and other surveyors of the political scene have had too limited a view of divided government' (1996: 1–2). This, he asserts, is because they 'have concentrated unduly on *divided partisan control* of elective institutions' (p. 2).[9] By contrast, Galderisi states that 'party may in itself be neither a sufficient nor even a necessary condition' (p. 3) for an understanding of divided government. Instead, like Sundquist and others, Galderisi equates the phenomenon with presidential/congressional confrontation and, consequently, with either gridlock or with 'the development of policy outcomes built on consensus'. Galderisi argues that divided government should

---

[9] Emphasis in the original.

be understood as 'more than just the outcome of divided party control', meaning divided government in an arithmetical sense. Indeed, he argues that it 'can operate even when partisan unity exists'. This is because the twin principles of the separation of powers and checks and balances ensure that 'quick and deliberate policy change' can be difficult to achieve at any time. Therefore, for Galderisi, like Sundquist, divided government is associated with divisiveness, but for Galderisi divisiveness is not necessarily confined to periods when the president's party fails to enjoy a majority in at least one house of Congress. Rather, it can occur whatever the congressional arithmetic. A similar line of reasoning has been adopted by both Brady and Volden (1998) and Krehbiel (1996) who both provide a formal model which shows that gridlock is just as likely to occur whether the president is supported by a congressional majority or not.

This interpretation, then, represents a quite different approach to the understanding of divided government from the arithmetical definition that was considered previously. Moreover, it represents an approach which can be applied quite uncontroversially to presidential regimes outside the US. There is no reason why inter-branch conflict, gridlock, or legislative compromise cannot occur in multi-party presidential regimes and, therefore, why divided government cannot manifest itself in this context as well. In this sense, the behavioural interpretation of divided government is totally transferable. Indeed, this approach to the concept can be applied to parliamentary and semi-presidential regimes just as easily. Here, though, writers tend to equate presidential-style divided government not so much with minority government, as in the arithmetical definition of the term, but with coalition government instead.

A number of writers have drawn comparisons between divided government in presidential regimes and coalition government in parliamentary regimes. For example, Fiorina argues that in both cases a single party wins only 'partial control of the full power of government' (Fiorina, 1991: 240). As a result, 'parties have to share governmental power, though we express that sharing in terms of ministries in one case, and in terms of branches of government in the other'. In either case, he states, 'policies cannot be adopted unless the parties can compromise their differences and agree upon a course of action'. Similarly, but from the opposite perspective, Peters has characterized coalition government as 'a form of divided government' (1997: 69). This, he argues, is because it entails a need for representatives of the executive to bargain, cajole, and propose side payments for legislators (pp. 69–70). In other words, it forces party leaders in parliamentary regimes to behave like the president and congressional leaders in presidential regimes. More explicitly still, Laver defines divided government as the situation where 'governance structures with independent sources of legitimacy have the potential to come into conflict' (1999: 6). While he argues that such conflict may occur during periods of minority government in parliamentary regimes, he goes on to add that coalition politics may also result in conflict between the legislature and the executive and that in this case it 'is the European equivalent of divided government' (1999: 7).[10] Finally, but from a different perspective, Pierce argues that 'cohabitation' is not a 'French version of divided government' (1991: 270–1). This is because the 'rival executive leaders in France did not avoid paralysis or crisis through compromise, but rather because of the pacifying effects of special conditions' (p. 271). In other words, Pierce argues that, as 'cohabitation' in France in 1986–8 did not lead to gridlock, the political system did not operate in the same way as the US system, or at least his interpretation of it, on the occasions when the president lacks a congressional majority.

The link between all of these examples is the type of political behaviour which is associated with the concept of divided government. In presidential regimes, divided government is associated with inter-branch conflict and compromise. In parliamentary and semi-presidential regimes, the same sort of behaviour is said to be associated with coalition politics. In both cases, divided government can occur whether or not there is a legislative majority in favour of the executive. In this way, there is a clear distinction between this interpretation of the concept and the previous definition of the term.

## The Concept of Divided Government in Comparative Perspective

In one of the first overviews of the topic, Bingham Powell stated that 'the application of the American concept of "divided government" in Europe forces a careful empirical definition and perhaps redefinition of the concept to place it in a functionally similar theoretical position' (1991: 232). There is no doubt that the review of the literature on divided government presented in this section merely confirms Bingham Powell's conjecture.

It is clear that the concept of divided government is used in different ways by different people. Moreover, it is also clear that this point applies to the study of the concept in the paradigm US case as well as to its application elsewhere. Against this background, there is little to gained from debating which of the competing conceptions of divided government is the most appropriate. Indeed, it might be argued that the discipline benefits from a plurality of definitions and interpretations, inciting people, as it may, into undertaking more varied and, hopefully, better quality research. It might also be argued that, in

---

[10] It might be noted that Laver's view on this matter appears to have changed over time. In the Laver and Shepsle (1991) article, they write that coalition majority governments in parliamentary regimes are 'neither really united, nor really divided in the strict US sense' (p. 267). Indeed, they go on to state that 'convoluted attempts to draw parallels' between coalition majority governments and divided government in the US 'are probably not very useful' (ibid).

the context of the present study at least, there are certain problems with adopting the behavioural interpretation of the term. Most notably, and in contrast to the arithmetic definition, there are no objective criteria which allow us to identify the various periods of unified (or party) government, on the one hand, and divided government, on the other, on the basis of this inter-pretation. For example, in the case of the US when does divided government become unified government, especially if, as Brady and Volden (1998) assert, the US system is characterized by 'revolving gridlock'? Similarly, in the case of parliamentary regimes, are all coalition governments to count as periods of divided government? Can there ever be purposive, coherent coalitions and, if so, are we to treat these examples as periods of unified government or not? Moreover, are all single-party majority governments to be counted as exam-ples of unified government under the behavioural interpretation? What if such a government is formed by a party which is internally divided and, as a result, has great difficulty in passing the legislation that its leader wishes? All of this is not to say that these issues cannot be resolved and, indeed, they may be with further conceptual refinement. It is simply to say that, as it currently stands, the behavioural interpretation of divided government leaves certain fundamental questions unanswered.

For these reasons the case-studies in this book have been chosen on the basis of an arithmetical definition of divided government. Here, divided gov-ernment refers to the situation where: 'the executive fails to enjoy majority support in at least one working house of the legislature'.[11] This definition has the advantage of being inclusive, allowing case-studies to be chosen which focus on the absence of simultaneous same-party executive and legislative majorities in both two-party and multi-party presidential regimes as well as the experience of minority governments and split-executive governments in parliamentary and semi-presidential regimes (see Figure 1.1). Moreover, it also has the advantage of making it easy to identify the periods when there is unified or divided government in each case; the simple criterion is whether or not there are simultaneous same-party executive and legislative majorities. Finally, it makes no behavioural assumptions. It does not imply that the examples of divided government which have been chosen are necessarily char-acterized by either conflict or co-operation between and/or within the execu-tive and legislative branches of government. On the contrary, as we shall see, this definition allows the causes of very varied types of political behaviour to be identified and the management of very different forms of political rela-tionships to be described.

---

[11] Here, the term 'executive' can, if necessary, comprise both a president and prime min-ister only one of whom (the president) actually meets the condition outlined in the defini-tion, as in the case of semi-presidential split-executive government.

TABLE 1.1. *Forms of divided government in the arithmetical sense*

| Type of regime | Form of divided government |
| --- | --- |
| Presidential | 1. A party (or parties) opposed to the president has (have) a majority in at least one working house<br>2. There is no majority in at least one working house |
| Parliamentary | The government (single-party or coalition) fails to command a majority in at least one working house |
| Semi-presidential | 1. The government (single-party or coalition) fails to command a majority in at least one working house<br>2. A party (or parties) opposed to the president has (have) a majority in the key house, leading to the appointment of a prime minister who is also opposed to the president |

## DIVIDED GOVERNMENT IN PRACTICE

The chapters which follow comprise detailed country case-studies of divided government. Each chapter comprises three substantive sections. The first indicates the frequency and form of divided government based on the arithmetical definition of the term provided above. The second examines the causes of divided government in each country. The third focuses on the management of divided government in each case. There are two reasons for structuring the case-study chapters in this way. The first is to deepen our comparative understanding of the causes of divided government. As noted at the outset, most of the work on divided government has been conducted on the US case. This work has generated a lively debate about the causes of divided government and has suggested that various factors may account for why it should occur so frequently. One of the main tasks of the country case-studies, therefore, is to establish a range of both country-specific and comparative reasons for the continuing presence of this phenomenon. The second aim is to begin a discussion about the political management of divided government. This issue is somewhat neglected in the literature, even in the vast amount of work that has been generated on this topic in the US. For the most part the question of how political leaders cope, or otherwise, with the challenges of divided government has been only addressed tangentially if at all. One purpose of the country studies, therefore, is to help redress this imbalance.

The rest of this section provides an introduction to the case-studies which follow. To this end, it focuses primarily but not exclusively on the US literature, highlighting a number of the potential causes of divided government and indicating some of the ways in which political leaders manage the problems of divided government. Needless to say, other causes will be proposed during the case-study chapters and other forms of political management will emerge, but the rest of this section provides a basis for the empirical work which follows.

## The Causes of Divided Government

The debate about the causes of divided government in the US has become a veritable cottage industry. The tone of the debate is usually, although not always, polite, but this should not mask the fact that the participants base their arguments on very different methodological assumptions and adopt radically opposed perspectives on the matter. Against this background, two general types of explanations can be identified: behavioural and structural/institutional.

### Behavioural explanations of divided government

In the US divided government can occur as a direct result of split-ticket voting, meaning the situation where at the same election voters vote for a president from one party and a congressperson from another party.[12] Various behaviourally based explanations have been proposed for why this form of voting should occur and two of the most influential of these explanations are outlined here. In both cases, though, it is clear that there are certain *prima-facie* difficulties in extrapolating from the US case to other cases. One of the tasks of the case-studies, therefore, will be to determine whether these explanations, variants of them, or other, quite separate, electoral accounts of divided government are at all appropriate in understanding the causes of the phenomenon.

Perhaps the most oft-cited electoral explanation of the cause of divided government in the US has been provided by Jacobson (1990). He attempts to explain why in the post-war period divided government has tended to be characterized by the election of Republican presidents and the return of a Democratic Congress, or at least a Democratic House of Representatives. For Jacobson, split-ticket voting of this sort is electorally rational for many voters. Indeed, writing about the phenomenon during the Reagan–Bush presidencies, he states that divided government 'faithfully mirrored the public's own divided and self-contradictory preferences' (Jacobson, 1996: 62). The public, he argues, wants both strong leadership at the national level and pork-barrel politics at the local level. It wants balanced budgets, tax cuts, and increased spending. It wants low inflation, high employment, and economic stability. In short, the public wants its politicians to exhibit a number of quite contradictory qualities. Split-ticket voting provides one way of at least partially reconciling these countervailing demands. Traditionally Republican

---

[12] It can, of course, also occur as a function of mid-term elections when the presidency is not being contested.

presidential candidates were rated positively on issues such as managing the economy. They were seen to be able to provide collective economic goods as efficiently as possible and in presidential elections, where voters are encouraged to think of the country as a whole, this was a distinct advantage. By contrast, polls showed that Democratic candidates were strong on special-interest politics. They were thought to be best placed to provide specific benefits to constituents, which was an advantage in congressional elections, particularly House elections, when the electoral constituency was local. Thus, Jacobson argues, 'the ticket-splitting which produced divided government . . . required neither cynicism nor even conscious calculation on the part of voters' (1996: 63). It was the simply the consequence of rational voting.

There have been a number of objections to Jacobson's thesis. Most notably, the fact that the 1992 elections returned a Democratic president and that the 1994 elections then delivered a Republican Congress seemed to undermine Jacobson's basic argument, although he did provide a trenchant defence (1996). On a different level, Jones has argued that Jacobson's thesis may well be valid in the US context but that fundamentally it is US-centric. Indeed, he states that it is one of a set of explanations whose applicability to presidential systems in Latin America is 'doubtful' (1995: 25). In particular, Jones argues that in Latin America 'the incentives to and the ability of congressional deputies to represent particular district interests is severely reduced' (p. 27) because of the multi-member PR electoral systems which predominate in contrast to the single-member plurality system in the US. Indeed, a further objection might be made concerning the transferability of this thesis. How can it be applied to parliamentary regimes where there is no opportunity for split-ticket voting, at least in the sense that there is only one source of electoral legitimacy? The present study provides at least the opportunity for Jacobson's theory to be tested more rigorously to indicate whether or not it really is US-specific.

An alternative, but equally influential, account of the cause of divided government in the US has been outlined by Fiorina. He proposes a 'balancing' explanation of divided government. According to this line of thought, 'the overall pattern of election outcomes is consistent with the notion of an electorate behaving *as if* it were consciously choosing or rejecting divided government' (1996: 65).[13] This model assumes that voters have some basic understanding of politics. They understand where parties stand on particular issues. They know whether parties are more or less left- or right-wing. They also know that the executive and the legislature collectively combine to determine the outcome of public policies. Assuming two parties, one left-wing and one right-wing, and assuming a large number of moderate centre-left and centre-right voters, there are incentives for people to engage in split-ticket

---

[13] Emphasis in the original.

voting. They do so as a way of balancing what they see to be the relatively extreme positions of the two main political parties, so forcing decision-makers to adopt policies which are closer to their own preferences.

As with Jacobson's thesis there is opposition to Fiorina's argument. In particular, a number of writers have suggested that the data simply do not fit with the theory. As Petrocik and Doherty state: 'to continue championing the policy-balancing theory is to tell a tale in conflict with the evidence' (1996: 104). Instead, the data they produce suggests that the incidence of unified or divided government has little to do with the policy distance between the two main parties in the system and that 'voters are not risk-averse cognitive balancers' (pp. 104–5). In the context of this book, there is, once again, a further problem concerning the comparative applicability of the concept. The Fiorina model assumes a two-party system, because this is the case in the country with which he is concerned. How does this theory stand up in the case of multi-party systems? Fiorina is one of those writers who makes an explicit link between US-style divided government and coalition government in parliamentary regimes. Does his 'balancing' theory have any relevance in explaining the causes of minority government and split-executive government? The country studies will again help to test the transferability of Fiorina's thesis and to suggest whether this model, or a variant of it, can be applied outside the US case.

### Structural/institutional explanations of divided government

In the US the main alternatives to behavioural explanations of divided government are structural/institutional ones. As before, certain elements of these explanations seem US-specific. However, in this case the opportunities for comparative extrapolation are arguably somewhat greater.

Structural/institutional explanations take many forms. For the most part these explanations try to explain why the Democratic party continued to enjoy a majority in the House of Representatives whatever the affiliation of the presidency, or, alternatively, why the Republican party continued to be successful at the presidential level whatever the makeup of Congress. Amongst these explanations are those which have stressed the advantages of incumbency. Incumbents, it is argued, can provide services for their districts. They may also gain the lion's share of campaign finance because they are seen as a 'safe bet'. Whatever the reason, these advantages supposedly helped to protect Democratic party candidates at the local level from swings against the party at the national level, thus helping to institutionalize divided government. Another argument has explained Republican presidential success at least partly in terms of how the Democratic party nominates its presidential candidates (Wattenberg, 1991). The fact that the party chooses delegates to its national convention on the basis of proportional representation means that candidates who lose primary elections still have an incentive to stay in the race. This increases the chances of a long and divisive nomination process, which damages the party's public image and reduces its chances of winning the subsequent presidential head-to-head. A further explanation suggested that the Democratic party in the House of Representatives deliberately gerrymandered electoral districts in order to maintain its majority. In this case, then, divided government was a function of deliberate party manipulation of the electoral process.

As with some of the electoral explanations of divided government, the empirical basis of some of the structural/institutional arguments, particularly those concerning gerrymandering and the advantages of incumbency, has been questioned by certain writers (see, for example, Fiorina, 1996: 14–23). Indeed, it has been suggested that these explanations are not be appropriate even in the US case. However, these explanations, along with the others considered here, do have the advantage of suggesting certain lines of enquiry which may be fruitful in a comparative context. There may be equivalent institutional reasons which account, perhaps more convincingly even, for the occurrence of divided government in other national contexts. Again, the search for such explanations is one of the key tasks of the country case-studies.

The second structural/institutional explanation focuses on the timing of elections and electoral formulae. One such explanation is quite straightforward. In the US mid-term elections provide voters with the opportunity to sanction decision-makers. Thus, these elections allow a majority opposed to the president to be returned during the chief executive's administration, so creating the conditions for unified government to be replaced by a period of divided government without the need for split-ticket voting. By contrast, in parliamentary systems where the opportunity for mid-term elections is absent, or in other presidential systems where executive and legislative elections are held only concurrently, the likelihood is that the incidence of divided government will be less (Shugart, 1995). The case-studies allow this line of reasoning to be tested more fully. Another explanation is somewhat more specific and has already been tested comparatively (Jones, 1995; Shugart, 1995). For one writer, 'electoral laws are the principal source of divided government in . . . Latin American presidential systems' (Jones, 1995: 155). Electoral systems, Jones argues, help to determine the degree of multipartyism and, hence, the likelihood that the president's party will obtain a legislative majority, there being, in effect, an inverse relationship between the two. In this context, plural electoral systems, Jones argues, are more likely, directly or indirectly, to provide the president with a legislative majority than proportional representation (PR) systems. In addition, he also argues that the type of PR system which a country uses is relatively insignificant in determining the level of legislative multipartism, although he does note that there is some link between effective district magnitude and legislative support. In the context of this book, this argument is important not just on its own right, but also because, like the other arguments outlined here, it provides a ready-made hypothesis which can be tested in a variety of contexts, presidential and otherwise, to determine the extent to which it is transferable across regime types.

## The Management of Divided Government

The literature on the management of divided government in the US is sparse. Few scholars have addressed this question at least directly. Indeed, only Cox and Kernell (1991: 242–3) have tried systematically to outline the various options with which decision-makers are faced in this respect. What is more, the same point applies to the study of minority governments in parliamentary systems (Strøm, 1990: 19). There have been a number of studies on the formation and collapse of minority governments, but there has been scarcely any work on how minority governments behave in office (*ibid.*). By way of an introduction to the case-studies, some of the options with which decision-makers are faced in the management of divided government will briefly be outlined.

According to Cox and Kernell (1991), decision-makers have three options when faced with divided government. The first option is for decision-makers to 'go it alone'. Here, the executive and legislative branch of government decide not to bargain with each other. Instead, each decides to use the constitutional and legal resources available to it in the pursuit of its own ends, whatever the consequences for the other branch of government. The attraction of this type of approach for political leaders is that they can be 'first to the game'. In other words, as Cox and Kernell state, 'the ability to pursue a policy unilaterally can present the other branch with a fait accompli that it is difficult or impolitic to overturn' (243). The danger associated with this option is that it is likely to lead to institutional conflict. There may be policy deadlock, constitutional crises, and/or open disputes, all of which may be sanctioned by the public at subsequent electoral consultations. Thus, the unilateral approach is a high-risk one, but one which may also appear appealing to decision-makers in a particular branch of government if they feel that they can turn the game to their advantage.

The second option is to 'go public'. For Cox and Kernell this type of behaviour is associated with the situation where leaders make 'public commitments to particular positions in order to raise the costs of reneging and thereby strengthen one's bargaining position' (p. 243). In this case, the public acts as the intermediary between the executive and legislative branches of government. Each institution tries to win voter support for its position in order to illustrate the potential electoral costs to those in the other branch of government if this position is not adopted. Although Cox and Kernell do not make this point, there is a sense in which it may be easier for the executive branch of government to play this particular game, in the context of presidential regimes at least. This is because the executive can, in general terms, speak more coherently than the legislature. In presidential regimes the executive is personified in the form of a president who can make clear public pronouncements. The legislature, by contrast, is a multifaceted institution which may find it difficult to speak with one voice. This option, therefore, may be one which the executive favours and which the legislature has to counter and try to negate.

The third option is 'to bargain within the beltway'. Examples of this type of behaviour for Cox and Kernell include 'delay and brinkmanship, careful attention to revision points, and the selling out of junior partners' (p. 243). Here, decision-makers in both branches of government know that they have to bargain and reach agreement. However, neither wants to make the first move and appear politically weak. Therefore, agreements are put off until the last minute, bluffing strategies are adopted, negotiations on certain policies are prioritized over others, and so forth until a compromise position is finally found at the eleventh hour. The risk in this strategy is that no agreement may be reached and that decision-makers are then blamed by the electorate. A further risk is that an agreement may be reached, but be unacceptable to the supporters of the various negotiators and, thus, cause substantial intra-party problems for the leaders in question.

These options were developed to help explain the politics of divided government in the US. However, there is no reason to suggest that they cannot be applied in some form or another to account for the management of divided government in other contexts, presidential and otherwise. That said, Strøm (1990) has already identified various ways in which minority governments go about building support for their policies in parliamentary systems, and he provides a good counterpoint to the US-centred studies considered previously. Building on his work, three examples of the way in which minority governments manage the problems of majority-building will be briefly outlined (see also Elgie and Maor, 1992). Some or all of these strategies may be identified in the chapters which follow. Indeed, there is no reason to suggest that they will be necessarily confined to the case-studies of parliamentary regimes alone.

The first example of how the divided government situation may be managed is by way of a 'formal' minority government (Strøm, 1990: 94–6). This type of government is one which meets the formal requirements of the arithmetical definition of the term, and hence can be classed as an example of divided government, but which is in fact guaranteed governmental office because it can count on the unequivocal support of a majority in the legislature. These governments come to power as a result of an explicit agreement between the party (or parties) represented in the executive and a support party (or parties) in the legislature. The reason why parties may wish to forego cabinet representation, but still officially support the government in parliament is that it can provide power without responsibility. The support party can shape legislation without having to defend that legislation as publicly as the government's representatives do. This can be an advantage if individual pieces of legislation, or the government's record as a whole, prove unpopular. Thus, it may be rational for a party to remain out of office and yet still be associated with the government of the day. In turn, it may also be rational for a government to accept this situation. This is because it is better placed to claim responsibility for the benefits of legislation, or for its overall achievements, than the support party in parliament. The number of parties who can justifiably claim credit for popular performace is, therefore, less. For both reasons, representatives in both the executive and legislative branches of government may have good reason to construct a 'formal' minority government in a parliamentary regime.

The second example is the situation where the government relies on 'shifting' legislative support parties. Here, rather than constructing a formal agreement with a fixed party (or set of parties) in the legislature, the government deals with the party which demands the fewest concessions for each item of legislation (Strøm, 1990: 97–8). Thus, the majority-building process is more *ad hoc* than in the previous case. The government wins the support one party (or set of parties) on one piece of legislation and another party (or set of parties) on another piece of legislation. The advantage of this approach for the government is that it maximizes its 'flexibility to exploit favorable issue opportunities' (p. 97). The disadvantage is that it also 'renders it maximally susceptible to defeat' because it has no stable support party.

The final example concerns the situation where the government takes a policy-centred approach to majority-building. Here, a government will attempt to construct a majority on a policy-by-policy basis. It will find that it is best to seek the approval of a particular legislative support party for one policy and that of another party for another policy. This is not the same as saying that the government is legislating on an ad hoc or day-by-day basis. On the contrary, there may be formal or informal agreements with individual parties in particular policy areas on a medium- or long-term basis. It is simply to say that in this case the government approaches the problem of managing divided government in a parliamentary context from an explicit policy perspective, searching out separate and perhaps stable partners for separate policy areas.

It is clear, therefore, that there are a number of strategies which minority governments may adopt as a way of managing the problems associated with the absence of a legislative majority in parliamentary systems. At first sight it may appear as if these examples are just as parochial as the US examples considered previously. In fact, though, there is a considerable degree of overlap between them. Presidents may try to build *ad hoc* coalitions of congresspersons in the attempt to win support and pass legislation when there is divided government. Alternatively, they may seek out support on a more coherent policy-related basis, knowing the policy concerns of individual legislators and appealing to them. In these ways, then, it would appear as if decision-makers potentially have common concerns and at least somewhat similar ways of responding to these concerns, whatever the institutional context within which divided government occurs. These are some of the issues on which the following chapters will concentrate.

## DIVIDED GOVERNMENT

To date, the study of divided government has largely been confined to the United States. However, as this chapter has shown, divided government is not confined either to the US or even to presidential regimes more widely. Instead, divided government can also occur in other types of political system in the form of minority government in parliamentary regimes and both 'cohabitation' and minority government in semi-presidential regimes. Against this background, this book examines the experience of divided government in a comparative context and identifies the similarities and differences between the various experiences of this undoubtedly common form of government. In particular, there are three studies of divided government in presidential regimes (the US, Mexico, and Ecuador), three studies of 'cohabitation' and/or minority government in semi-presidential regimes (Finland, France and Poland) and three studies of minority government in parliamentary regimes (Denmark, Germany and Ireland). In the conclusion, the various causes of divided government will be reviewed and the different ways of managing divided government will be reassessed in the light of these examples.

# 2

## Divided Government in the United States

### Alan Ware

Discussion of divided government usually begins with the United States: it was the country in which analyses of the phenomenon started; there is a large and growing literature on divided government in America, and this is a literature that can stimulate similar research on other political systems. It has been a common form of political arrangement at the federal level of politics for over 160 years, and it also occurs frequently in state government. The factors that have brought about divided government have changed over time, and the ways of managing its effects have also varied both between the state and federal level and over the years. This means that there are a number of different kinds of relationship between the two branches of government that have developed, and this is of importance for comparative analysis. This chapter concentrates mainly on the federal level of government, although some attention is also given to the state level. It considers the impact of structural and institutional factors in bringing about divided government, before examining the effects of changes in electoral behaviour at that level. The third section of the chapter focuses on how divided government is managed at federal and state levels. First, I shall examine the extent to which divided government has been evident at the federal level.

### THE FREQUENCY AND FORM OF DIVIDED GOVERNMENT IN THE US

It is widely agreed that a competitive party system, consisting of two well-organized parties, had become established in the US by the second half of the 1830s. Both the Democrats and the Whigs had built up mass organizations by the end of that decade, and, for the purposes of this chapter, the beginning of the era of competitive party politics is taken to be the election of 1836. Between the elections of 1836 and 2000 (exclusive) there were eighty-two national elections—forty-one for the presidency and Congress, and a further forty-one mid-term elections for the Congress. Of these eighty-two elections, thirty-five (or 43 per cent of the total) resulted in the presidency being held by one party while control of one or both chambers of the Congress was held by the other major party. It has been slightly less common for just one chamber to fall into the hands of the president's opponents—this happened on sixteen occasions (18 per cent of all election results)—with the more usual pattern of divided government being that of both chambers being led by party leaders who were from a different party from the president (23 per cent of all election results).

Nevertheless, beyond alerting us to the point that divided government is a relatively common occurrence in the US, aggregating the data in this way conceals quite distinct patterns apparent in different eras. Three clearly differentiated periods are evident. In the first period, from 1836 to 1896 (exclusive), divided government was common—of the thirty elections precisely one half yielded instances of divided government. This was followed by a period from 1896 to 1948 (exclusive) in which unified government was the much more usual result of an election—85 per cent of elections in these years produced unified government. Finally, in the years from 1948 to 2000 (exclusive) divided government occurred even more frequently than in the nineteenth century—of these twenty-six elections, sixteen (62 per cent of the total) produced divided government. Given these data, it might appear as if national politics in the second half of the twentieth century was rather similar to the politics of most of the nineteenth century, but there are important differences between the two periods to which attention should be given.

One of the significant features of the nineteenth-century experience was that divided government was a very common result following mid-term elections, whereas it was much less common after a presidential election. Two-thirds of all mid-term elections led to divided government, but only one third of presidential elections did so. This is not the pattern in the period since 1948; in these years 70 per cent of all mid-term elections have brought about divided government, the same incidence found in the nineteenth century (67 per cent), but the pattern for presidential years is dissimilar. From 1948 to 2000 seven of the thirteen presidential elections (54 per cent of total) ensured divided government, compared with 33 per cent of such elections from 1836 to 1896.

Another difference between the contemporary era and the nineteenth century is that since 1948 it has been much more common for both chambers to be controlled by the party that does not control the presidency than for just one of them to be in the hands of his partisan opponents. Three-quarters of the instances of divided government have seen a president faced by the opposing majority parties in both House and Senate; by contrast from 1836 to 1896 on only 40 per cent of the occasions of divided government was it both chambers that had fallen into the hands of the party opposing the president.

Typically, when it has just been one chamber that the president's party does not control, that chamber has been the House. This pattern has been especially evident in the contemporary era; only once among these four instances (in 1954) has it been the Senate that has a majority nominally hostile to the president. Of the ten instances of single-chamber divided government in the nineteenth century, seven involved the House and three involved the Senate. Here, too, a quite distinct nineteenth-century pattern can be observed, the significance of which is discussed in the next section. Of the seven occasions between 1836 and 1896 in which it was the House alone that created divided government, six emanated from mid-term election results; 1876 was the only presidential year when a president's party had control of the Senate but not the House. On the other hand, of the three instances in which the Senate was the only chamber not controlled by the president's party, two occurred in presidential election years. There is no such pattern in the relatively few instances of single-chamber divided government since 1948—two of the three instances involving the House occurred in presidential election years (1980 and 1984), while the sole instance involving the Senate occurred in a mid-term year (1954).

Another way of thinking about the different roles played by House and Senate respectively in the division of government in the nineteenth century is to consider all instances of divided government. Of the twelve occasions on which an election produced a majority in the House for the party opposed to the president, only two (17 per cent) occurred in presidential election years; of the eight occasions involving the Senate, three (38 per cent) occurred in presidential election years. There is no such difference between the chambers since 1948. Indeed, since that date presidential election years have been rather more likely to produce a House majority composed of the party opposed to the president (54 per cent of all presidential election years) than Senate majorities opposed to the President (39 per cent of all presidential election years).

How are such variations over time to be explained? Answering this question takes us to matters that lie at the very heart of the transformation of American political parties since the nineteenth century. I begin by examining the impact of structural and institutional factors.

## THE CAUSES OF DIVIDED GOVERNMENT IN THE US

### *Structural and Institutional Factors*

The single most important factor accounting for divided government in the nineteenth century was the non-coinciding terms of office for the members of the House and the Senate, on the one side, and for the president on other. Since the ratification of the Constitution in 1789, members of the House of

Representatives have been elected every two years, with every seat being subject to election; Senators are elected for six-year terms—all seats being
directly elected by voters since 1914—with one-third of the seats being subject
to election every two years. The president is elected for a four-year term. The
significance of this becomes evident if we imagine this institutional framework operating in a polity in which the vast majority of the electorate are
fierce partisans who vote for the same party from one election to the next; voters are motivated to vote for a party rather than for particular candidates. We
may also imagine that in this political world there is a relatively small minority of voters that might switch its vote from one election to the next, and that
the share of the total vote that each of the two major parties can expect to
obtain in an election is very similar. In such a world, what would we expect to
happen in successive elections?

First, in a presidential election year we would expect the party that won the
presidential election also to win the House of Representatives; we have
assumed that voters vote a straight party ticket, so that the party that wins the
presidential election would also win the House election. Two years later, however, that House majority might be overturned by the opposing party if the
administration has (for whatever reason) become less popular. Given that
administrations cannot expect their popularity to be consistently high, we
might expect that divided government of this kind could be common. With
the Senate, though, we might expect there to be less responsiveness to shifts
in public opinion. Depending on which of the Senate seats were being contested, an otherwise unpopular administration might maintain its Senate
majority at a mid-term election; if the seats being contested that year happened to be disproportionately in areas of it main electoral strength, national
voting trends working against the party might have relatively little impact on
the composition of the Senate.

Secondly, given the possible unrepresentative character of the Senate seats
being contested in a particular year, it is more likely in the case of the Senate
that, in a presidential election year, the party winning the presidency may fail
to win the Senate. Consequently, even in an electoral universe of voters who
never split their tickets, it is possible that the majority party at a presidential
election might be faced with divided government in the Senate.

In fact, this imaginary world is not that dissimilar from the real world of
nineteenth-century politics. Parties penetrated American society very deeply
after the 1830s, there was close competition between the parties, and most
voters were strong partisans; split-ticket voting, at least at the highest levels
of the party ticket, was not common.[1] Not surprisingly, therefore, the data

---

[1] Split-ticket voting was more common for lower levels of office because of the difficulties
the parties had in controlling local party activists who were working in support of unofficial
party candidates. See Ware (2000).

cited earlier for the period 1836–96 demonstrate a pronounced tendency for divided government to occur in mid-term elections. In the case of the House, ten of the twelve instances of divided government emanated from mid-term elections—the two exceptions being 1848 and 1876. In the Senate a majority of the eight instances of divided government were the result of mid-term elections, but divided government after a presidential election was relatively more common than it was with the House—occurring in 1840, 1848, and 1884.

Before passing on, it is worth raising the question of why divided government involving the House should have happened at all in either 1848 or 1876. After all, in such a highly partisan world as the US in the nineteenth century it might be thought that finding even two instances of this form of divided government is unexpected. In fact, both instances are not as deviant as they appear at first sight.

Divided government arose after 1848 because, for much of the nineteenth century, congressional elections were not held at the same time as presidential elections. While some states held the former a few months before the November presidential contest, other states did not hold them until the spring or summer of the year following that contest. This arrangement was possible because a new Congress did not meet until thirteen months after the presidential election. If a new administration ran into trouble early on, it was possible that the president's party might fare so badly in the later congressional elections that the party would fail to control the Congress. This happened in 1848–9 when the incoming president, Zachary Taylor, alienated major factions of his Whig party over the distribution of patronage. Having won 57 per cent of the 141 House seats contested in 1848, the Whigs won only 30 per cent of the ninety contests held in 1849; this enabled the Democrats, with the aid of the Free Soil Party, to take over the Speakership (Holt, 1999: 455 and 470–2).

Moreover, 1876 is also an odd case in that there is a strong argument for reclassifying it as an election won by the Democrat, Samuel Tilden. This was the notorious 'stolen election' in which the election result hung in the balance; a post-election deal was struck between some Southern Democrats and the Republican party in which the former supported the Republican Rutherford B. Hayes. (In return, the Republican administration formally ended Reconstruction in the South.) But for this deal Tilden would have won, given the party votes cast, and it would have produced divided government in the Senate—a form of divided government that, we have seen, was not infrequent in the nineteenth century.

From 1836 to 1894 not only was divided government a regular occurrence but there were frequent shifts in control of Congress, especially the House. In a fifty-eight-year period the House majority changed on thirteen occasions, while control of the Senate switched between the parties seven times in those years. This contrasts with the era that followed—in the fifty years from 1896 to 1948 only four elections produced divided government, and there were only four switches of control of the chamber in the case of both House and Senate. Unified government became the norm. The main difference between the two periods lies in the much lower levels of competition between the parties. Whereas close contests characterized most of the nineteenth century—with the important exceptions of the years immediately following the Civil War, when many white Southerners were disenfranchised—only in the period 1910–16, and again in 1946, were the two parties evenly matched at the national level. One party dominated national politics. In 1896–1910, and also 1918–32 that party was the Republicans. After 1932 Franklin Roosevelt took advantage of the opportunity presented by the Republicans' collapse that year, in the wake of the Great Depression, to build a majority coalition for the Democrats.

The result of this change in the balance of electoral coalitions was that mid-term elections did not play the significant role in dividing government that they had in the nineteenth century. Nevertheless, this was not the only respect in which politics was now different, and this is important in relation to developments later in the twentieth century. There is considerable evidence that, early in the twentieth century, levels of ticket-splitting for higher offices—such as between president and Congress—started to increase (Reynolds and McCormick, 1986: 853). They did not reach anything like the levels they were to attain in the second half of the century, but they were rather higher than they had been in the nineteenth century. This had an impact on the election of 1916, which was by far the closest presidential contest in the years from 1896 to 1946, although there had been many much closer contests in the nineteenth century—including all four of the elections held in 1880–92. Yet 1916 produced a result that none of those four elections did—a president of one party and a House majority of the other. Indeed, as we have seen, only in 1848, and in the unusual circumstances of 1876, had this occurred at all in the earlier era.

From 1948 a new pattern emerged; the frequency of divided government increased greatly—it became even more common than it had been from 1836 to 1896—but this was not accompanied by frequent shifts in control of Congress. Many mid-term elections produced divided government, but majority parties in Congress rarely lost their majorities at these elections. In the House there were only two switches of control (1954 and 1994) in mid-term years, and with two occurring in presidential years (1948 and 1952) this meant that there were the same number as in the previous period (1896–48) that was characterized by low levels of party competition. Change of control was slightly more frequent in the Senate (six occasions in total), but, again only three mid-term elections (1954, 1986, and 1994) resulted in new majority parties. The distinctive feature of the contemporary era, therefore, is that the single most important institutional factor bringing about divided government in the nineteenth century—non-coinciding terms of office—plays a much more limited role now.

As we have seen, the high level of frequency of divided government today is associated with the fact that presidential elections often do not produce majorities in Congress for the party winning the presidency. More frequently presidents win office without carrying their congressional party with them than actually carrying them (seven out of thirteen instances). Nor is this the product, as it was between 1896 and 1948, of infrequent switches of party control in the presidency. The presidency changes hands between the parties now almost as frequently as it did in the years from 1836 to 1896—47 per cent of elections produced a change in party control from 1948 to 2000, compared with 53 per cent of elections in the first period. (The corresponding figure for the years 1896–1946 is 31 per cent.) Moreover, the seeming weakness of party in its ability to produce unified government at presidential elections appears to be growing; since 1952, there has been only one occasion on which a change of party control of the presidency has been accompanied by a similar change in party control of at least one chamber of Congress. In 1980 Republican Ronald Reagan was elected president while the Republicans regained control of the Senate.

That divided government in the second half of the twentieth century appears to have been very different from divided government in earlier periods prompts two related questions: why do parties no longer connect presidential candidates and congressional candidates in the ways that they used to, and why has the current pattern of divided government developed? To answer these questions involves raising matters of change in electoral behaviour as well as institutional and structural matters, and it is to the former that we must now turn.

### Electoral Factors

During the first half of the twentieth century voters continued to vote primarily on party lines: party identification remains the starting-point for understanding electoral behaviour until at least the 1950s. But, even at the beginning of the century, changes in party politics were starting to affect how potential voters were linked to parties and to candidates. Four main changes are relevant in understanding the transformation in divided government. First, as McGerr (1986) has shown, between the 1860s and the 1920s political campaigning moved from being a form of extensive mass participation to being an activity in which most potential voters were passive spectators. Secondly, between the end of the nineteenth century and 1950 there was a massive change in the structure of local government, so that party patronage no longer played the role that it had in helping to keep together a whole army of people who, in various ways, owed loyalty to their party. Thirdly, from

1896 onwards, presidential candidates in both parties started to play a much more active role in election campaigning than had been typical earlier in the nineteenth century; together with other factors, this was to create a cleavage between the president and his party that would lay the basis, in the 1930s, for Franklin Roosevelt to transform American government, not by moving towards a stronger form of party government but to a form of *administrative government* (see Milkis, 1993). Fourthly, a series of reforms in the states at the beginning of the century, including the direct primary, helped to weaken seriously party structures in the western states and to render party structures even less relevant in the one-party South. (In the rest of the country these reforms had relatively limited effects on party structures at the time.)

By the 1950s parties still played a rather similar role to the one they had in the nineteenth century, but they could play that role much less effectively. That was to change radically in the 1960s. The availability of new campaigning techniques, especially television, interacted with the direct primary to produce a style of politics below the level of the presidency that was much more candidate-dominated than it had been. As money became more important in politics, enabling candidates to purchase the new techniques, so the resources parties had available to them became relatively less important. At the presidential level, as the macro-economic management of America became the main criterion on which presidents would seek to be judged by voters, and would be judged by them, so parties became less relevant in the eyes of both politicians and voters (see Coleman, 1996). Consequently, there was a decoupling from parties at both the congressional and the presidential levels. Parties mattered less in both kinds of election campaign than they used to, and, with this, the old nineteenth-century form of divided government passed away. As an explanation of divided government, non-coinciding terms of office became far less important as a factor.

Nevertheless, the decline of American parties takes us only so far in accounting for the form of divided government evident today. Voters are less attached to parties than they used to be, and levels of ticket-splitting are much higher, but why does this produce so much divided government? One explanation might be that some voters favour divided government and vote accordingly to bring it about. There is absolutely no evidence to support this hypothesis. An alternative version, discussed by Robert Elgie in Chapter 1, is that voters have had contradictory preferences. They want lower taxation and smaller levels of government expenditures, and have voted for Republican presidential candidates to effect this, while at the same time they want the government programmes from which they benefit personally protected, and so they voted for Democratic members of Congress (Jacobson, 1996). Leaving aside the obvious problem that this account cannot explain how a Democratic president (Clinton) ended up with a Republican Congress for six of his eight years in office, there is relatively little evidence that this is what was driving those key sectors of the electorate who were Republican in presidential elections and Democratic in congressional elections.

One factor that takes us part of the way towards accounting for the contemporary form of divided government is the incumbency effect. In the nineteenth century not only was there close electoral competition in a number of states, but in many places public officials would serve only a term or two in office. An informal convention in many localities was that the holding of a public office should rotate between different places within a constituency. Such a convention was incompatible with political careerism based on elective office. However, in the last two decades of the nineteenth century, length of service in Congress started to increase and it continued to rise during the first half of the twentieth century (Polsby, 1968). Because party still mattered a great deal as a voting cue in these decades, a newly elected member of Congress from a marginal district could not expect to be able to hold on to a seat that had been won during a major swing of support to his or her party. Incumbency started to have an independent effect on his or her ability to hold the seat as he or she became more senior, for it was then that the member would have the leverage to deliver 'pork' (and other policies) for which there was demand in their district. The hierarchical nature of the congressional committee structure really started to benefit them after they had reached its middle rungs.

The decline of this hierarchical structure is tied up with the rise of candidate-centred campaigning in congressional elections. Divorced as they were becoming from their parties in electoral campaigning, newly elected members of Congress were much less willing to go along with internal structures in the chamber that gave them little. These members provided the main push for congressional reform in the early 1970s—reforms which decentralized power in their favour. The change in congressional tenure was remarkable. Many of the Democrats elected in unpromising districts in the landslide years of 1958 and 1964 lost their seats two and four years later; yet many of the 'freshman class' of 1974 were still in office in the 1980s. Over the years, members of House and Senate started to vote themselves resources that helped to boost their chances of re-election—staffers to assist with problems raised by constituents, allowances for airfares to travel back to their districts so as to 'keep in touch with them', and so on. In short, incumbency became a factor working for all members of Congress, not just for those in safe party districts.

The incumbency effect can help to explain, for example, why the Democrats held control of both House and Senate during the Nixon–Ford years and of the House in the Reagan years. However, it is evident that, by itself, it is an incomplete explanation. There are two obvious limitations. First, it might help explain why some Democrats elected in 1974 or 1976 were still in Congress in 1984, but it cannot explain longer term Democratic dominance, that is, why the

Democrats, having regained control of the House in 1954, were still controlling it after the 1992 elections. Secondly, it cannot account for major electoral revolts against Democratic incumbency in 1946 and 1994, and the absence of such a revolt in, say, 1978. We need to know why Democratic congressional control endured for so long, and why it could not be revived after 1994 as it was after 1946.

The explanation for this lies in the dynamics of coalitional politics and of party realignment in the US. Party realignment may not involve mere shifts in the voting behaviour of key groups of voters. It is also to be connected to the structure of incentives facing politicians: whether they stay in the same party, or switch to another party (possibly a new one) is affected by how they view their own prospects for political influence or advancement, by comparison with the alternatives available. For example, John Aldrich (1999) has described the dynamics of party change in the rise of the Republican party in the mid-1850s. In that case, those politicians who had continued to operate in the, now much smaller, Whig party, or who had participated in the American party, found a strong incentive to cast in their lot with the relatively new Republican party. Once the Republicans had made an electoral breakthrough in the western states in 1854, the incentive not to join them became much higher, and a rapid transformation of party politics was thereby effected in 1853–7. The situation was very different, though, with party realignment in the second half of the twentieth century.

The New Deal had created a majority party that contained many inconsistent elements; most especially it included white Southerners whose antagonism to the party nationally surfaced as early as 1948 when the Democratic party adopted a civil rights platform at the National Convention. However, for individual Southern politicians building a career for themselves, there would continue to be advantages for decades after this in pursuing that career within the Democratic party. It was the majority party in their states as well as in Congress, and with majority status in Congress came a number of benefits for the members in relation to their ability to defend constituency interests. That the Democrats did not look like losing their majority status in the House was one of the factors that helped to keep conservative white Southern politicians in the party for so long. Despite the fact that liberals and black politicians in the South were also using the Democratic party as their vehicle, individually white conservatives found little incentive to move to the Republican party. The result was that there was no equivalent to the rapid transformation of the party system evident in the 1850s. Instead, there was a slow process of Republican gains in the South until the 1990s. When the Republican party finally regained control of the Congress in 1994, the change in the incentive structure for Southern politicians enabled the process of realignment to be completed—nearly fifty years after it had started.

The separation of presidential from congressional electoral politics in the South helped to bring about an extended period of divided government. Democrats kept control of the House for forty years, with the incumbency effect often protecting them from one election to another. However, given that revolts against incumbent politicians do occur from time to time in American politics, there remains the question of why the Democrats should have enjoyed forty years without such a revolt against them. Of course, part of the answer is that divided government makes it less likely that just one party in Congress will suffer from voter discontent with the political establishment. Nevertheless, the Republicans were also hampered by the effects of Watergate at a time when they might have expected to have consolidated their position. In the 1970s voter disillusionment with Congress tended to be directed towards the Republicans, thereby helping to extend the duration of their minority status. The 'emerging Republican majority' that Kevin Phillips (1969) had predicted failed to materialize in congressional politics partly because the party was weakened at precisely the time when it might have hoped to take advantage of one of the periodic voter revolts against the political establishment. Had this not happened, it is quite possible that the process of Southern realignment would have been completed more quickly, and the pattern of Republican presidents and Democratic Congresses may well have been broken much earlier.

The division of government since 1994 is different from what preceded it in two respects other than the obvious one—namely, that it is the Republicans that now control both House and Senate. The first is that the process of Southern realignment has been completed, so that it is no longer the case that a majority in the legislature partly reflects a disincentive for legislators to shift to a (minority) party closer to their own ideology. Secondly, the House majorities have been smaller than at any point since 1956–8; even in the Senate, the 55–45 Republican majority in the 1998–2000 Congress was as small as any party majority since the 1958 mid-term elections; and the results of the 2000 election confirm the view that the US has entered a period of close electoral competition at the national level. This is significant in relation to a point to be discussed in the next section, namely, the problem of managing divided government in the contemporary era. It should be noted that the relationship between institutional and electoral forces in providing for divided government has been rather similar, though not quite the same, at the state level as at the federal level.

Divided government has been, and still is, a common phenomenon in the states. Indeed, the incidence of it has increased. In the 1950s V. O. Key observed that, in states that had genuine two-party competition, unified government occurred on about half the occasions possible. Key argued that two factors accounted for the high frequency of divided government in the states. One factor was non-coinciding terms of office, which we have seen was also important at the federal level. The other factor was not significant at the federal level—the malapportionment of legislative districts in many states. Key claimed that reapportionment of electoral districts would remove many instances of divided government, and he argued that only in about half a dozen instances in thirty-two states over a period of twenty-two years did voters appear deliberately to have brought about divided government (Key, 1956: 71).

However, court-ordered reapportionment from the early 1960s onwards did not have the consequences that Key had predicted. In an earlier study this author compared two-party competitive states in two rather similar periods, 1954–8 (before reapportionment) and 1970–4 (just after reapportionment), and found that the incidence of divided government was almost exactly the same in the two periods (Ware, 1985: 44–7). Key had not been incorrect in attributing divided government in the earlier period to malapportionment but the behaviour of both voters and candidates had changed in the mean time, so that straight ticket voting was now less frequently practised than it had been. These changes paralleled the change discussed earlier in relation to federal elections.

As two-party competition increased in the South so the total number of states experiencing divided government increased. In the forty-nine state legislatures between 1965 and 1976 the mean number of instances each year of divided government was twenty-one.[2] Between 1977 and 1988 the mean rose to twenty-five, and it increased again between 1989 and 2000 to twenty-eight.[3] In other words, in the most recent period, typically divided government has occurred on about 57 per cent of all occasions. The incidence of divided government at the state level is now very similar to the incidence at the federal level between 1948 and 2000 (62 per cent of all occasions).

THE MANAGEMENT OF DIVIDED GOVERNMENT IN THE US

The state in America did so little before the New Deal that managing divided government was a much less serious problem than it was to become later. Like two dogs divided by a chain-link fence, there was a limit to the harm that president and Congress could do to each other. There were disputes over the distribution of patronage, so that, for example, before the Civil War even Supreme Court justices might find their nominations had been blocked for partisan reasons. Some inter-branch disputes did have more serious consequences for American public policy—possibly the best example of this was the Republican Senate's refusal to back Democratic President Woodrow

---

[2] Nebraska's unicameral legislature is elected on a non-partisan ballot.
[3] Data recalculated from Jewell and Morehouse (2000: 222).

Wilson's proposal that the US participate in the League of Nations. However, the massive expansion of government activity from the New Deal onwards meant that managing relations between the two branches became far more important than it had been earlier.

Some political scientists, notably Mayhew (1991), have emphasized the point that as much substantive legislation appears to have been passed under divided government as under unified government. Nevertheless, it is only in particular kinds of circumstances, that the relationship between the two branches under divided government can be described as being one of constructive engagement.

The first period of divided government since the New Deal occurred in 1947–8 when a Republican Congress, often with Southern Democrat support, passed a number of major bills—including the Taft–Hartley labour relations bill—that were opposed by President Truman. Truman knew that he lacked the votes to sustain his presidential vetoes in many cases, and his strategy was not to engage in a 'guerrilla fight' against the legislation, but to stand back, and then use the Republican legislative record against the party in the 1948 presidential election. The tactic, which was entirely successful in re-electing Truman and regaining control of Congress for the Democrats, differed from the one Bill Clinton was to deploy in 1995–6, but in neither period were relations between the parties other than antagonistic.

The situation from 1955 to 1960 was rather different, in that Republican Dwight Eisenhower had a limited legislative agenda of his own and had not been a partisan politician prior to his nomination in 1952. Bipartisan co-operation was also possible in this era because of the skill of the Democratic leaders in the two chambers, Sam Rayburn and Lyndon Johnson. Both Texans, they led from the centre, complementing Eisenhower's restricted vision of the role of the modern presidency; for that reason this period can be regarded as something of a 'golden age' of divided government. It was a period of cross-party coalition-building in Congress under majority party leaders who were prepared to compromise in order to get legislation enacted.

The same cannot be said of the Nixon years. Nixon failed to pass much of his legislative agenda, including welfare reform, through Congress in 1969 and 1970 and he then turned to other means to achieve his goals. In foreign affairs he by-passed Congress, stretching presidential prerogatives beyond their usual limits in matters such as the secret bombing of Cambodia. In domestic policy he used the (constitutionally dubious) impoundment of funds to achieve ends that he could not achieve otherwise in view of the Democratic-controlled Congress's very different policy agenda. The Nixon resignation in 1974 brought to office a president, Gerald Ford, who was determined to rebuild congressional–presidential relations, but even his policy agenda was radically different from that of the Democratic Congress. His term of office saw an extensive use of presidential vetoes of legislation.

Somewhat more constructive relations between the president and Congress were evident from 1980 to 1986, but two factors contributed to this. On the one hand, the Republicans controlled the Senate as well as the presidency. On some major legislation—for example, tax reform in 1986—the Senate could act as an important bridge between the Democratic House and President Reagan, thereby preventing legislation from being mired in controversy. On the other hand, substantial Democratic losses in the House in 1980 (thirty-four seats, meant that a number of Southern and border-state conservative Democrats were less willing to submit to the pressure of their party leadership than they might otherwise have been, and on a number of key votes in 1981 and 1982 they could be recruited to vote with the Republican minority.

The remaining two years of the Reagan administration, the four years of the Bush administration, and the Clinton administration all saw a far more conflictual relationship develop between the branches. Especially because of the constraints on public expenditures imposed by the budget deficits, it became much less possible to reconcile the differing policy agendas of president and Congress. There were partial shutdowns of the federal government, following disputes over the federal budget, under both Bush (1990) and Clinton (1995). Divided government became much more a matter of confrontation between the president and the party leaderships in the Congress; in many ways, it resembles the conflicts of 1947 and 1948 but on a more intense level. Nevertheless, confrontation did ebb and flow—for example, the budget shutdown of 1995 was followed by a more co-operative mode of interaction between president and Congress in the election year of 1996. However, at least until the conclusion of the impeachment proceedings against Bill Clinton, the trend was towards a ratcheting up of conflict between the two branches.

In some respects, therefore, the Clinton impeachment proceedings can be understood as the culmination of a long-term movement towards partisan warfare operating through divided government. The vote in the House to impeach Clinton was split on strongly partisan lines, and represented a major shift from the bipartisan approach to divided government evident in the 1950s. Furthermore, associated with this much greater party-based hostility between president and Congress, there has been a decline of comity within Congress itself (Uslaner, 1993). Since the early to mid-1980s the House has become a badly divided body, with much worse personal relations between its members. Members of opposite political parties in the House dislike each other in a way that was not typical of the 1950s, nor even of the 1970s. This has tended to 'raise the stakes' in disagreements between the White House and the congressional majority party on policy issues. Quite simply, governing has become that much more difficult.

It is important to ask whether the aftermath of the failed attempt at impeachment is likely to produce a change in both institutions to effect more constructive presidential–congressional relations. For example, should the choice of Dennis Hastert as the Speaker (succeeding Newt Gingrich) be seen as an attempt by the House Republicans to move towards a less confrontational style? Undoubtedly it should, but, as noted earlier, the road to the intense form of inter-branch confrontation of the mid–late 1990s was not one of continually escalating conflict, for, as in 1996, there were periods when it suited both sides to attempt conciliation. Perhaps the immediate post-impeachment period might best be interpreted as just one of these interludes. Obviously, it is difficult to predict how congressional–presidential relations will develop in the longer run under divided government. On the one side, it could be argued that the likely sobering effect of the impeachment experience, together with the elimination of the federal budget deficit, may help to reduce the drive to exploit partisan advantage through presidential–congressional confrontation. On the other side, it could be argued that many of the factors that gave rise to this confrontation—including the greater concentration of powers in the hands of House party leaders after the 1970s—will still be present under future presidents.

For all the arguments to the effect that under divided government major pieces of legislation can still be enacted, it remains the case that the division of government under America's system of separated powers makes governing a likely conflictual experience. Only in three periods since the New Deal has divided government worked reasonably well. First was under Eisenhower, when there was a president who had a restricted policy agenda of his own. Secondly, relations between Gerald Ford and the Congress were reasonably amicable, partly because both sides wished to display that American government could still work after the Nixon years, but these were exceptional circumstances. Thirdly, in the first six years of the Reagan administration, the impact of divided government was reduced both by the president's party regaining control of the Senate in 1980 and also by the scale of his defeat of incumbent Jimmy Carter in 1980. In those circumstances it was less easy for the Democrats to use their control of the House in ways that would provoke the highest levels of inter-branch antagonism. With the exception of these three instances, divided government has tended to produce confrontation. If we exclude the exceptional case of Ford, and the Reagan experience of having to deal with only one chamber controlled by the opposition, we are left facing the conclusion that divided government tends to produce confrontation, unless the president has limited public policy objectives. The experience of Truman (1947–8), Nixon (1969–74), Reagan (1987–8), Bush (1989–92), and Clinton (from 1995) suggests that there is an inherent tension between the separation of powers and party power when government is divided.

One of the main problems is that the two institutions (the president and Congress) are too evenly matched. Unlike France under *cohabitation*, when the president's role is reduced significantly by comparison with unified government and where a form of constructive engagement between the two sides is possible, in the US the roles of the two institutions do not change radically. In a political system that was less firmly established, or in one that was not federal, it is likely that the result of these regular periods of conflict would have been the destabilizing of the regime. As it is, American government goes on as it has always gone on—leading some to claim, as they did after the Clinton impeachment proceedings finished, that all this showed was that the 'system had worked'. However, there has still been a serious cost to the persistent conflict generated by divided government, and that has been a dramatic decline in public confidence in America's political institutions. Opinion polls reveal a consistent downward shift in confidence since the 1960s—a shift that coincided with an era dominated by confrontation between the two branches of government under divided government.

Overall, we must conclude that divided government in the post-New Deal era has added significantly to the difficulty of governing a country that was already difficult to govern—partly because of its size and diversity, and partly because of the dispersion of political power created by the Constitution. Parties, which were so important in helping to link separated institutions, have generally had a much more negative effect on the governing process in periods of divided government since 1946. Changes in the parties themselves, and especially the weakening of both the conservative southern wing of the Democratic party and the liberal north-eastern wing of the Republican party, has led to greater antagonism between them in Congress. The cross-party alliances that were possible in the 1950s have become less easy to create since the 1970s, and parties are now not so much vehicles that can help to create majority coalitions in support of particular public policies, as vehicles used in support of either presidential or congressional party leaderships. It is far from clear that anything can prevent a repetition of the discord seen in recent decades, in five, ten, or twenty years' time. However, might the experience of divided government in the states shed light on the problems facing the federal government?

Generalizing about the management of divided government in the states is difficult because of considerable variations in their institutional arrangements. In most states the governor, unlike the US president, is not the only directly elected executive officer. Various positions (such as state treasurer) are directly elected, and their executive responsibilities can intrude on the areas of autonomy for a governor within the executive branch. On the other hand, many states have granted their governors a form of line-item veto that, in effect, gives them considerably more power over the state legislatures than the similar veto only recently granted to the president (1996). Moreover, arrangements within the legislatures can weaken the potential for co-ordinated party action; for example, some states provide for the most senior members of the chamber, irrespective of party, to hold certain key positions (such as chairs of legislative committees). Finally, the resources and power available to the majority leader in a chamber may be so extensive that he or she might be able to hold on to office even when the party has lost its majority at an election. Willie Brown, the Speaker of the California State Assembly, was able to do just that after the 1994 elections. As Richardson (1996: 382) notes: 'Willie Brown and his Democratic caucus . . . succeeded for a solid year at keeping the Republican leaders from controlling the Assembly. His experience and intelligence overwhelmed the Republican opponents in 1995, keeping them constantly off guard and in chaos.' In particular circumstances a few Republicans found it to their advantage to co-operate with Brown, even though they did not change parties, and Brown was able to use this to prevent the Republican leadership from actually controlling the chamber. Brown's ability in keeping the nominal majority at bay reflected also the long history of weak party organization and cohesion in California: it was one of the states in which a form of candidate-centred politics had developed during the first two decades of the twentieth century.

Given this great variation between the states, comparing the experience of divided government in the states with that at the federal level is complex. Nevertheless, there are two factors which tend to facilitate a less confrontational relationship between the two branches of government at the state level. The first factor is that the persons who become state governors have often been central actors in state politics for some years, and thus they have long-established relationships with legislative leaders, and they know how it might be possible to work with them under divided government. Correspondingly, the state legislative leaders will usually know both the opportunities and difficulties in working with a new governor of the opposing party. Of course, exceptions can be cited, but in many instances establishing gubernatorial–legislative relations usually involves building on existing relationships, and that makes management of divided government easier. By contrast, most presidents have had limited experience in Congress, or in working closely with members of Congress. Of the presidents since Harry Truman, only Johnson and Ford had served for a long period in Congress before coming into office. Eisenhower, Carter, Reagan, and Clinton had never been elected to Congress; Kennedy, Nixon, and Bush had only relatively short service in Congress, and none of them had been influential members of the legislature, although both Nixon and Bush did have the benefit of eight years as vice-president, thereby providing them with some links to the Congress when they entered the White House.

To the extent that knowledge of the 'other side' helps both a chief executive and a legislative majority leader, it is evident that divided government is likely to be more difficult to manage at the federal than at the state level. In some states there is a second factor at work. Several state constitutions have not imposed term limits on the governor. Knowing that the same person may be governor in, say, ten years' time affects the strategy of legislative leaders.

There is potentially a much higher cost to sustained opposition to an incumbent governor. Indeed, the prospect of long-term divided government is not just a theoretical possibility at the state level. For example, the Republican party controlled at least one chamber of the Colorado state legislature, and usually both, every year from 1974 to 1998, but during that entire period two Democrats were governors—first Richard Lamm and then Roy Romer, each of whom served three terms. In these circumstances neither the governor nor the majority leaderships in the state legislature could afford to embark on too many destructive confrontations with each other. Part of the problem in realizing inter-branch co-operation at the federal level is that, in no more than eight years, presidents are seeking to build a record of achievement by which they will be remembered, while congressional leaders know precisely the maximum period with which they must deal with a particular incumbent.

The evidence from the states suggests that divided government can work reasonably well in a system of separated powers, and, certainly, the difficult experience at the federal level is not repeated in all the states. However, at the very least, massive institutional reforms would be required to make it more likely for divided government to work more constructively at the federal level as it tends to at the state level; these reforms would include repealing the 22nd Amendment to the Constitution, and radical reform of the parties' presidential nominating procedures to increase the likelihood that senior members of Congress would become presidential nominees. The likelihood of anything like this happening, of course, is tiny, so that the problems of presidential–congressional relations under divided government are likely to continue.

## CONCLUSIONS

Divided government in the US has been the prevalent political arrangement in recent decades, at both the federal and state level. To what extent can any failings in the workings of modern American government be attributed to divided government? One possible line of argument is that, if there is such a flaw, it lies in the separation of powers itself, and not in divided government. That is, tension between the branches is manifest irrespective of whether different parties control Congress and the presidency. Evidence for this argument can be found in the inability of the Carter administration to pass major legislation (including energy and welfare reforms) and of the Clinton administration to pass legislation on health care reform in 1994. Democratic control of Congress did not prevent Democratic presidents from experiencing legislative failure on the bills to which they had given the highest priority. Furthermore, the way in which the Senate is organized, emphasizing the role of the individual senator, means that, unless the majority party has at least sixty of the hundred seats, the minority party is in a strong position to force compromises on legislative proposals. Consequently, even unified government may be insufficient to ensure that a president can enact his policy agenda in the form that he wants.

Convincing though these arguments are, they do not take into account the fact that, in many instances of divided government at the federal level, there have not been mere obstacles to the initiation of radical policy reforms, but often also overt conflict between the two branches that has its origins in partisan politics. The partisan dimension evident under divided government converts the tension inherent between the two branches of government in the separation of powers into more overt conflict. Furthermore, several factors—including both the term limiting of the president and the fact that most presidents have had rather limited personal experience of Congress—have meant that the problems of divided government often appear more severe at the federal level than at the state level. It is difficult to see how the situation might be improved during the twenty-first century. Divided government may well persist, but anything short of the most radical kind of institutional reform is unlikely to reduce the potential for inter-branch confrontations under divided government. Since the prospects for that kind of reform are slim, the problems associated with divided government will surely persist well into this century.

# 3

# Squaring Off: Executives and Legislatures in Ecuador

## Monica Barczak

Laver and Shepsle note that the constitutional separation between the executive and the legislature is 'quintessentially American' (1991: 250). The statement is true in the broadest sense—political regimes throughout much of the Americas follow the US model of presidentialism. Indeed, the two cases of presidentialism outside the US included in this volume come from Latin America. Drawing from the US experience, one can reasonably ask whether, and to what degree, presidential regimes elsewhere exhibit characteristics of divided government. As this chapter shows, divided government, like presidentialism, is not unique to the United States.

It is the task of this chapter to discuss divided government in Ecuador. I will argue that divided government is virtually the norm in Ecuador and has been since the demise of the last military regime in 1979. Divided government can appear in different forms, but typically involves the lack of any majority in the single house of the legislature. I point to historical experience and political institutions, particularly electoral rules, as the main causes of divided government in Ecuador. As for managing divided government, I suggest that 'muddling through' more appropriately describes executive–legislative relations. The president does have a few tools, however, which allow him to 'go it alone'. These include the ability to issue decrees of urgency as well as convoke public referendums when matters become tied up in the legislature. The legislature, for its part, may express its displeasure with the executive by submitting cabinet members or the president himself to intense scrutiny that may lead to impeachment. Finally, the president may take an ad hoc approach to coalition-building, depending on the legislation at hand.

## THE BACKGROUND TO POLITICS IN ECUADOR
### The Historical Context

Ecuador attained its independence from Spain in 1822, but its politics for almost the next century were dominated by military or civilian *caudillos* (strongmen) rather than organized political parties. The country was split roughly along the lines of religion and region. The Sierra, consisting of inland provinces where economic power centred on the haciendas, became the centre of the Conservative party. The Conservatives favoured a large role for the Church in political and social life. The coastal provinces, on the other hand, developed a secular politics and commercially based economics that triumphed with the 'Liberal Revolution' in 1895.

As the twentieth century began, regional polarization intensified as the emerging bourgeoisie, consisting largely of exporters and financiers and represented by the Liberal party, grew even stronger on the coast. Other political parties began to form in a more organized manner, but the electorate remained tremendously restricted. According to the earliest data available, registered voters represented less than 10 per cent of the population and actual voters less than 5 per cent well into the 1930s (Juárez and Navas, 1993).

Politically, the first half of the twentieth century in Ecuador is best described as a period of great instability. Between 1925 and 1948 the executive changed hands twenty-three times. Military *coups d'état* occurred in 1925 and 1937 (and later, in 1963 and 1972). Populism emerged as an important element on the political landscape as well. José María Velasco Ibarra, a populist leader whose influence spanned four decades, occupied the presidency for the first time in 1933.[1] He would hold that position four additional times, finishing a full term only once. The Velasco Ibarra phenomenon exemplified the weakness of political parties during the first seven decades of the twentieth century. Despite the organization of Liberal and Conservative parties, and eventually their offshoots, political conflict in Ecuador was generally waged on a personal level. This was due partly to the fact that restricted suffrage rights excluded most of the masses from politics, but also because people like Velasco Ibarra amassed considerable political might without institutionalizing parties or forging connections to groups in society (Conaghan, 1994).

---

[1] It is important to note, however, that populism in Ecuador did not look much like the Perón-style populism of Argentina or the Vargas-style populism of Brazil in the 1940s and 1950s. Under Perón and Vargas, populism was an urban phenomenon. These leaders sought support of workers and poor urban dwellers, often combining nationalist rhetoric into their appeals. Velasco Ibarra, in contrast, maintained ties with traditional élites, even while employing anti-oligarchic rhetoric (Quintero, 1980). Moreover, populism in Latin America differs from what was known as populism in the US, where it was a rural movement.

While many new parties formed between 1930 and 1970, middle and lower class groups remained largely excluded from political competition. Parties failed to develop roots in corporate groups and these operated through independent interest groups instead. Literacy requirements for voting, in effect until 1978, prohibited many from participating in politics. Indeed, as late as 1960 only 23.4 per cent of the population was registered to vote, and only 17.8 per cent actually voted (Juárez and Navas, 1993). Moreover, the large indigenous population remained outside of the formal political arena, as a result of both illiteracy and lack of broad-based organization.

The key point is that during these decades much of the population remained disconnected from the operations of political parties. People either pursued their political interests through other channels, or they did not have the means to pursue them at all. This experience severely delayed, if not outright impeded, the formation of ideologically based, programmatic parties that could clearly occupy roles of party in government, party of the opposition, or coalition partner. Moreover, citizens lacked the opportunity to form lifelong allegiances to parties for whom they might vote election after election.

On the eve of the 1972 military *coup*, the ubiquitous populist Velasco Ibarra occupied the presidential palace. He had been elected in 1968, but in June of 1970 declared his government a 'civilian dictatorship' after an extreme battle with his opponents in the legislature. This *coup* ushered in the longest period of military rule in Ecuador's history. The military junta, suspicious of politicians, banned political parties but allowed corporate groups and interest groups to continue functioning. This decision exacerbated the gap between citizens and parties while increasing ties between citizens and interest groups. Planning for a return to civilian rule began in 1976, and by 1978 a new constitution had been drafted and approved in a popular referendum.

The new constitution made a serious attempt to force the institutionalization of Ecuadorian politics and the party system. Some scholars mark 1978 as the year that Ecuador finally developed a 'modern' party system (Verdesoto, 1991; Conaghan, 1995). In understanding why divided government so dominates Ecuadorian politics, one must surely bear in mind the historical lack of connection between parties and citizens. Indeed, the most important factors in the Laver and Shepsle (1991) model of divided government are political parties and political institutions, neither of which developed in Ecuador in the way that they did in the United States. For this reason, most of this chapter will be concerned with the period after the 1978 Constitution.[2]

---

[2] Another problem with analysing the period before 1978 is lack of data on the party composition of the legislature. In one widely used source of electoral data in Latin America, Dieter Nohlen's *Enciclopedia Electoral Latinoamericana y del Caribe*, the Ecuador chapter has patchy data on voting returns, 1947–70. For example, data for the elections of 1956, 1960, 1968, and 1970 are missing, while data for the 1958 election only identify parties by a number or letter instead of by party name. No data are reported for the seat distribution in the

## Political Institutions in Ecuador

Before addressing the forms divided government takes in Ecuador, it is useful to understand the institutional layout and some of its variations over time. While Ecuador mirrors the US in the use of a presidential regime, it differs in other respects, creating different kinds of divided government.

The Constitution of 1978 was the nation's eighteenth national charter. Significant institutional changes in the document, compared to the previous constitution, included collapsing the previously bicameral legislature into a unicameral body, and enfranchising illiterates for the first time. Politicians enacted major constitutional reforms in 1984 and 1995. The latter set of reforms came as a result of a series of two popular referendums convoked by the president. An elected constituent assembly approved a new constitution in 1998.

With so many constitutions and reforms, it is not surprising to find that rules pertaining to the presidency have taken various forms over time. For example, the president's term length has generally been four years, although eight-, six-, and five-year terms have also been tried. The Constitution of 1978 originally stipulated a five-year term, to be served concurrently with legislators holding five-year terms. Currently, however, presidents hold office for four years.

Only the Constitution of 1869 allowed a president to run for immediate re-election. Others mandated a president to wait one or two terms before running again, while both the 1929 and the 1978 Constitution prohibited any kind of re-election. As a result of reforms enacted in 1996, however, sitting presidents may run for (re)-election after waiting out one term. From 1861 until the 1972 *coup*, citizens elected presidents directly by a plurality vote. The 1978 Constitution introduced a majority run-off presidential formula to Ecuador.[3] The president and vice-president run on the same ticket, but they

legislature during this period. The data on both vote and seat shares are much more reliable and consistent between 1978 and 1990. The chapter's authors report their original source for data was the Supreme Electoral Tribunal of Ecuador (Juárez and Navas, 1993). Indeed, one of the Tribunal's publications presents a table of presidential candidates and the number of votes received by each. In the column that would normally be titled 'Party', however (as in the party affiliation of the candidate), appears instead the word 'Tendency' (*tendencia*). Examples of such tendencies are liberal, *conservador*, *socialista*, and even *velasquismo*. The term 'Party' is not used consistently to identify an organized entity until 1978 (TSE, 1989: i). In terms of the timing of the transition, the referendum on the Constitution, the first round of the presidential election, and local elections were held on 16 July 1978. The second round was held concurrently with elections for the national legislature, on 29 Apr. 1979.

[3] Originally, the rules stated that if no ticket received a vote share of 50% + 1, a second round of competition between the top two finishers would determine the winner. The 1998 Constitution altered that formula, allowing tickets to win with only 40% of the vote, provided they beat the second-place ticket by 10 percentage points.

do not have to be from the same party. The Constitution grants the president sole authority to name his cabinet as he sees fit.

The rules governing the composition of the Ecuadorian legislature have varied over time. The legislature typically has been comprised of two houses, although the Constitutions of 1830, 1851, 1945, 1978, and 1998 all specified unicameral legislatures. The 1945 and 1978 documents distinguished between two kinds of deputies (representatives) in the unicameral house. The 1945 charter classified deputies as either provincial (representing provinces) or functional (representing professional or social groups). The 1978 charter outlined a two-tier legislature, with a small group of 'national deputies', elected from the nation-at-large, and a larger group of 'provincial deputies', elected to represent the provinces. The number of representatives allotted a province (similar to a state) depends on the province's population. Since 1996, every province has been guaranteed at least two deputies. Each province, then, comprises a multi-member electoral district. While the Constitution originally called for national and provincial deputies to hold office for five years, the 1984 reforms shortened the term length of the former to four years and the latter to two years. With a presidential term length of four years, Ecuadorian presidents, like their US counterparts, faced typically punishing mid-term elections. The new 1998 Constitution alleviated this problem by eliminating the national deputies, and setting the term length for all deputies at four years.[4]

The Largest-Remainders Hare formula converts votes into assembly seats. The use of proportional representation formulas, such as the LR-Hare, is generally thought to be associated with European parliamentary systems (Laver and Shepsle, 1991: 251), but they are actually quite common in the presidential systems of Latin America.[5] Proportional representation formulas, as has been well established, tend to facilitate the formation of multi-party systems more frequently than do single-member plurality systems. This has most assuredly been the case in Ecuador, where between fifteen and twenty-two parties commonly contest elections. The combination of presidentialism and extreme multi-partism contributes heavily to the pervasiveness of divided government in Ecuadorian politics.

Electoral rules have permitted deputies to run for immediate re-election, apart from the 1978 Constitution, which, until 1996, required them to wait a term before running again. Deputies currently may run for immediate, indefinite re-election. With the exception of the founding elections, held in 1978 and 1979, legislative elections have been scheduled concurrently with the

---

[4] This provision of the 1998 Constitution will not actually take effect until the 2002 election. The legislature at the time of this writing contained 101 provincial deputies and twenty national deputies, with every member elected for a four-and-a-half-year term.

[5] See Jones (1995) for detailed information on regime types and electoral formulas in the Americas.

first round of the presidential election. Candidate lists have been closed and blocked (meaning voters cannot select which candidate/s they prefer from the list, nor can the order of candidates be altered), although the 1998 Constitution will allow voters to select individual candidates from the same list or across lists beginning in 2002. Since 1996 independent candidates have been permitted to run for office, whereas prior to that year only political parties could place candidates on the ballot. The Supreme Electoral Tribunal assigns each party an identification number upon its attaining legal recognition. This number does not change until the party loses legal recognition. Parties appear on the ballot in numerical order.[6]

Several other constitutional provisions merit attention, since they contribute to the tension between the legislature and executive. On the legislative side, deputies have the power to submit cabinet ministers to a *juicio político*, or interpellation. This process targets ministers for questioning periods, frequently backed with the threat of impeachment. Because a vote of impeachment carries with it the punishment of not being able to hold public office for almost two years, ministers who fear they would not survive the vote have a clear incentive to step down if such an action is pending. High ministerial turnover, not to mention time spent in session accusing and questioning ministers rather than passing legislation, antagonizes relations between the executive and legislative branches. As I show in a later section, deputies have constantly taken advantage of this provision. While they may not always succeed in removing ministers, the process itself occupies the president's time (if he decides to defend his cabinet) and sends him a hostile message.

On the executive side, a president has several ways by which he can virtually leave the legislature out of the law-making loop. First, the president may issue an 'urgent' economic decree. This means the assembly has a very limited time in which to consider the legislation, and if they fail to do so, the president can proclaim the decree as law. Second, a president may call popular referendums on constitutional reforms and matters deemed of extreme importance. Results are binding with the approval of an absolute majority of those who voted. Both of these tools diminish the role of the legislature. A president who uses them risks provoking irritation and *juicios políticos*.

## THE FREQUENCY AND FORM OF DIVIDED GOVERNMENT IN ECUADOR

Divided government has been endemic to Ecuador. In this section I use the arithmetic definition of divided government outlined in Chapter 1 to speak more precisely about the form and frequency of divided government in

---

[6] e.g., the Social Christian Party is identified by the number 6, and it always appears in the sixth position on the ballot.

Ecuador. Divided government in presidential regimes is manifest when either a party or parties opposed to the president hold a majority of seats in at least one working house or when there is no majority in at least one working house. Because Ecuador has a unicameral legislature, the executive's party would need only a majority in that single chamber to avoid divided government.

While institutions prohibit the emergence of one form of divided government, then, rules in Ecuador create the opportunity for a kind of divided government not seen in the US, a parliamentary-style division, in that the president and vice-president may represent two different parties. In this case, the executive is akin to a coalition executive seen often in parliamentary systems. When this coalition fails to command a majority in the house in Ecuador, that must be counted as an instance of divided government.

Given political institutions in Ecuador, then, there are four possible scenarios: (1) unified government (the president's party controls a majority in the legislature); (2) parliamentary-style divided government (the coalition of the president's party and vice-president's party fail to command a majority in the legislature); (3) a party (or parties) opposed to the president has (have) a majority in the legislature; and (4) no majority in the legislature. Situations 1 and 3 assume a president and vice-president of the same party.

The other important variable to consider is the party system, which is a highly fragmented. In the post-1978 period, at least twelve parties have competed in each legislative election. Until 1996, when the legislature numbered between sixty-nine and eighty-two, seats were distributed across at least ten parties. While it is not the purpose of this chapter to explain why so many parties survive in Ecuador, a brief list of important factors would include: proportional representation; a majority run-off presidential formula with legislative elections held in the first round; the continued salience of regional divisions; the fact that until 1996 only parties could put candidates on the ballot; and the history of personal grievances among political élite reverberating in the party system.[7] These points will be discussed in more detail in the following section.

Returning to the four scenarios listed above, what can election results tell us about unified and divided government in Ecuador? Let us consider unified government first. Electoral return data show that it is rare for a president's party to hold a majority of seats in the legislature. While it is difficult to match the results of legislative and presidential elections for individual parties in elections prior to 1978 (see n. 2), available data do indicate that no individual party won more than a 35 per cent vote share between 1947 and 1970 (Juárez and Navas, 1993). Given these results, it is unlikely that any elected president

---

[7] See Lijphart (1990, 1994) on the effects of proportional representation. See Jones (1995) and Shugart and Carey (1992) for discussions of the majority run-off formula. See Conaghan (1994, 1995) on the effects of no independent candidates and personal grievances.

enjoyed a majority in the legislature, although it is possible that a coalition of parties in opposition to the president combined to form a majority.[8] Data limitations make it impossible to confirm seat shares.

Since 1978, data show that this trend continued—no single party has held a majority in the legislature. Table 3.1 reports the vote shares of winning presidential tickets in the first- and second-round elections, along with the vote share of the presidents' parties and the parties that supported the pair *in the first round*. Certainly if one is looking for unified government, one can only consider the proportion of the legislators that share the president's party affiliation. Since each party's seat share is determined in the first round of voting, under the provisions of the arithmetic definition of divided government it makes the most sense to evaluate the eventual president's legislative bloc at this point, before the president has even been chosen. (This becomes more complicated when we begin to classify different types of divided government.) It should be noted that the legislative seat shares appearing in the table were recorded at election time—in most instances these figures changed during the president's term, as a result of party defections or mid-term elections.

According to Table 3.1, Ecuador has not experienced a single period of pure unified government in the post-1978 period. Indeed, divided government is the norm in Ecuador. So what form does divided government take? One possibility is what I have dubbed the parliamentary-style form, where the president and vice-president represent two distinct parties but still fail to hold a legislative majority. Table 3.1 shows that winning presidential tickets rarely contain two individuals from the same party.[9] Despite this, the two parties tend not to have a majority in the legislature. Ecuador most frequently experiences a similar kind of divided government to parliamentary regimes, a 'coalition government' that fails to command a majority in the single house.

A president (or coalition) may in fact enjoy a majority of support in the legislature, if the parties that support the winning ticket in the second round of competition continue to ally with the executive once in office. In other words, once parties' presidential candidates fail to advance to the second round, they typically, although not always, endorse one of the remaining tickets. These alliances tend to be short-lived, however, since a president, once elected, does not need to maintain the 'confidence' of the legislators in the way a prime minister in a parliamentary system must. Legislative support in a parliamentary system can be 'guaranteed' via the distribution of cabinet portfolios. This has not been the case in Ecuador, although there is nothing precluding presidents from doing it.

---

[8] Electoral rules may have converted a 35% vote share into a majority of legislative seats.

[9] When the presidential and the vice-presidential candidate represent two different parties, the party of the latter has not, at least so far, also run a presidential candidate.

TABLE 3.1. *Presidential elections in Ecuador, 1979–1998*

|  | Winners (Party) | First round[a] | Second round | Total party support in legislature (% of seats)[b] |
|---|---|---|---|---|
| **1979** |  |  |  |  |
| President | Roldós (CFP) | 27.7 | 68.5 | 42.0 |
| Vice-Pres. | Hurtado (DP) |  |  |  |
| **1984** |  |  |  |  |
| President | Febres (PSC) | 27.7 | 68.5 | 22.5 |
| Vice-Pres. | Peñaherrera (PLRE, supported by PCE, PNR) |  |  |  |
| **1988** |  |  |  |  |
| President | Borja (ID) | 24.4 | 54.0 | 42.2 |
| Vice-Pres. | Parodi (ID) |  |  |  |
| **1992** |  |  |  |  |
| President | Durán (PUR) | 31.9 | 57.3 | 22.1 |
| Vice-Pres. | Dahík (PCE) |  |  |  |
| **1996** |  |  |  |  |
| President | Bucaram (PRE) | 26.3 | 54.3 | 26.8 |
| Vice-Pres. | Arteage (FRA) |  |  |  |
| **1998** |  |  |  |  |
| President | Mahuad (DP) | 35.3 | 51.3 | 28.5 |
| Vice-Pres. | G. Noboa (DP) |  |  |  |

[a] The figures for first and second-round support refer to the percentage of the vote won by the presidential/vice-presidential ticket in each case.

[b] Support can change if deputies leave their parties or as a result of mid-term elections

*Key*: DP; Popular Democracy; FRA; Radical Alfarist Front; ID: Democratic Left; PCE: Ecuadorian Conservative party; PLRE: Ecuadorian Radical Liberal party; PNR: Nationalist Revolutionary party; PRE: Ecuadorian Roldósist party; PSC: Social Christian party; PUR: United Republican party.

There are two other possible scenarios to consider: the president and vice-president represent the same party and an opposition party (or parties) holds (hold) a majority in the legislature; or the legislature lacks a majority altogether. Since Ecuador has a multi-party system rather than a two-party system, it certainly would not be valid to assume that, when the president's party lacked a majority, the opposition enjoyed one, as is typically true of the US.

In the immediate aftermath of elections, whether the president and vice-president represent the same party or not, the most common result in Ecuador is for the legislature to lack any kind of formally constituted majority. This is particularly true because of the electoral timing, described above, which encourages parties to run their own presidential candidates in the first round. After the first round, parties may be concerned with electing one of the remaining tickets, or with preventing one of the remaining tickets from being elected, or be indifferent. After the president is elected, parties' interests may shift, altering their relationships. In other words, the fluid nature of partisan politics and alliance or coalition formation in Ecuador pushes analysis of divided government there into the behavioural realm.

One other important element of Ecuadorian politics reinforces this conclusion, and it pertains to intra-party dynamics (Laver, 1999). Hopefully it has become clear how inter-party conflict, intensified due to the high number of political parties, contributes to divided government in Ecuador. We cannot assume, however, that parties will behave as coherent entities, particularly where parties are as weak as they are in Ecuador. Under such conditions, party members may vote against their party line and alter the arithmetic dynamic. In Ecuador, it is not uncommon for deputies to relinquish their party affiliation after being elected.[10] This behaviour was, in part, a result of the rule stipulating candidates run only under party sponsorship (eliminated in 1996). When deputies leave the party that elected them, they can alter the strength of the president's legislative support, for better or for worse. The important point is that the constant state of flux of the legislature presents difficulties when analysing divided government arithmetically. While in general Ecuador exemplifies divided government regardless of changes in the composition of the legislature, the form of divided government can vary over time.

The common scenario in post-1978 Ecuador, then, is that ten to twelve parties win seats in a legislature that is small enough and fragmented enough to ensure that a two-seat or even one-seat bloc can disrupt smooth relations between the legislature and the executive. Meanwhile, the two presidential candidates who move on to the second round of voting struggle to reach agreements and form alliances with other parties for electoral support. While parties generally do sign on to support one of the two remaining contenders, these informal alliances have proved short-lived. With a constitutional ban on re-election, loyalty to an incumbent president does not provide the same career advancement opportunities that it might otherwise offer. Members from outside the president's party, even if they supported the president during the second-round campaigning, begin setting their sights on the next presidential contest. Relations between the executive and legislative branches disintegrate into politics of opposition, gridlock, and occasionally, outright

---

[10] An adviser to the Popular Democracy party told me in an interview that such practice was common. While individuals must report alterations in party affiliation to the Electoral Tribunal, they may become 'independent' without informing anybody. The president may entice deputies to become 'independent' by offering material incentives, in effect, urging these deputies to vote pro-government. In a search of shelved legislative bills, I found sixteen, written between Aug. 1979 and Apr. 1996, seeking to curb this behaviour by removing deputies who abandoned the party under which they were elected.

*Monica Barczak*

hostility and violence. In some instances, mid-term elections weaken the president's party in the legislature even further.[11]

### THE CAUSES OF DIVIDED GOVERNMENT IN ECUADOR

There are two main reasons why divided government has become almost a given in Ecuadorian politics: political institutions (especially rules governing elections) and historical experience. I address the second cause first.

Given the very slow expansion of the electorate in Ecuador and the success experienced by political leaders such as Velasco Ibarra without having to form ideologically grounded parties, political competition remained stunted and in the hands of the élite until the late 1970s. As mentioned previously, politics did not generally include peasants, workers, or most of the population. Aspiring leaders sought political victory by building clientelist networks rather than organizing parties and competing on ideals or platforms. Small groups of intellectuals, families, or individuals dominated party structures (Cohaghan, 1995).

If party leaders failed to offer effective channels of representation to individuals, individuals failed to demand it from party leaders. Indeed, actors in society advanced their political interests through corporate groups such as business associations. Chambers of industry, agriculture, and commerce held privileged status inside economic policy-making entities (Conaghan, 1994). Before 1978, the legislature often included functional representatives— deputies who represented corporate groups rather than political parties. During the authoritarian period from 1972 to 1979, interest groups were permitted to continue operating, while political parties were not.

Thus, with the introduction of the new constitution and Law of Elections in 1978, disdain for parties—not to mention the lack of experience in organizing mass-based parties—was well engrained among Ecuadorian political élites (Conaghan, 1994). There was little commitment to developing programmatic parties with strong bases of social support, which might have narrowed the number of parties or at least promoted the formation of longer lasting coalitions. At the same time, the new electoral rules themselves, while designed to advantage programmatic parties and reduce clientelistic practices, created incentives that only exacerbated the situation.

---

[11] Mid-term elections did not take effect in the post-1978 period until 1986. In that year, the incumbent's party actually performed marginally better than it had in 1984. Rodrigo Borja's Izquierda Demócrata (ID, Democratic Left), on the other hand, was soundly beaten in the 1990 mid-term election, as was Sixto Durán Ballén's Partido Unidad Republicana (PUR, Republican Unity Party) in the 1994 mid-term. The man elected president in 1996, Abdalá Bucaram, was no longer in office by what would have been mid-term elections in 1998.

One such law required all candidates to belong to a party to get on the ballot. The idea was to promote the institutionalization of parties and the development of national party organizations and platforms by forbidding the participation of independent candidates. Individuals who might have otherwise run as independents, however, joined parties not on an ideological basis but as a way of getting on the ballot. Moribund parties, in particular, accepted such candidates, especially if they were well-known personalities, in the hope of providing the party with victory. Other parties accepted these candidates as well, such as the Partido Social Cristiano (PSC, Social Christian Party), which gave León Febres Cordero a place on the 1979 legislative ballot despite his lack of ties to the party. In 1984, Febres would claim the presidency for the PSC. The success of outsiders, however, irritates senior party militants and exacerbates intra-party conflict. Moreover, such manœuvring does little to alleviate the 'party-as-electoral-vehicle' mentality mastered by past politicians such as Velasco Ibarra.

The second important law that keeps the number of parties high and therefore increases the likelihood of divided government is the majority run-off presidential formula. Jones (1995) has written extensively on the problems that arise with use of this formula. The main point to remember is that parties have very little incentive under such a system to co-operate and ally in support of a single presidential candidate. Parties which hope to do well in legislative elections fear being seen as less than serious if they do not also run a presidential candidate. Presidential races are more visible, and can promote party name recognition more than legislative elections. In addition, the bigger the candidate field, the lower the threshold parties must attain to move to the second round. These are fertile grounds for dark-horse, outsider candidates.[12] Finally, in a two-round system, voters are less able to predict the eventual winner. While they may vote a straight ticket in the first round, eventually they may be forced to select a president from a different party than their legislative choice, increasing the likelihood that a president will have a minority in the legislature.

The third rule that prohibits parties from joining forces to support a single presidential candidate is the stipulation that candidates appear under only one party's heading on the ballot (Conaghan, 1995). This produces an incentive akin to that produced by the majority run-off—no party wants an empty slot on the presidential ballot. The problem is particularly serious when the presidential and vice-presidential candidates are from different parties. Voters who support the legislative ticket of the vice-presidential candidate's party have higher informational costs than other voters who can simply look at the ballot and select whichever candidate appears in the slot of their favoured party.

---

[12] Schmidt (1996) explains how the majority run-off formula helped the ultimate dark horse, Alberto Fujimori, win the presidency in Peru in 1990.

Finally, rules designed in 1978 to restrict the number of parties by eliminating small parties and parties that failed to develop a national structure were either poorly implemented or suspended. For example, the Law of Parties originally contained a provision whereby a party failing to win 5 per cent of the vote in two consecutive national elections would lose its legal status. The Constitutional Court suspended the provision in 1983 (with legislative approval), before two consecutive elections had even been held.[13]

## THE MANAGEMENT OF DIVIDED GOVERNMENT IN ECUADOR

Ecuador, to this point, has not so much 'managed' divided government as simply survived and muddled through it. Executive–legislative conflict has hamstrung many an administration, with some disputes resulting in violence. Legislative paralysis has been common. Interestingly, however, as serious as some of these crises have been, the democratic regime has not toppled in the post-1978 period.[14] A brief description of presidential administrations illustrates the point.

In the founding election, the military prohibited likely front-runner Assad Bucaram of the Concentración de Fuerzas Populares (CFP, Concentration of Popular Forces) from running for president. To circumvent this rule, Bucaram picked Jaime Roldós to run in his stead, with the idea that Bucaram would hold the real presidential power (Conaghan, 1995). In an effort to establish his autonomy, however, Roldós selected Osvaldo Hurtado of Democracía Popular (DP, Popular Democracy) as his vice-presidential running-mate, much to Bucaram's chagrin.

The pair's victory heightened the emerging struggles over the leadership of the CFP, which were reflected in increasingly tense relations between the executive and the legislature. For example, Bucaram accused Roldós of passing over older party faithful in the distribution of cabinet posts. The president chose to fill these positions with independents and individuals who had worked for him during the campaign. The sizeable CFP bloc in the legislature, which should have helped Roldós implement his agenda, withered as deputies sided with either Bucaram or Roldós. Bucaram himself held considerable power as the President of Congress for the first year of the administration. In retaliation, Roldós created a new party, the Pueblo, Cambio, y Democracía (PCD, People, Change, and Democracy). Tragically, the president died in a plane crash not long afterwards. Roldós's brother-in-law,

---

[13] The measure reappeared in 1992 with a 4% threshold. The 1998 Constitution includes the 1978 version, with a 5% threshold.
[14] On 21 Jan. 2000 the military did hold power for a few hours following the ousting of President Mahuad. However, Vice-President Gustavo Noboa was quickly named president.

Abdalá Bucaram, founded the Partido Roldosista Ecuatoriano (PRE, Ecuadorian Roldósist Party) in his memory.

In the wake of the president's death, vice-president Hurtado ascended to the presidency. Hurtado, resented by CFP loyalists, had a very difficult time assembling support in the legislature. He tried to win allegiance through the distribution of ministerial posts and by making appeals to populist and centre-left parties. Such tactics did not work well, however, as these parties often sided with the right and centre-right to remove ministers. Indeed, from 1979 to 1983, fifty-eight different individuals occupied the thirteen ministry positions, with an average stay of just 11.5 months (Conaghan, 1994).

One of the most vocal opponents of Hurtado was a businessman-turned-legislator from Guayaquil named León Febres Cordero. Febres won his seat on the PSC list, although he had not been a party militant and selected this ticket to comply with electoral rules (Conaghan, 1995). By 1984, Febres had become powerful enough to compete for the presidency. He united a group of parties, including the PSC, the Partido Conservador Ecuatoriano (PCE, Ecuadorian Conservative Party), the Partido Liberal Radical Ecuatoriano (PLRE, Ecuadorian Radical Liberal Party), the Partido Nacionalista Revolucionario (PNR, Nationalist Revolutionary Party), and the Coalición Institucionalista Demócrata (CID, Democratic Institutionalist Coalition), to support him. The loose alliance became known as the Frente de Reconstrucción Nacional (FRN, National Reconstruction Front). With the help of all these parties he advanced to the second round, where he faced the candidate from Izquierda Democrática (ID, Democratic Left), Rodrigo Borja. For this second round, Febres won the tacit support of the CFP (*LARR*, 18 May 1984).

After Febres's victory, conflicts over patronage and positions erupted and the FRN faded away. For example, Febres filled many cabinet posts with economists and businessmen from Guayaquil rather than members of the Front (*LARR*, 27 July 1984). Meanwhile, parties on the centre and left, joined by several populist parties, formed the Bloque Progresista (Progressive Block). For a time, the Bloque held a majority of seats. The development of a legislative majority is rare—in this instance, the majority was anti-government. The first four months of Febres's term, from August to December 1984, were marked by legislative stalemate. Deputies walked out of sessions, physical fights broke out on the floor, and there were even tear-gas bombs lobbed into the chamber (Conaghan, 1994). Throughout Febres's term, his efforts to block impeachment resolutions against ministers exacerbated his conflict with the legislature.

Febres's heavy reliance on urgent economic decrees, which essentially make an end-run around the legislature, added to the inter-branch hostility. He issued twenty-six such decrees in 1984–5 to implement the core of his neo-liberal programme (Conaghan, 1994). The tactic excludes parties from important aspects of the 'legislation game' as well as the 'nomination game' (in Laver and Shepsle's terms). Instead of simplifying these games, however, party members tried to make their voices heard however they could, whether that meant protesting legislation or bringing impeachment motions against ministers.

A temporary truce, negotiated between Febres and the president of the assembly, Raúl Baca Carbo of the ID, helped calm the situation. The Bloque lost its majority for a time, but regained it in the 1986 mid-term elections. Further opposition to Febres came from the ranks of the air force. General Frank Vargas, in fact, led two failed uprisings in which he sought to expose government corruption. Congress granted amnesty to the general, but Febres refused to recognize the decree. In response, air force paratroopers kidnapped the president and held him for a day. Days later, the Bloque passed a motion requesting Febres resign but it failed to generate the necessary two-thirds votes majority to impeach. The president limped to the end of his term.

As the end drew near, Febres threw his efforts into getting Jaime Nebot nominated as the PSC's presidential candidate. But the incumbent's aggressive political style alienated many of the party élite. Sixto Durán Ballén, a PSC founder who opposed Febres, became the candidate for the PSC and the centre-right, aided by support from the PCE.

The centre-right lost the 1988 elections, however, giving the centre-left its turn with a victory for ID's Rodrigo Borja. As shown in Table 3.1, Borja began his term with considerably more support in the legislature than Febres had enjoyed. Moreover, in the second round the informal coalition backing Borja included the DP, the CFP, the Movimiento Popular Democrático (MPD, Popular Democratic Movement), the Frente Radical Alfarista (FRA, Radical Alfarist Front), and the Frente Amplio de Izquierda (FADI, Broad Front of the Left). Borja began his presidency will at least informal support, then, from forty-nine of seventy-one deputies, or 69 per cent.[15] In June 1988, Borja talked about solidifying this support by forming a more united government, and said he would create a 'pluralist' cabinet (*LARR*, 23 June 1988). Despite his rhetoric, he filled eight spots with members of the ID and four spots with independents. Only the Minister of Trade and Industry, Juan José Pons, came from another party (*LARR*, 8 Oct. 1988).[16]

In the 1990 mid-term elections, the ID lost over half its legislative seats. Febres Cordero began orchestrating the opposition from behind the scenes. He

---

[15] This is the only potential instance of non-divided government for the period under consideration. There is no majority opposition coalition, nor is there a lack of majority in the legislature. The alliances in the 'government' coalition, however, are not at all formal, nor are they long-lasting. Given this, I hesitate to label the period as unified government.

[16] While the *Latin American Regional Reports* list the names of cabinet members after presidential elections, this was the only instance in which I found they had included party identifications as well.

urged the parties to unite in opposition regardless of ideology. Indeed, the PSC, PRE, and the Partido Socialista Ecuatoriano (PSE, Ecuadorian Socialist Party) began making some noise about working together at least in the short term, to initiate impeachment proceedings against the ministers of the interior, of education, of public works, of agriculture, and of mining. Such co-operation would signify true discontent with Borja, as the PSC and PRE, headed by Jaime Nebot and Abdalá Bucaram respectively, were long-time enemies (*LARR*, 2 Aug. 1990). President Borja responded by describing the opposition legislators as a gang of 'ill-mannered, irresponsible people who do not understand how to live in a democracy and do not respect other people's honour' (*LARR*, 11 Oct. 1990: 3).

The ID's poor performance in the 1990 elections also threatened Borja's ability to influence the selection of the president of the legislature. To solve his problem, Borja awarded non-cabinet government posts to PLRE members in exchange for favourable votes from the three PLRE deputies when it came time to fill this office. The PLRE deputies agreed, stipulating that they were not joining any kind of formal pro-government alliance, but were only acting to 'rescue the parliament' in the wake of tremendous conflict (*LARR*, 20 Dec. 1990).

The PLRE bloc's co-operation did not prevent the impeachment of two ministers, and four others had to step down under threat of impeachment. The legislature subsequently began the process to dismiss sixteen members of the Supreme Court. When Borja refused to allow this to happen, Averroes Bucaram of the CFP, president of the legislature and the brother of Abdalá, announced the legislature would initiate impeachment proceedings against the president. At the height of the crisis, the three PLRE deputies joined pro-Borja forces to remove Bucaram from the presidency, charging that he had been plotting a 'legislative coup' against the president (*LARR*, 15 Nov. 1990). But Borja's troubles did not end there. As his term drew to a close, the legislature pursued the impeachment of both Vice-President Parodi and the president himself. This time Borja was being punished for calling his opponents a 'gang of layabouts' when they failed to act on a bill deemed of economic urgency (*LARR*, 21 May 1992).

While Rodrigo Borja ultimately escaped impeachment, the effects of divided government tarnished much of his term. Indeed, the intensity of conflict between the executive and the legislature from 1988 to 1992 illustrates the possible consequences of minority government, particularly when battles become personal. Even so, conflict was marked during these years by inter-party, rather than intra-party, conflict. In the months leading up to the 1992 presidential elections, intra-party conflict would also escalate.

Sixto Durán Ballén competed again for the PSC nomination at the party convention in February 1991 but lost by a narrow margin to Jaime Nebot. In response, Durán formed the Partido Unidad Republicana (PUR, United

Republican Party). This move turned out to be wildly popular among the PSC's anti-Febres wing. In a puzzling move, however, Durán decided to ally the new PUR to the old PCE, so he selected Alberto Dahík as his running mate. Dahík had been Febres's economic minister and was known as a hard-core neo-liberal. When the PUR director and militants tried to prevent Dahík from joining the ticket, they were expelled. The PUR, born of conflict, remained engulfed in it.

While Durán won the presidency in the name of the PUR, the party fared quite poorly in the legislative elections. Even with the addition of the PCE legislators, the president was very far from a legislative majority. Although the president might have hoped for support from like-minded centre-rightists in the PSC, early conflict foreshadowed that personal rivalry between PUR and PSC leaders would overpower ideological similarity.

The president did receive some help in the beginning of his second year when independent action by a few members of the DP and the PRE increased the pro-government coalition in the legislature. In a battle over who would be President of Congress, nine deputies from the DP and PRE broke party ranks to support Durán's choice. After the vote, DP and PRE leadership expelled the nine members from their respective parties, and the PRE charged the president of buying votes (*LARR*, 2 Sept. 1993).

Early in 1994, the vice-president announced Durán was considering holding a *consulta popular* (referendum) on constitutional reforms to resolve the governability crisis. In particular, the administration appeared willing to support a reform extending the term length of provincial deputies from two to four years, to take effect immediately. Only months before, the president had claimed he was not in favour of allowing incumbent provincial deputies to 'reappoint' themselves in this way. With mid-term elections rapidly approaching, however, the president found himself in a difficult position. Analysts were predicting the PUR–PCE coalition would not win any of the sixty-five seats in the mid-term elections. Moreover, due to the ban on re-election, the twenty-two deputies who had defected from their parties to become 'independent' (i.e. pro-government) would disappear as well, closing the door on any chance the president had of pushing his neo-liberal economic policies through the legislature (*LARR*, 10 Mar. 1994).

Proving the analysts wrong, the governing coalition won seven seats in the mid-term election (*LARR*, 26 May 1994). The PSC and PRE, traditional enemies, worked together to name Heinz Moeller of the PSC as the President of the National Congress. These two large parties pledged to block the government's legislative programme, sending a clear message to Durán that his final years in office would not be easy (*LARR*, 8 Sept. 1994).

In August 1994 the president held an eight-question *consulta* on constitutional reform, to which voters responded favourably. The reform package moved on to the legislature, where opposition from both left and right made it obvious that deputies would not be able to act on the matter in the 100 days allotted them. Additionally, opposition deputies continued to subject ministers they did not like to interpellations and threats of impeachment. For example, the legislature impeached the foreign minister for undermining Ecuador's international prestige by changing his mind several times on his vote for a new secretary general of the Organization of American States (*LARR*, 17 Oct. 1994).

During most of 1995, executive–legislative conflict slowed to a simmer as Ecuador became entangled in a war with Peru over territory in the Amazonian region. While the legislature managed to pass part of the 1994 constitutional reform package into law, the president convoked another *consulta popular* for 26 November 1995. Voters used the occasion as a referendum on the president's administration, however, and handed him a resounding defeat. Compounding the president's problems was the fact that vice president Dahík had been accused of misusing approximately $10 million in secret funds. After an investigation headed by Carlos Solórzano, the President of the Supreme Court, Dahík fled to Costa Rica. As previous presidents had done, Durán hobbled to the end of his term.

With the 1996 presidential election approaching, the centre-left appeared to be in a state of disarray. On the right, Jaime Nebot stood as the clear front-runner, representing the PSC. His opposition, however, split support between Rodrigo Paz of DP, and Freddy Ehlers, a television host turned presidential candidate who carried the banner of the newly formed Movimiento Unidad Plurinacional Pachakútik—Nuevo País (MUPPNP, Pachakútik Plurinational Unity Movement—New Country). The new movement attempted to bring indigenous and environmentalist interests into the formal political arena. What happened instead was that the division on the left opened the door for a charismatic candidate from the populist PRE to advance to the second round. Abdalá Bucaram, the former mayor of Guayaquil, then proceeded to woo much of the centre-left and secure the presidency for the PRE.

Bucaram both campaigned and ruled with a flair all his own. Campaign promises to build local roads, increase teachers' salaries, increase the health and police budgets, subsidize basic staples such as rice, milk, meat, and oil, and provide cheap medicines and free maternity care, amounted to approximately US$2.35 billion, or two-thirds of Ecuador's budget for 1996 (*LARR*, 1 Aug. 1996). Upon taking office, he declared a state of emergency, fired 6,000 bureaucrats, accused the outgoing president of lying to the people about the state of public finances, and antagonized both his vice-president and newly elected MUPPNP deputies from the Sierra. Despite campaign promises, Bucaram's aggressive energy minister, Alfredo Adoum, introduced a measure to repeal subsidies, threatening to push the price of cooking oil up 500 per cent. In response, the MUPPNP block threatened to impeach Adoum (*LARR*, 10 Oct. 1996).[17]

Bucaram's economic programme would prove to be his undoing. Once in office, Bucaram jettisoned his populist promises and announced a 'convertibility plan' to link the Ecuadorian *sucre* to the US dollar. Part of the plan called for the elimination of subsidies and increase in rates on public services, particularly electricity, which would be privatized. Bucaram threatened to hold a plebiscite on the plan if the legislature failed to approve it (*LARR*, 21 Jan. 1997).

By early February, before Bucaram had completed six months in office, the president had alienated his own vice-president, the legislature, and the indigenous groups and unions that had helped get him elected. The first wave of price increases triggered massive street demonstrations, culminating in a national strike on 5 February. Called by a broad coalition of workers, social movements, and indigenous groups, and supported by parties such as the PSC, the DP, the ID, the MPD, and the MUPPNP, the strike ended after the legislature determined Bucaram to be mentally incompetent and declared the presidency vacant. While Bucaram at first rejected the legislature's ruling, he quickly fled to Guayaquil, and within a few days left Ecuador for Panama. A power struggle between Vice-President Rosalía Arteaga and the President of the National Congress, Fabián Alarcón, ended with the latter's ascension to the presidential office.[18]

Bucaram's ouster must be understood in great part as the result of his own personality in addition to institutional shortcomings. Certainly he swept the executive and legislative branches into a tremendously stressful relationship, but this had more to do with his dramatic swing in economic philosophy after the election, the questionable decisions he made regarding his cabinet and staff, and his own erratic behaviour and aggressive rhetoric. While factors

[17] The controversy surrounding Bucaram and his cabinet produced political surrealism. I was in Ecuador in Oct. of 1996, and each day the newspapers printed bits of the secretary of education's doctoral thesis, alongside the text she allegedly had plagiarized. Accusations flew that Adoum had physically assaulted a female energy worker and routinely brandished a pistol during debates. Bucaram, who referred to himself as El Loco ('the crazy one') gave televised singing performances (he had recorded a compact disc) and theatrically shaved off his moustache during a telethon for sick children. He distributed plastic bags of milk called 'Abdalact', with his picture on the label, to the poor, and he used his president's budget to charter a private plane to fly his son to Miami for obesity treatment (also see *LARR*, 14 Nov. 1996).

[18] As the legislature declared the presidency vacant, both Arteaga and Alarcón claimed the office for themselves. The Constitution stated the vice-president served as resident upon temporary incapacity or absence of the president, but was silent on the protocol of permanent incapacity. Alarcón won the support of fifty-seven deputies (out of eighty-two) in his quest to become 'interim' president. On 9 Feb. he resigned that position, and Arteaga was named 'temporary' president. She stepped down from this post on 11 Feb., and Alarcón was again seated as 'interim' president until a new election could be held in 1998 (*LARR*, 25 Feb. 1997).

outlined in this chapter as important causes of divided government, such as the majority run-off presidential election formula and Ecuador's history of populism and clientelism, helped put Bucaram in office, the intensity of executive–legislative tensions escalated as a result of Bucaram's behaviour.

As interim president, Alarcón took power hampered by the serious weakness of a shortened term. With elections scheduled for 1998, large parties had little incentive to co-operate with the new president and more incentive to launch their campaigns. In an effort to demonstrate his power, Alarcón held and won a plebiscite confirming that voters not only agreed with the decision to remove Bucaram, but also supported Alarcón as president. Plebiscite results additionally showed voters favoured more constitutional reform (*LARR*, 17 June 1997).

The legislature spent its time creating headaches for the administration. For instance, deputies voted to dismiss thirty Supreme Court judges, plus the institution's president, Carlos Solórzano, who was one of the most highly (if not the only) respected members of government. Solórzano dubbed Ecuador a 'country of madmen' and outside observers seemed to agree. The US ambassador to Ecuador accused judges there of trafficking in drugs, the international press issued warnings to investors that Ecuador was 'insecure' and British and French officials expressed fears that Ecuador had become 'high-risk'. Within Ecuador, the Church declared Alarcón's government unable to govern (*LARR*, 22 July and 28 Aug. 1997).

As 1997 drew to a close, elections were held for a constituent assembly while the popular and indigenous groups that had demonstrated against Bucaram threatened to hold their own alternative assembly. Strikes, protest marches, and criticism against the president grew. Under attack from all sides and facing a corruption suit filed by a former colleague, Alarcón threatened to assume emergency powers. Meanwhile, the administration failed to make any progress on its privatization programme (*LARR*, 4 Nov. 1997).

Plans for constitutional reform, however, lumbered forward. In October 1997, indigenous and social groups convoked their Alternative Assembly in Quito, during which they hammered out reform proposals such as collective rights, decentralization of power, and declaring Ecuador a plurinational society. They would take these demands to the official assembly, inaugurated on 20 December, with limited success (Andolina, 1999). Constitutional reform remained in the hands of the large political parties, especially those of the PSC.

The assembly provided yet another body ready to fight with President Alarcón. The assembly was to finish its work by 30 April 1998. As the deadline approached, members calculated they would need eight more days to complete their task, an extension that Alarcón refused to grant. The assembly ignored the president's refusal, and continued to meet until 8 May. Both the president and the legislature initially declined to recognize any text approved after 30 April. By mid-June, Alarcón announced he was ready to talk about accepting the text in full, although with national elections approaching, it was not clear under which constitution the new administration and legislature would be seated. Opinion polls, meanwhile, showed that 71 per cent of the people doubted constitutional reforms would matter anyway, that almost 82 per cent felt Ecuador was in worse shape than it had been in the immediate aftermath of the Bucaram crisis, and that just over half would prefer an authoritarian government to what existed at the time (*LARR*, 19 May and 23 June 1998).

In the electoral arena, the presidential race shaped up into a contest between Jamil Mahuad, a former mayor of Quito from DP, and Alvaro Noboa, a multi-millionaire businessman from Guayaquil running for the PRE. A moderate and skilled politician, Mahuad secured support from Freddy Ehlers, former vice-president Rosalía Arteaga, the ID, and the national indigenous association for the second round. In true PRE style, Noboa deployed populist methods, using his wealth to hand out food, clothing, and medicines to coastal populations devastated by El Niño (*LARR*, 19 May 1998).

Mahuad won the race, but his party did not secure a majority in the newly expanded legislature. He selected a cabinet comprised mostly of technocrats, including only a few DP faithful. Early legislative activity indicated a potential coalition of DP and PSC deputies, much to the consternation of the ID and the PRE.[19] The new 1998 Constitution took effect on 10 August, nine days after the inauguration of the new government (*LARR*, 28 July 1998).

President Mahuad managed to maintain a lid on executive–legislative tensions for almost an entire year by relying heavily on the PSC. His troubles instead stemmed from increasing popular protest, civil unrest, and urban violence, in addition to severe economic crisis. By mid-July, street demonstrators shouted out slogans such as 'Bring back Bucaram' in the streets of the capital city. In Guayaquil, León Febres Cordero, ever the spoiler, led marches demanding Mahuad change his economic policies, and Defense Minister General José Gallardo warned of the danger of a military *coup d'état* (*LARR*, 27 July 1998).

Gallardo's warnings were not unfounded. As the year 2000 opened, protesters took to the streets of Quito to demand an end to neo-liberal economic policies and the proposed 'dollarization' of the sucre. The Confederation of Indigenous Nationalities of Ecuador organized a 'national uprising' beginning on 15 January. Centred in Quito, the uprising attracted the support of tens of thousands of people. By 21 January, some sectors of the military broke

---

[19] The DP held thirty-two seats and the PSC held twenty-seven. On the opposition, the PRE occupied twenty-four seats and the ID eighteen. The assembly had grown to a total of 121 deputies (*LARR*, 28 July 1998).

ranks to join the protests. Activists seized the National Congress building and announced the formation of a 'Government of National Salvation', stripping Mahuad of the presidency. Within hours, however, top military officials had installed Vice-President Gustavo Noboa as the new president. Meeting in an emergency session in Guayaquil, the National Congress voted to approve this transition. At the time of writing, Noboa remained in the presidency and the dollarization programme had moved into its final stages.

## CONCLUSION

Divided government has been endemic to Ecuador. It appears in several different forms, thanks to electoral rules that allow a mixed-party presidential ticket, the survival of many parties, and a small assembly. It simply has become very difficult for parties to capture legislative majorities on their own.

Some of the more important electoral rules contributing to divided government are the majority run-off formula in the presidential election, the rule that forced candidates to run on party lists (until 1996), and the inconsistent implementation of rules designed to reduce the number of parties. At the same time, presidents wield considerable formal powers that permit them to by-pass the legislature, while legislatures can needle ministers with impeachment threats. Historical experience has also shaped divided government in Ecuador by retarding the development of a coherent party system in which parties can occupy clear positions as 'the government' and 'the opposition', not to mention build voter allegiance.

Solutions to divided government in Ecuador exist, at least in theory. One way presidents could try to build legislative support would be through the distribution of cabinet portfolios.[20] A president could exchange a cabinet portfolio for a formal commitment to pro-government voting in the legislature. Of course, the parties that might be included in such an agreement would have to share some kind of programmatic affinity with the president's party.

Typically, however, cabinet positions are either reserved for rewarding loyal supporters or are intentionally depoliticized. In the first instance, new presidents name ministers who worked on their campaigns. In the second, presidents select 'independent' ministers, chosen for their technocratic abilities rather than partisanship. This has increasingly been the case with financial and economic ministries since 1978. When party leaders and long-time party stalwarts are left out of ministerial positions, policy-making falls out of the hands of parties, and, in a broader sense, the legislature (Conaghan, 1995). As with urgent economic decrees and popular referendums, the

---

[20] See Geddes (1994) on the more extreme case where presidents, fearing for their own political survival above else, distribute political posts based on these kinds of calculations.

'technocratization' of the cabinet increases the sense of frustration felt by parties and exacerbates tensions between the two branches. On the other hand, these tools allow a president to 'go it alone' in some policy areas.

Divided government has been a difficult problem for Ecuador because the tensions between the legislative and executive branches have been so acute. Clearly other factors have contributed to political instability in recent years— most notably, the exclusion of indigenous people and peasants. Still, political paralysis has stymied the search for solutions to the problems of economic growth and improved social welfare. While other states may be able to manage divided government productively, so far Ecuador has mainly managed simply to avoid a return to sustained military rule.

# 4

# Divided Government in Mexico's Presidentialist Regime: The 1997–2000 Experience

## Joseph L. Klesner

Divided government at the national level came to Mexico after the 1997 federal congressional elections. Prior to that year, Mexico displayed one of the most unified national governments in the world. Indeed, the dominance of Mexico's president led one scholar to characterize the position as a limited-term dictatorship, writing, 'Mexicans avoid personal dictatorship by retiring their dictators every six years' (Brandenburg, 1964: 141). From 1988 onward, however, the emergence of opposition parties and their representation in the Chamber of Deputies (the lower house) began to put constraints on hyper-presidentialism. In the 1997–2000 Congress, the opposition parties' majority in the Chamber of Deputies forced President Ernesto Zedillo (1994–2000) to act like presidents in many other presidential systems, namely, he had to build coalitions to pass the legislation that he needed to govern. Mexico's new president, Vicente Fox (2000–6), the first president from a party other than the Institutional Revolutionary Party (Partido Revolucionario Institucional, PRI) since it was founded in 1929, will also face a legislature in which his party, the National Action Party (Partido Acción Nacional, PAN), lacks a majority in either house.

To understand the operation of divided government in Mexico we must first appreciate the remarkably unified government that had characterized the nation from the mid-1930s until 1988.[1] With divided government has come

[1] As I will detail below, divided government can be thought to involve either a situation in which the opposition has a simple majority in one house and can thereby block bills presented by the president or his party or a circumstance in which the president's party does not have two-thirds of both houses and thus cannot pass constitutional amendments. The former situation obtained only after 1997, but the latter has been the case since 1988. The former is obviously a clear case of divided government, but as I will suggest, the latter becomes an issue more than might be expected at first sight because the Mexican constitution is amended so frequently.

the end of Mexican presidentialism, or *presidencialismo*, as it is known there. As I will outline below, some scholars and public intellectuals have traced the roots of *presidencialismo* to Mexican political culture. Others see it emerging from the constitutional arrangements created at the end of Mexico's revolution (1910–17). However, the most convincing explanation for *presidencialismo* comes by examining the structure of incentives posed to politicians seeking elective office, given Mexican electoral rules and the long existence of a hegemonic party. This electoral explanation of *presidencialismo* will show then how divided government could emerge in Mexico once the electoral circumstances ceased to favour the PRI. Relations between the executive and the legislature and the internal operations of the Congress changed once the conditions that had created *presidencialismo* ceased to exist.

In its many years of unified government, the PRI developed institutional arrangements for managing executive–legislative relations that made passage of presidential initiatives relatively painless for all involved. Opposition deputies had opportunities to speak against executive-sponsored bills, but no power to control the agenda of the Congress nor even slow down the passage of the president's bills. With divided government, managing executive–legislative relations has required reinvention of the internal structure of the Chamber of Deputies. Greater conflict with the executive has resulted, although Zedillo succeeded in working with the Chamber to pass important legislation. Even more prominently, conflict within the Chamber has grown dramatically to include physical struggles among legislators as well as verbal assaults on one's political enemies. The incoming government of Vicente Fox will certainly want to develop means to control conflict with the Congress if it truly wishes to reform the Mexican regime.

In this chapter, I will first describe the record of unified and divided government in Mexico, providing evidence about both the arithmetic and the behavioural manifestations of each. Then I will review the major modes of explaining unified government, using the insights developed there to explain how divided government came to Mexico in the 1990s. Finally, I will explore the management of divided government in the 1997–2000 Congress, describing how the internal organization of the Chamber of Deputies has changed as well as the coalitions that have been formed to support presidential initiatives. To provide a better insight into coalition formation, I will review the 1997–2000 Chamber's experience in passing the three budgets sent to it by President Zedillo.


## THE FREQUENCY AND FORM OF UNIFIED AND DIVIDED GOVERNMENT IN MEXICO

One can hardly discuss Mexico's brief experience with divided government without placing it in the larger historical context of unusually unified government in both the arithmetic sense and the behavioural sense, as Robert Elgie has defined those terms (see Chapter 1). I will begin by briefly describing the institutional context and the record of party representation in the Mexican Congress. That discussion must start with a short discussion of the party system.

## The Record of Unified Government

Although opposition parties have existed in Mexico since the 1930s, from the founding of PRI as the National Revolutionary Party in 1929 until the 1990s Mexico had a hegemonic party system, to use Giovanni Sartori's term (1976). The election of Vicente Fox of the PAN as president in 2000 marks the first time the PRI has lost the presidency since its founding. Until 1989 it had not lost a gubernatorial race. Before 1988 the PRI had won every senatorial race it had contested. Prior to 1988 the PRI seldom lost elections in the 300 single-member federal deputy districts. Only from 1988 onward has the PRI's hegemony been contested, and only in 1997 was it broken.

Mexico's presidentialist regime mirrors that of the US in many of its constitutional features. The president, elected for a six-year, non-re-electable term (or *sexenio*), serves as head of the executive branch, as head of state, and as commander-in-chief of the armed forces. The bicameral Congress has a Chamber of Deputies with 500 members who serve three-year terms and a Senate with 128 members who serve six-year terms.[2] The Congress is charged with the responsibilities of auditing the public accounts of the previous year, approving the budget of the coming fiscal year, and voting on all bills introduced to it by the president, or by members of the Chamber of Deputies or the Senate, the two houses of the bicameral legislature, or by state legislatures.[3] In the formal rules about making laws established in the Mexican constitution, a bill becomes a law there in ways similar to the US: bills must pass both houses of Congress; they can be approved or vetoed by the president; and if they are vetoed, the veto can be over-ridden by a two-thirds vote of both houses.

The annual federal budget is an exception to the rules just described (see Weldon, forthcoming). The president must submit the budget initiative to the Chamber of Deputies, which has the sole responsibility to pass it (that is, the Senate does not vote on the budget). The Chamber may revise the president's initiative in any way, but it must do so before the beginning of the fiscal year, which begins on 1 January. The president typically does not

[2] Both chambers of the Congress have had their membership increased and redefined in recent decades, as I will detail below.

[3] Very few bills have been submitted to Congress by state legislatures in recent years even though the Constitution permits the practice, although the number increased significantly in 1997–9 as the number of opposition-controlled state legislatures grew (Casar, 2000: 40).

submit the budget initiative before 15 November, but the ordinary session of
the Chamber ends on 15 December, giving the Chamber only a month to
consider, to debate, and to approve some version of a federal budget. The
president must then accept the budget as passed by the Chamber. What
would happen if the president found the budget unacceptable or if the
Chamber failed to pass a budget bill by 31 December (in extraordinary session) remains unclear (see Carrillo and Lujambio, 1998). Although only the
Chamber votes on the budget bill, both the Chamber and the Senate must
approve the revenue bill (Weldon, forthcoming).

The president has been blessed during most of this century by an unusually
co-operative Congress because of the PRI's hegemony. Tables 4.1 and 4.2
show the distribution of seats in the Chamber of Deputies since 1961 and the
Senate since 1964. An explanatory comment is in order. Political reforms led
to changes in the composition of the Chamber of Deputies in 1977 and 1986
and the Senate's composition changed in 1994. Prior to the 1977 political
reform, the Chamber included less than 200 single-member district seats and
a small and variable number of seats for 'minority deputies'.[4] In 1977, the
Chamber's composition was changed to 300 single-member district seats and
100 proportional representation seats reserved for minority parties, a total of
400 deputies. In 1986, an additional 100 PR seats were added to the Chamber,
bringing the total to 500, but the PR seats became available to all parties, with
much political wrangling about limits to the size of the largest party's representation as well as demands by the PRI for a 'governability clause' that
would guarantee it a majority of seats even if it failed to get a majority of
votes.[5]

The Senate, meanwhile, had been composed of two members from each
state and the Federal District, both chosen in presidential election years until
1988. Thereafter, one senator from each state was to be chosen during presidential election years and the other chosen in mid-term elections (hence
thirty-two senators were elected in 1991). In 1994, however, the Senate was
doubled in size to include 128 seats, three awarded to the party receiving the
first plurality of votes in each state, one to the party finishing second in each
state. In 1997, Senate representation was changed yet again so that the 128
seats were distributed in the following manner: the party receiving the first
plurality in each state would receive two seats and the party finishing second

---

[4] In 1963, recognizing the under-representation of opposition parties in the Congress
and concerned about the democratic image of the regime, the Adolfo López Mateos administration (1958–64) introduced a political reform that gave up to twenty seats in the
Chamber of Deputies to each minority political party that exceeded 2.5% of the vote. The
bar was lowered to 1.5% for the 1973 election. Nationally, there were 178 electoral districts
until 1970, 194 for the 1973 congressional election, and 196 for the 1976 election. Mabry
(1974) assesses the 'party deputy' system.

[5] See below for details of the evolution of the 'governability clause' over time.

TABLE 4.1. *Seats in the Mexican Chamber of Deputies, 1964–2000*

| Year | PRI | PAN | PCM, PSUM, PMS, PRD | PT | PVEM | Others |
|------|-----|-----|---------------------|-----|------|--------|
| 1964 | 175 | 20 | — | — | — | 15 |
| 1967 | 177 | 20 | — | — | — | 15 |
| 1970 | 178 | 20 | — | — | — | 15 |
| 1973 | 189 | 25 | — | — | — | 17 |
| 1976 | 195 | 20 | — | — | — | 22 |
| 1979 | 298 | 41 | 18 | — | — | 43 |
| 1982 | 299 | 51 | 17 | — | — | 33 |
| 1985 | 289 | 41 | 12 | — | — | 58 |
| 1988 | 260 | 101 | 139 | — | — | * |
| 1991 | 320 | 89 | 41 | 0 | 0 | 50 |
| 1994 | 301 | 119 | 70 | 10 | 0 | 0 |
| 1997 | 239 | 122 | 125 | 6 | 8 | 0 |
| 2000 | 209 | 208 | 53 | 9 | 15 | 6 |

*Source*: Instituto Federal Electoral.
* Several of the parties of the left supported the candidates of the National Democratic Front (FDN) in 1988. Their totals are listed under the PRD column.

TABLE 4.2. *Seats in the Mexican Senate, 1964–2000*

| Year | PAN | PRI | PRD | Other |
|------|-----|-----|-----|-------|
| 1964 | 0 | 60 | — | 0 |
| 1970 | 0 | 60 | — | 0 |
| 1976 | 0 | 63 | — | 1 |
| 1982 | 0 | 64 | — | 0 |
| 1988 | 0 | 60 | 4 | 0 |
| 1991 | 1 | 61 | 2 | 0 |
| 1994 | 24 | 96 | 8 | 0 |
| 1997 | 32 | 76 | 15 | 5 |
| 2000 | 46 | 60 | 15 | 7 |

would receive one; thirty-two seats would be chosen by proportional representation with a single national constituency.[6]

Tables 4.1 and 4.2 demonstrate that until 1988 the PRI held super-majorities (greater than two-thirds of the seats) in both houses. Super-majorities serve the

[6] Hence, in 1994, the thirty-two senators elected in 1988 left office. They were replaced by ninety-six senators chosen so that the party receiving the highest vote in a state received two seats, the second-placing party receiving one. In 1997, the thirty-two senators elected in 1991 left office. They were replaced by thirty-two senators chosen for a three-year term by proportional representation. See Lujambio (2000).

key role of allowing the party holding them not only to pass ordinary legislation, but also to promulgate constitutional amendments. Because the Mexican
constitution of 1917 not only dictates the institutional structure of the polity
but also includes articles that stipulate relatively specific goals of government,
it has been amended frequently. Presidents who cannot count on congressional
super-majorities cannot expect to undertake ambitious policy agendas because
major policy changes typically require that some articles of the Constitution be
amended. Indeed, the Constitution has been amended over 300 times since it
became Mexico's Magna Carta in 1917 (Casar, forthcoming).

Prior to 1988, then, the PRI majorities in both houses could produce both
normal legislation and constitutional amendments easily, without worrying
about defections. In the period when the PRI's dominance barely was contested—the mid-1930s until the mid-1960s—the effect of the PRI majority
was overwhelming. According to Mexican sociologist Pablo González
Casanova (1970: 201), no presidential initiatives sent to Congress between
1935 and 1964 were rejected. Furthermore, presidential initiatives dominated
the legislative agenda. Bills presented by legislators amounted to fewer than
half of those proposed by the executive during this period (cf. González
Casanova, 1970: 201; Casar, forthcoming). Moreover, defections were few.
González Casanova reports that in most of the years he selected to examine
between 1935 and 1964, at least 75 per cent of bills proposed by the president
were passed unanimously. Of those bills not passed unanimously, the average
number of votes against presidential initiatives was about three (1970: 201).

## The Record of Divided Government

Mexico's experience with divided government began in 1988 when the PRI's
Carlos Salinas won a much-questioned presidential election with only 50.7
per cent of the vote. Because the Chamber of Deputies had been expanded by
the addition of 100 PR seats (thus, 200 PR seats in all) after a 1986 political
reform, because the new electoral legislation laid down rules of representation
that yielded near perfect proportionality, and because there were few ticket-
splitters among PRI voters, the Chamber of Deputies produced by that election gave the PRI only 260 seats out of 500. Salinas, however, entered office
with ambitious plans to restructure the economy which would require constitutional amendments so that he could privatize many of the state-owned firms
that dominated the stagnant Mexican economy, particularly the banking system that had been nationalized in 1982. Salinas also sought to change Article
27 of the Constitution that dealt with land reform so as to permit commun-
ities that held land in common to distribute it to their members as private
property. Finally, seeking to bolster his legitimacy, Salinas regularized relations with the Roman Catholic Church, which involved amending Article 130
that deals with the Church's juridical status. Thus, he was forced to negotiate

with the PAN in order to pass the amendments by which his neo-liberal economic restructuring package could be implemented (Loaeza, 1999: 482–5). Not all of these measures were accomplished in the 1988–91 Congress, but Salinas did not gain a super-majority in the 1991–4 Congress either (the PRI had 64 per cent of the seats in that legislature), and he looked to the PAN to help amend the Constitution in the second half of his presidency too.

The near loss of the majority in the Chamber of Deputies in 1988 caused the PRI and the Salinas government to reform the electoral rules so that even if a party with the highest plurality of votes only received 35 per cent of ballots cast for federal deputies, it would be guaranteed a majority of seats in the Chamber. A complex formula for representation limited the share of seats in the Chamber to 70 per cent if a party (presumably the PRI) received 70 per cent or more of the votes and guaranteed the majority party proportionality of seats and votes if it received between 60 and 70 per cent of votes. This agreement was only in place for the 1991 mid-term elections, in which the PRI received 61.5 per cent of the votes, and, hence, fewer seats than the two-thirds needed to pass constitutional amendments, as mentioned above. Subsequent reforms to the 'governability clause' reduced the over-representation of the party receiving the first plurality and limited the representation of the largest party to 60 per cent of total seats. Hence, in 1994 the PRI received 300 deputy seats (60 per cent) but in 1997 it failed to gain a majority of seats because it did not reach the 42 per cent of valid votes then required to be given a majority.

In sum, the record of divided government in arithmetic terms has been that the PRI commanded a majority of both houses of Congress until 1997 and it had the super-majority necessary to pass constitutional amendments until 1988. However, from 1988 forward, the PRI required the co-operation of another party if it sought to pass constitutional amendments. Indeed, the PRI required over seventy opposition votes in the Chamber to amend the Constitution in 1988–91, only fourteen in 1991–4 (which could be acquired from a parastatal party rather than a true opposition party),[7] and thirty-four in from 1994–7. During the Salinas presidency (1988–94), major constitutional amendments were passed to alter Church-state relations, to bring land reform to an end, and to permit the sale of state-owned enterprises. To pass those amendments, Salinas turned to the largest opposition party, the PAN, often considered to be the 'loyal opposition' (Loaeza, 1999).

---

[7] Several of the parties of the left that contested elections before 2000 could be considered para-statals, parties encouraged by the government to form to give the appearance of pluralism in the party system. Prominent examples were the Popular Socialist Party (Partido Popular Socialista, PPS) and the Socialist Workers Party (Partido Socialista de los Trabajadores, PST, which later changed its name opportunistically to the Party of the Cardenista National Renovation Front and then to the Cardenista Party). These parties were generally thought to be financed by the Ministry of the Interior (*Gobernación*) and they often chose to vote with the PRI to support presidential initiatives.

## THE CAUSES OF DIVIDED GOVERNMENT IN MEXICO

The easiest way to understand how divided government came to Mexico is by explaining the conditions under which unified government was produced. Unified government, in the behavioural sense, is equivalent to what is known as presidentialism (or *presidencialismo*) in Mexico, a circumstance in which the president has metaconstitutional powers and is effectively able to rule without legislative constraints, sure that his initiatives will pass the Congress with little more than token opposition and marginal amendments to the main bills. Luis Javier Garrido (1989: 422) argues that the Mexican presidency was granted greater powers by the 1917 Constitution than existed under the earlier 1857 Constitution. However, these constitutional powers are not more extensive than those held by most presidents in other Latin American political systems (Mainwaring and Shugart, 1997*b*). Beyond the constitutionally designated powers, however, Mexican presidents have enjoyed 'metaconstitutional powers', a 'series of prerogatives [that] corresponds to the "unwritten" norms of the Mexican system. They allow the president to centralise his power progressively through a distortion of constitutional mechanisms' (Garrido, 1989: 422). Garrido identifies ten such metaconstitutional powers, the most important of them being the effective capacity to amend the Constitution, the role of 'chief legislator', the capacity to designate one's successor to the presidency, and the domination of lower levels of government in the Mexican federal system. The president's anti-constitutional powers, in Garrido's view, are a capacity to violate the legal code and immunity from prosecution (powers that arguably no longer exist). Thus, as Roderic A. Camp (1999: 11) suggests, 'Presidencialismo is the concept that most political power lies in the hands of the president and all that is good or bad in government policy stems personally from the president.' *Presidencialismo* has been not only the normal practice, these scholars suggest, but also a norm in Mexican politics.

### The Bases of Unified Government

A number of students of Mexican politics have developed cultural explanations of the dominance of the Mexican Congress by the president. This view is articulated by Mexico's Nobel Laureate in Literature, Octavio Paz, as summarized by Alicia Hernández Chávez (1994: 217):

According to Paz, the roots of presidentialism can be found in the specific nature of the Mexican political tradition, characterized by a process whereby the different cultural molds —Indian, Spanish, mestizo, and creole —are synthesized. The result of this process is a political tradition 'lacking an ideology' which leads to 'a respectful veneration by Mexicans of the figure of the president'.

In a political system with a great respect for a dominant leader, the argument goes, Congress plays a secondary role.

In keeping with this perspective, early scholarly treatments of the Congress tended to attribute largely symbolic functions to it. González Casanova, for instance, argued that 'the legislative power has a symbolic function. It sanctions the actions of the Executive. It gives them a traditional and meta-physical legitimation' (1970: 20). Rudolph de la Garza similarly argued that the Chamber of Deputies 'plays an important role in legitimizing the government and the political system' (1972: 2). Other scholars, while putting less emphasis on the cultural sources of the legislature's relative weakness before the executive, sought to find functional explanations for the Congress's continuing importance in the political system. Alejandro Portes (1977), for instance, focused on the role of the Congress as a route for political recruitment and on the communication and political brokerage functions of legislators (see also Smith, 1979: 223). Portes argued, 'The three functional sectors of the PRI and their legislative delegates attempt to symbolically integrate the poor into a system of political and economic privilege' (1977: 198).

Another way of explaining the weakness of the Congress *vis-à-vis* the president has been to focus on the institutional sources of presidential power (see Hernández Chávez, 1994; Casar, 1996). Scholars note the elimination of the vice-presidency in the 1917 Constitution (thereby making the removal of the president by impeachment more threatening to political order than when a vice-presidency existed). Also, the president can appoint and remove cabinet ministers without congressional approval. Very important to presidential power has been the political management of the economy, particularly because of the large number of state-owned enterprises, a realm in which the president has had autonomy. However, Mexican presidents have not enjoyed nearly such great institutional bases of power as some other Latin American presidents, particularly those in Brazil, Ecuador, Paraguay, and Uruguay (Shugart and Carey, 1992).

Instead of relying on cultural or institutional explanations of legislative weakness, one can develop an electorally based explanation of *presidencialismo* and unified government (in the behavioural sense) and thereby predict its demise. As Jeffrey A. Weldon (forthcoming) states: 'There are three necessary conditions that create the meta-constitutional powers of the presidency in Mexico: unified government [in the arithmetic sense], party discipline, and the recognition of the president as party leader. If any of these conditions are relaxed, the president should lose some or all of his extraordinary powers.' In the past six years, each of these conditions has eroded or ceased to exist. Let us first explore how each of these conditions functioned to create unified government in the behavioural sense.

Unified government in the arithmetic sense was created in the 1930s when PRI had its origins, a theme too complex to describe here (see Garrido, 1982).

The three key factors allowing the PRI to maintain its arithmetic domination of Congress were its corporatist structure, its incumbent advantages, and its indirect control of the national and state-level electoral authorities. The PRI's corporatist structure was built by Lázaro Cárdenas during his presidency (1934–40), with the party being organized into three 'pillars', the official labour movement, the official peasant movement, and the 'popular sector', a diverse group of urban organizations the most important of which were bureaucrats and teachers. Once the numerical majority of Mexicans, those organized into the corporatist pillars of the party could be mobilized or coerced to vote for the PRI at all levels of government. Very few voters split their tickets, PRI presidential candidates won by extraordinarily wide margins, and hence PRI congressional candidates were swept into office in almost all of the single-member constituencies across the country. Once in office, PRI presidents could use incumbency advantages to reward those whose votes had to be bought—not peasants or manual workers, but those in the 'popular sector', especially white-collar workers in urban areas. To ensure that the party did not split and to encumber those who would attempt to create credible opposition parties, the PRI passed a new electoral law in 1946 that gave it control over the electoral authorities, that prohibited candidacies not postulated by registered political parties, and that gave the electoral authorities control over party registrations (Molinar Horcasitas, 1991).

Unified government in the arithmetic sense would not have ensured unified government in the behavioural sense if there had not been unusual party discipline within the PRI. Party discipline within the PRI resulted from two institutional features of Mexican politics, one an electoral law, the other a party rule. Mexico's no re-election clause, which applies to all elected posts in the country, inhibits legislators from establishing independent bases of support in their constituencies and discourages their development of expertise in the issue areas in which they are given committee assignments (Nacif, 1997). Unable to seek re-election, legislators must constantly look toward their next political opportunities, either new elected posts or administrative assignments which they hope will promote their careers (Smith, 1979: 221–2). The PRI party rule that has made nominations for elected positions a closed list (only in the past three years has the PRI begun to hold primaries for gubernatorial and presidential nominations), when combined with the no re-election clause, promotes party discipline of the highest order. Who would seek to confront the party leader(s) in a context in which one's political future could be stymied by angry superiors?

Of course, if the president is not the head of the disciplined majority party in Congress, he cannot be assured that his legislative initiatives will pass. However, Mexican presidents since the 1930s have been understood to be the leaders of their party. Lázaro Cárdenas created the institutional arrangements of the modern PRI during his presidency and by its end had become effectively both president of the republic and head of the PRI. He passed this dual power on to his successor, and each president from then until the beginning of Zedillo's administration also held *de facto* leadership of the party (Weldon, forthcoming).

## The Erosion of the Bases of Unified Government

These factors, then, have been the bases of *presidencialismo*, or unified government in the behavioural sense. If one or more ceases to operate, unified government will be eroded or destroyed. The PRI's capacity to produce electoral super-majorities was the first factor to go by the wayside. Two separate processes contributed to the PRI's decline. First, the demographic and socio-economic bases upon which PRI electoral hegemony had been built gradually eroded due first to the successes of the development model pursued by the PRI and then later to the colossal failures of the model in the 1980s. As Mexico modernized, a smaller and smaller share of the population remained in the peasantry, the official labour movement, and other captive organizations (see Klesner, 1993). As Mexicans became better educated, they increasingly sought to exercise political independence. The vote shares of opposition parties thus grew in the 1960s and early 1970s, albeit slowly. Then, when the excesses of Mexican populism produced an insurmountable foreign debt crisis in the 1980s, forcing the government to yield to the structural adjustment demands of the international financial community, the nation endured its 'lost decade of the 1980s', nearly ten years in which the economy either did not grow or actually declined. Many voters fled from the PRI as early as the local elections in 1983, a phenomenon that accelerated during the middle of the decade, when opposition challenges led the PRI to engage in blatant vote-stealing to ensure its victories in congressional elections in 1985 and in state elections in Chihuahua in 1986. The electoral culmination of the voters' first rejection of the PRI came in 1988, when the PRI's Carlos Salinas de Gortari won a fraud-tainted election over Cuauhémoc Cárdenas, son of the president who had given the PRI its modern form but who had bolted from the party in 1987.

Second, two major events produced legitimacy crises for the one-party regime. The first came in 1968 when a student movement emerged in the run-up to the Summer Olympic Games, held that year in Mexico City. The government, seeking to avoid the spectacle of protests telecast around the world, repressed the movement, killing hundreds and jailing many more. In so doing it alienated the intelligentsia and a sizeable share of the youth population, leading some student leaders to form unregistered political parties and others to engage in political violence. To incorporate the new left into the official electoral arena, thereby hoping to relegitimate the regime, the government sponsored a political reform in 1977 that relaxed many of the registration barriers imposed in 1946 and that created 100 seats reserved for the opposition in an expanded 400-seat Chamber of Deputies. In 1986, responding to further opposition demands for representation, the government added 100 more PR seats to the Chamber.

The second political trauma came with Salinas's tainted victory in 1988. Cuauhtémoc Cárdenas's near-defeat of the PRI standard-bearer and the defections from the PRI that made Cárdenas's candidacy viable allowed the formation of a major party of the left in the form of the Democratic Revolutionary Party (Partido de la Revolución Democráta, PRD). In addition, Salinas's narrow victory margin meant that the PRI held a narrow congressional majority, as mentioned above. Relying on the PAN to support major policy initiatives, Salinas was forced to negotiate additional electoral reforms which helped to make the electoral playing field more level by increasing the degree of independence of the electoral authorities (thereby guarding against PRI-perpetrated electoral fraud) and improving the opposition's access to public financing of campaigns and to the broadcast media (Klesner, 1997).

As the result of these economic developments and the regime's crises of legitimacy, by the early 1990s the PRI's super-majorities had become mere majorities, and barely that—Salinas and Zedillo each won just a whisker more than half of the votes in 1988 and 1994, respectively. However, since opposition parties on both the left and the right had developed, the PRI could divide and conquer, particularly in the senatorial elections and the 300 single-member lower-house districts where the first-past-the-post rules favoured the PRI (see the top of Table 4.1 and Table 4.2). By the mid-1990s, however, the PRI's decline suggested that another major crisis might provide the opposition with an opportunity to take the lower house of Congress. The political crises of 1994—the peasant uprising in the southern state of Chiapas and the assassination of the PRI's first presidential candidate, Luis Donaldo Colosio—provided the opposition parties with the chance to pressure the PRI to engage in further electoral reforms (in 1994 and 1996) that finally freed the electoral authorities from PRI control and limited the over-representation of the PRI in the Chamber of Deputies to no more than 8 per cent (meaning that a party had to obtain 42 per cent of the vote to take half of the seats). These reforms, one preceding the economic collapse of 1995, the other following it, allowed the opposition parties to take advantage of voter anger at the PRI for the sharp economic downturn in 1995 to deny the PRI a majority in the Chamber of Deputies in 1997. Hence, unified government in the numerical sense ended in 1997 after a long, at first gradual, then accelerating erosion of PRI hegemony.

The PRI maintained remarkable party discipline during the economic restructuring of the 1980s and 1990s, with members of Congress voting for legislation to dismantle the large state sector of the economy that many surely did not personally support. But even the PRI's remarkable party discipline began to show some strain in the first half (1994–7) of the Zedillo presidency. In particular, members of the PRI objected to some of the electoral reforms proposed by Zedillo as a part of his 'definite electoral reform' package that was finally approved in 1996. PRI congressional leaders significantly amended those aspects of Zedillo's reform package that dealt with campaign finance reform and the parties' access to the media (Klesner, 1997), elements of the electoral system the loss of which PRI deputies felt would greatly compromise the ability of the party to win elections. Other elements of Zedillo's legislative agenda that were stalled or significantly modified by the PRI-controlled Chamber of Deputies in the first half of his term included social security reforms, the sale of petrochemical plants owned by the state oil firm PEMEX, and the creation of the new position of federal controller (Weldon, forthcoming).

This evidence of PRI legislators' opposition to presidential initiatives suggests that the PRI congressional delegation's recognition of the president as head of party declined during Zedillo's term too. At the beginning of Zedillo's term his own preference for a 'healthy distance' between the PRI and the presidency can be identified as a major factor in weakening executive dominance over the legislature. Indeed, Weldon (forthcoming) argues that when Zedillo began to act in a more partisan way during the 1997 congressional campaign, his party began to respond by exercising greater discipline in the Congress. Casar's data (2000: 45–6) indicate that the PRI was still by far the most disciplined party in the 1997–2000 legislature.

In addition, the president's capacity to wield the threat of withholding nomination to future offices has lost some of its former power. As other parties have become more competitive, especially since 1994, those PRI members who have failed to get the nominations they sought from the executive and the party leadership have increasingly exercised their 'exit option' (see Casar, forthcoming). While some of these PRI members have defected to the PAN, the majority have gone over to the PRD, a phenomenon that led to several PRD victories at the state level in 1998 and 1999 (Klesner, 1999). Hence, the capacity of the presidency to compel legislative discipline has diminished as the PRI's electoral margins have narrowed.

I have sought to emphasize that the unusual power of the Mexican presidency during the PRI's heyday owed much more to electoral factors than to either cultural or institutional ones. As the PRI's electoral majority faded, the operation of forces that had produced the unusual party discipline and the willingness to concede to presidential leadership began to weaken. When it lost its majority in the Chamber of Deputies in 1997, *presidencialismo* could no longer operate as it had, even though Mexican institutional arrangements had not changed and arguably the culture had not either. With the PRI's loss of the presidency to Vicente Fox of the PAN in 2000, *presidencialismo* is dead.

How have executive–legislative relations evolved with the PRI's loss of the Chamber? How will they likely operate under a non-PRI president?

## THE MANAGEMENT OF DIVIDED GOVERNMENT IN MEXICO

### *The Operation of Unified Government*

Once again, the operation of unified government provides the best context for understanding how divided government has worked. When the PRI held a majority, it directed the Chamber of Deputies through a committee-of-committees called the Gran Comisión, on which one representative of each of the thirty-two states was seated. For years the state delegations only elected PRI members to this oversight committee. Then, in 1979 a law on parliamentary procedures provided that the Gran Comisión should be composed only of members of the majority party (Nacif, forthcoming). The Gran Comisión made appointments to other committees and controlled the agenda of Chamber. Likewise, a Gran Comisión existed to manage the Senate's business (Camp, 1995). Because of these committees' power to control the agenda and to make committee assignments, the head of the Gran Comisión in each house was the effective leader of each body and was chosen by the president (Camp, 1999: 165–7).

As has been mentioned, most legislation originated in the executive branch and came to the Congress in the form of presidential initiatives. Ordinarily bills are submitted to committees before reaching the floor of either house, except when the chamber suspends that rule by a two-thirds vote because a bill is of 'urgent or obvious resolution' (Weldon, 1998: 1). Although committees are supposed to report bills out within fifteen days, they seldom meet this goal. Bills that eventually make it to the floor of a chamber must receive an absolute majority of votes from the committee members considering it, with the committee chair getting a second vote (a *voto de calidad*) in the event of ties (Weldon, 1998: 2). Those holding committee chairs, because of their *voto de calidad* and their control of the committee's meeting agenda, thus have been able to exercise some real power. Amendments to bills can be made in committee and on the floor, but technically any amendments to a bill on the floor are supposed to send a bill back to the committee (unless the committee agrees to an amendment on the floor). So, as Weldon concludes, 'The rules give the committee a veto over any amendments to its own [report]' (1998: 5). However, as Weldon's evidence suggests, during the period of the PRI's virtual monopoly of congressional seats (1930–64), the vast majority of public bills were not amended either in committee or on the floor of the Chamber of Deputies (1998: 17). Here the logic of the system that allowed presidential dominance can be seen: even though the formal institutional arrangements, both the relationship of the legislature to the executive in regard to law-making and the internal procedures of the Chamber of Deputies, would have allowed the Congress to exercise independence *vis-à-vis* the president, the Chamber rarely even amended presidential bills (Casar, 1996). That the Congress did not exercise the institutional prerogatives it enjoyed by the Constitution must be attributed to the legislators' subservience to the partisan powers of the president, particularly his capacity to make next career step available to those PRI legislators.

To appreciate how much PRI legislators depended on the president to make their career move forward, consider Table 4.3, which presents a list of positions that PRI deputies might regard to be attractive as next moves in their political careers. In the period from 1979 to 1997, approximately 300 PRI deputies would be leaving office at the end of each three-year term. For them, about 1,030 political appointments (elective offices, party posts, and administrative positions in the federal and state governments) would be appealing subsequent jobs. Of course, they would be competing with governors, senators, and mayors leaving their posts because of the clause forbidding re-election and with those party and state officials who would want to rise within the party or the state. Hence, having the support of the president or those close to him would be essential for career advancement. Therefore, the Gran Comisión placed the most reliable and experienced PRI legislators in the chairs of committees and the committees reported out presidential initiatives with few if any amendments. With an overwhelming numerical advantage, the PRI then passed the president's bills by near-unanimity.

The PRI's control of committees came to an end in a 1991 reform of the Chamber of Deputies by which the parties represented in the lower house would

TABLE 4.3. *The structure of opportunities for PRI deputies in Mexico*

| Position | Approx. no. |
| --- | --- |
| *Elective offices* | 322 |
| Governors | 32 |
| Senators | 128 |
| Mayors of major cities | 100 |
| Top positions in state legislatures | 62 |
| *Party offices* | 84 |
| National Executive Committee | 30 |
| Top State-level party posts | 64 |
| Sectoral offices | not known |
| State administration | 624 |
| Federal bureaucracy | 500 |
| Top State-level party posts | 124 |
| Total | 1,030 |

*Source*: Ugalde (2000: 120).

receive committee chairs in proportion to the size of their delegation (Nacif, forthcoming). This reform came in reaction to the opposition parties' demands to be given greater voice in the internal organization of the Chamber after their unprecedented success in the 1988 election when they received 240 of the Chamber's 500 seats. Giving committee chairs to opposition legislators did not significantly change the legislative process at that juncture, however, because most important legislation emanated from the executive departments and the PRI still held committee majorities that could vote down opposition bills.

### The Management of a Divided Chamber of Deputies

Once the PRI lost its majority of the Chamber of Deputies, the procedures described above could not function as they had before. To begin, with no party in a majority, the Gran Comisión did not have to be formed, indeed could not be formed according to the 1979 law on the Chamber's internal organization. The four parties that denied the PRI its Chamber majority in 1997 effectively formed a negative coalition that united mainly for the procedural purpose of denying the PRI control of Congress, or to put it another way, to produce divided government. At the outset of the 1997–2000 legislature, the PRI held 239 seats and the other four parties 261.[8] Although many observers worried that the two smallest opposition parties, the Labor Party (Partido del Trabajo, PT) with seven seats and the Green Party (PVEM) with eight, would be bought off by the PRI so it could retain its majority, that did not transpire. The procedural coalition held against the PRI when it tried to claim that, because it was the largest party (even if not the majority), it should be given the leadership posts in the Chamber (Dillon, 1997a). The coalition refused to form a Gran Comisión and instead shifted power to the Internal Rules and Political Coordination Committee (CRICP), on which each party had a representative. To deal with the obvious point that all parties on the CRICP had different sized congressional delegations, the parties arrived at a weighted voting arrangement (Weldon, 1998). Then, after a highly confrontational opening to the legislative session that included heckling, fisticuffs, and broken chairs, the procedural majority granted chairs of the most important committees to the PRD and the PAN and agreed to rotate the leadership positions among the opposition parties in the Chamber (de la Garza, 1997).

Given that the PRI retained its majority in the Senate and that Zedillo continued as president in 1997–2000, the opposition majority in the Chamber could hardly expect to embark on a major legislative programme, even if the PAN and the PRD had been able to agree on one. As it was, they tended to disagree strongly on economic policy and to see each other as rivals for second

---

[8] Several deputies defected from their parties during the 1997–2000 legislature. The PAN lost four members, the PVEM two, and the PRI one by Sept. 1999. See Weldon (2000: 1).

place in electoral politics. Therefore, a PAN–PRD–PT or PAN–PRD–PVEM coalition (either would have been sufficient to pass bills) was unlikely on substantive grounds because the two larger parties in such combinations disagreed on the policy prescriptions in most areas. So, with presidential legislating being the norm and no other substantive majority likely to form in the Chamber, the 1997–2000 term became marked by the efforts by President Zedillo to find majorities on an issue-by-issue basis, luring opposition parties into temporary alliance with the PRI to keep the government working.

María Amparo Casar has produced the most extensive published evidence about the parties' voting patterns in the period from September 1998 to August 1999 (electronic voting did not begin until then, and, thus, role-call data was less available). Table 4.4 summarizes her findings about coalitional patterns in four substantive areas: economic policy, public security and the judiciary, political issues (organization of the Congress, political reforms, and so forth), and all others. As her data indicate, the PAN ended up voting with the PRI on economic issues, which is not surprising given the closeness of the two parties on economic policy. Those two parties also allied on political matters, although the majority of votes on political issues dealt with congressional rules, the most important of which had been changed the year before. In the other issue areas, the most frequent coalitions were of all parties—perhaps predictable on the less confrontational issues grouped under 'other' and even so on public security issues, given the salience of concerns about public safety in Mexico in recent years.[9]

TABLE 4.4. *Coalitions in the Mexican Chamber of Deputies, September 1998–August 1999 (%)*

| Coalition | Economy | Public security | Politics | Other | Total |
|---|---|---|---|---|---|
| All parties | 37 | 33 | 11 | 89 | 37 |
| PRI-PAN | 47 | 0 | 49 | 0 | 30 |
| PRI-PAN-PVEM* | 8 | 22 | 3 | 6 | 9 |
| PRI-PAN-PVEM-PT* | 3 | 38 | 0 | 0 | 9 |
| PRI-PAN-PRD* | 0 | 0 | 17 | 0 | 5 |
| PRI-PAN-PRD-PVEM* | 0 | 0 | 2 | 6 | 2 |
| PRI-PRD-PT | 0 | 7 | 0 | 0 | 2 |
| PRT-PT | 0 | 0 | 2 | 0 | 1 |
| All opposition | 5 | 0 | 14 | 0 | 6 |
| Total | 100 | 100 | 100 | 100 | 100 |

* Sometimes including independent legislators
*Source*: Derived from Casar (2000: 42–4).

[9] Weldon (2000), using different techniques for determining coalition formation patterns, arrives at the same general conclusions as Casar.

The party that tended to be marginalized in the 1997–2000 legislature was the PRD, which Casar found had been excluded from far more winning coalitions than any other party—the PRD was excluded from 49 per cent of winning coalitions, while the PAN was in on all but 2.5 per cent and the PRI all but 6 per cent of the coalitions that passed legislation (Casar, 2000: 44). The PRD's intransigent refusal to co-operate with the PRI on many issues meant that it was infrequently sought by the PRI or by Zedillo to support presidential initiatives. The PRD proved to be a less disciplined party too, although all parties showed relatively high levels of discipline among their Chamber delegations, particularly in situations in which a vote was seen as a party-line ballot (see Casar, 2000; Weldon, 2000).

So, in the 1997–2000 legislature Mexican parties dealt with political cohabitation in two ways. On one hand, the opposition parties allied to deny the PRI participation in procedural issues. This they did because they explicitly sought to weaken the PRI and the power of the presidency. On the other hand, many legislators recognized that, for the government to perform its functions, legislation must be approved by the Congress. Particularly on issues of government finance—raising government revenues and deciding how those revenues would be spent—the Congress had no choice but to approve legislation. Therefore, a revenue bill would have to be passed each year as well as a budget bill. To achieve passage of a budget bill and other bills to which he attached great importance, President Zedillo had to find allies in the Chamber. Typically he found them in the PAN. Moreover, he continued to need the discipline of his own party. This he won. Those who have analysed the roll-call data (such as it is) have concluded that PRI deputies less frequently voted against their party (Casar, 2000: 45–6; Weldon, 2000).

I should emphasize that the Zedillo administration followed a strategy of building coalitions on a case-by-case basis. Although the PAN more frequently allied with the PRI than did other parties, there was no permanent coalition between the PRI and the PAN. Indeed, Weldon's analysis suggests that, as the electoral campaign heated up in the latter half of 1999, the PRI and the PAN allied less frequently than they had the year before, suggesting that each had begun positioning itself for the presidential race. Further, the PAN allied more frequently with the PVEM, its eventual electoral coalition partner, than with any other party, and the PRD did likewise with the PT, with which it formed an electoral coalition in late 1999 (Weldon, 2000).

This type of coalition formation is not atypical of presidential regimes. The Chamber has no need to support a government, as in parliamentary regimes, hence it has no reason to have a permanent coalition to conduct its business. Although it supported the Zedillo government in much of its legislative agenda, the PAN did not do so because it was part of that government—although a PAN member served as Zedillo's first attorney-general. Policy convergence between the PAN and the technocrats in Zedillo's administration may explain the legislative alliance better than any other factor. Indeed, many legislators in the PRI probably disliked the president's initiatives more than did PAN deputies, but Zedillo could still impose discipline on those PRI members.

### *Divided Government and Budget-Making: A Brief Case-Study*

The budget bills passed during Zedillo's term offer excellent insight into the management of divided government. As mentioned above, the Chamber of Deputies has the sole authority to pass the budget, which the president must submit to it by 15 November. The ordinary legislative session closes on 15 December, so haste is necessary to complete the budget proceedings on time. Historically, the Chamber barely modified the presidential initiative at all. James Wilkie (1970: 17–20) found that during the PRI's heyday, the approved budget rarely differed from the presidential bill by more than 0.2 per cent.

In December 1997, the Chamber of Deputies took up Zedillo's 1998 budget proposal. As is normal, they first considered the revenue bill. Both the PAN and the PRD had promised in their congressional campaigns to lower the nation's value-added tax (IVA) from its 15 per cent level if elected, the PAN because its middle-class and business constituency simply did not support taxation, the PRD because it felt the IVA fell disproportionately on the poor, the PRD's major support base. On 4 December 1997, the two parties plus their coalition partners voted to lower the IVA from 15 to 12 per cent. This vote was largely symbolic, or at least their leaders must have known it was largely symbolic, because the president refused to accept that action—it threatened to widen the budget deficit, which Zedillo was trying to reduce to 1.25 per cent of GDP. The revenue bill, which had to pass both chambers, was changed in the Senate to remove the IVA reduction. The PAN then decided to acquiesce to the president's revenue bill so that the government could continue to operate (Sarmiento, 1997).

The PAN joined with the PRI to pass the budget bill in the Chamber. Although many observers called the PAN decision a 'definitive split in the opposition alliance', PAN legislators argued otherwise. As Francisco José Paoli, a PAN congressional leader, argued during the budget debate, 'In the PAN we never conceded nor accepted that the election on the 6th of July [1997] was a vote to change economic policy—that's false!' Another PAN deputy said that his party 'is co-responsible for the governability of the nation' (Camacho Guzman and Pérez Silva, 1997). However, the PAN's vote in favour of Zedillo's 1998 budget was hardly based on its sense of responsibility for the country's governability alone. In the negotiations that yielded the 1998 budget, the PAN was able to reduce the size of a secret fund controlled by the president by two-thirds and to place limits on how the executive could disburse many line items in the budget, thereby 'significantly reducing the President's discretionary authority', according to the *New York Times* reporter who investigated the budget talks (Dillon, 1997*b*). In addition, the PAN successfully urged the PRI to move US$800 million from a fund to bail out failing banks and instead directed it to federal distributions to municipalities (Dillon, 1997*b*). The latter move was significant because by December 1997 PAN mayors governed most of the nation's largest cities but had relatively weak revenue bases for dealing with urban problems.

In the 1997 budget process we see patterns emerging that were to characterize subsequent budget processes and that provide insight into the management of divided government in Mexico. To begin, the convergence of policy perspectives between the executive branch and the PAN created opportunities for deals to yield the necessary majorities to pass budget bills. Indeed, one carefully designed study (Estévez and Magaloni, 1998) suggested that the PAN–PRI–executive branch alliance found its basis in the centre-right tendencies of the electorates that voted those two parties into the Chamber. Not to vote together on fiscal matters would have threatened either party's electoral base. Second, the PAN used its strategic position to wrest important concessions from the Zedillo government. The PAN intended that some of those concessions would weaken presidential powers, for example, the reduction in the size of the president's secret slush fund and greater constraints on his discretion in spending allocated monies. Other deals benefited specific PAN constituencies—as a result of the 1998 budget, those living in PAN governed cities would be better served because of the increased federal disbursements to municipalities. Finally, the president used the occasion of budget negotiations—where, after all, more than just symbols are on the table—to split the opposition parties and to keep the PRD, which the PRI for years regarded as more dangerous than the PAN, marginalized. The PRD's frustration with the whole process was evident when the party marched out of the Chamber *en masse* after the budget vote. A PAN congressional leader characterized the PRD's behaviour: 'They wanted to control and annul the executive. Our [PAN's] idea is that Mexico needs a strong but contained executive with enough flexibility to operate efficiently' (Preston, 1997).

In 1998, the PAN again joined with the PRI to pass Zedillo's proposed 1999 budget. This round of budget talks had a complicating factor too—not the IVA this time, but the bank bailout fund (known as FONAPROA). The bank bailout grew to unexpected proportions in 1998, and the PAN and the PRI developed a plan to finance FONAPROA, but the PAN wanted a symbolic gesture from the government so that it would not seem as though the PAN had colluded with the PRI in bailing out bankers who had extended questionable loans to family members and political cronies. The price the PAN asked was the resignation of the head of the Banco de Mexico, Guillermo Ortiz, who had been finance minister when the size of the bailout ballooned (Preston, 1998). In the end, the PAN did not get Ortiz's resignation, but it did get an agreement that he could not serve on the board of FONAPROA (Tangeman, 1999). This deal the PAN saw as its effort to limit the powers of the executive in the 1998 budget process.

Substantively, Zedillo again sought a budget with a deficit of no more than 1.25 per cent of GDP, a goal with which the PAN agreed. The issue was how to achieve it in a year in which oil prices (oil revenues account for about one-third of Mexican state revenues) had dropped. Zedillo had wanted to avoid cutting government expenditures, instead proposing to increase revenues so as to hit his targeted deficit. However, the tax increase he proposed—a 15 per cent tax on telephone bills—was unpopular with the public and with foreign telephone companies, and therefore with the PAN. The PAN instead urged the president to cut expenditure, succeeding in getting a US$1.4 billion cut in expenditures while agreeing to a modest increase in some tariffs, a phasing-in of a corporate tax reduction, and the cancellation of a reduction in taxes on alcoholic beverages (Downie, 1999). So again in the process of joining with the PRI in passing the 1999 budget, the PAN forced the president to make substantive concessions and to recognize some limitations in his latitude for action—in this case, constraining his ability to appoint a political ally to an important post on the FONAPROA board.

In December 1999, as the Chamber debated Zedillo's 2000 budget proposal, all parties had an eye on the July 2000 presidential election, for which candidates had already been named. To emphasize the independence of the Chamber *vis-à-vis* the president, the four opposition parties had drafted an alternative to the president's budget. However, the PRI managed to lure away a handful of the opposition's deputies, and their bill was defeated at the end of the Chamber's regular session. However, the PRI's first attempt to pass the presidential budget initiative also failed during an extraordinary session, forcing a second extraordinary session. Substantively the opposition's budget and the presidential bill differed little—about 0.3 per cent—suggesting that the parties were positioning themselves in electoral politics rather than debating real differences in budget philosophy (Dillon, 1999).

Again, issues associated with the budget but not formally part of the budget bill played large roles in the inter-party conflict. In particular, the PRI was able to narrowly avert the passage of a bill supported by all of the opposition parties that would have cut funds to the bank bailout fund when several opposition legislators failed to appear for that crucial vote. However, in the end, the budget initiative passed by an overwhelming margin as the opposition parties won from the PRI additional funds for states and municipalities, pensions, health care, and other social programmes (Hernández *et al.*, 1999).

The struggles between the president and the opposition in the Chamber of Deputies over the budget, the most public of their battles, have thus ended with budgets passed that have been little different from those initially proposed by the president. Each year the Chamber has passed the budget in time for it to be put in place for the coming fiscal year. The debates have been long and loud, and the opposition has endeavoured to win symbolic victories over the president that suggest that the Chamber is now the president's equal. However, the bottom line is that, so far, divided government has not forced government to shut down in Mexico as it sometimes has in the US. By giving up some symbolic victories to the opposition and yielding some material gains to their constituencies, Zedillo saw his budgets passed.

## EPILOGUE

In the last years of the PRI's control of the presidency, Ernesto Zedillo was able to manage executive–legislative relations by forging alliances with opposition parties on a issue-by-issue basis, usually turning to the PAN on the economic policy issues so central to his government's agenda. A member of the PAN now sits in the presidential chair. Will Vicente Fox be able to manage divided government as well as Zedillo? Given an ambitious agenda of reform of governmental structures, he must hope to do so.

Working in Fox's favour is that, in the past legislature, the PAN formed the centre of the coalitional system. Weldon's research (2000) indicates that the five parties represented in the Chamber arrayed themselves on a single ideological dimension that ran, from left to right, PRD–PT–PVEM–PAN–PRI. The PRI and the PRD very seldom allied in a coalition that excluded the PAN. Thus, as in the 1997–2000 legislature, Fox might hope to win PRI legislators over to join with the PAN to support his economic policy initiatives while turning to the left to win the PRD and the other parties to his side on issues of state reform. Much depends on the willingness of these parties and their leaderships to co-operate with Fox. Since he will only have 208 PAN votes, or 223 votes from his electoral coalition with the PVEM, Fox will be far short of the 251 votes needed for a majority. If the PRI and the PRD wish simply to obstruct Fox, they could, unless Fox can buy the votes of PRI and PRD legislators who, after all, will need new positions after July 2003.

A key political reform issue will be re-election of legislators. Even some PRI leaders have come out in favour of eliminating the ban on re-election of members of Congress (Rossell and Gutiérrez, 1999). If re-election of legislators is re-established, two weaknesses of the Congress can be remedied. First, the capacity of party leaders and of the president to coerce or to buy the loyalty of legislators will be greatly diminished as members of Congress build their bases of support in their districts. Of course, this will not apply to those deputies and senators elected on PR lists, so another political dynamic may develop between the party leaders elected on the PR lists and those back benchers with safe constituencies. Second, members of Congress who serve several terms will develop legislative and policy expertise that will bolster the capacity of Congress to openly debate with the executive branch on policy issues and to pose more credible policy alternatives. No political reform could more effectively promote Mexican democracy than permitting re-election of legislators.

# 5

# Divided Government in Finland: From a Semi-Presidential to a Parliamentary Democracy

## *Heikki Paloheimo*

In cross-national comparisons the Finnish political system has been classified as one of the semi-presidential systems where executive power is divided between an elected president and a government responsible to the parliament (Duverger, 1980). According to the old Finnish constitution that was in force from 1919 to 2000 (Act 94/1919 with later amendments) the president appointed governments, presented government bills to parliament, ratified laws accepted in the parliament, issued decrees, led Finnish foreign policy, appointed judges of the Supreme Court, the Supreme Administrative Court, and Courts of Appeal, as well as senior civil servants, was the head of the armed forces, could grant pardons, had the right to dissolve the parliament and to convene extraordinary sessions of the parliament. Thus, these duties included legislative, executive, and judicial powers.

However, the constitution did not accurately reflect the real division of power between the president and the government. It is typical of many parliamentary democratic systems that presidents are armed with constitutional powers they do not actively use. In Finland different presidents have used their constitutional prerogatives in highly different ways. The Finnish semi-presidential regime has been, as Dag Anckar has put it, for the presidents like a 'buffet table' (1999). It has been up to the president to choose which constitutional powers they want to pick up from the constitutional buffet table. Some presidents have been quite moderate in using their powers, leaving much room for the parliamentary side of the executive body. Others have used their powers more actively. President Urho Kekkonen (1956–81) was, as Anckar puts it, a *gourmand*. But none of the Finnish presidents have been really ascetic, not even the presidents who have had a highly parliamentary ethos.

The division of power between president and government established a system of divided government in Finland. However, divided government was also present in another sense. The frequency of minority governments and the qualified majorities that were needed to pass legislation often made it necessary for the governments to co-operate actively with the parliamentary opposition in order to implement their policies. In this sense, divided government has manifested itself in terms of the 'cohabitation' between the government and the legislature in the Finnish system.

## AN OVERVIEW OF POLITICS IN FINLAND

### *The Division of Power: Four Periods*

Based on the styles and frequency of divided government, Finnish political history may be divided into four periods: the First Republic, 1917–39; wartime, 1939–44; the Second Republic, 1944–82; and parliamentarization, 1982–2000. Divided government was common during the first decades following the independence of the country in 1917 and in the period immediately after the Second World War. However, since the 1980s Finland has moved towards a normal parliamentary system and divided government has almost totally disappeared.

The search for democratic traditions in the First Republic occurred in the circumstances where the cleavage between different social groups was sharp and the party system was polarized and fragmented. Conservatives expected strong, almost monarchical leadership, while Liberals and Social Democrats were more sceptical towards a strong executive.

Although the monarchical features of the Swedish Gustavian constitutions had to some extent been copied to the Finnish constitution, the first president, Kaarlo J. Ståhlberg, did not rule like a king. As a liberal, he had a parliamentary ethos. He did not, however, resign himself to being merely a figurehead. He carried out his duties in conditions where the party system was polarized and fragmented, no single party had a majority in the parliament, the coalition capability of the parties was low, and government coalitions were both fragile and unstable. In these conditions, Ståhlberg was active in the process of government formation. Besides two majority coalitions and four minority coalitions, Ståhlberg's presidency also included two caretaker governments that took the form of quasi-presidential governments. When the young, party-based parliamentary system was unstable, a president elected for a fixed term gave stability to the executive.

Ståhlberg established a model for the Finnish semi-presidential system. He wanted to stabilize the functioning of the parliamentary system, but was also ready to lead and rule in order to make the system work. Thus, beginning with Ståhlberg's presidency, Finnish presidents have been active political leaders and decision-makers with their own preferences and policy styles, arbitrators of political conflicts, opinion leaders in public life as well as representative figureheads of the state (Nousiainen, 1998: 206). The typical features of the First Republic were that the party system was fragmented and polarized and the capability of the parties to form coalitions was low; governments were weak, unstable, and short-lived; governments were mainly minority governments; the parliamentary opposition was strong enough to overthrow governments but too weak to form new coalitions; when governments were weak and unstable presidents had to use their prerogatives quite actively.

During the Second World War, governments were all-party governments or at least they enjoyed a qualified majority in parliament. Actual decision-making was very centralized. Decisions were made by the president, prime minister, a couple of ministers, and Marshal Mannerheim, Commander of the Finnish armed forces, in a kind of war cabinet.

In the First Republic and during wartime, the president's public role was monarchical. After their election they handed over their party membership cards and no longer participated in party activities. They were supposed to be above party disputes and they were not publicly criticized in the newspapers (Nousiainen, 1985).

The third phase of executive power began after the Second World War. During this period, often called the Second Republic, presidents Paasikivi and Kekkonen took foreign policy leadership into their own hands. Moreover, when Kekkonen was president he gradually increased his power in domestic affairs too. The Finnish semi-presidential system was becoming presidentialized (Arter, 1981; Anckar, 1990). Kekkonen involved himself so actively in party disputes that over time he was openly criticized. Since the latter half of Kekkonen's presidency, successive presidents have been criticized in the media just as much as any other politician.

The typical features of the Second Republic were that the coalition capability of the parties gradually increased; over time majority governments became common; the life-span of governments became longer; internal disagreements were the most common cause of government resignations; all majority coalitions were still 'connected' coalitions on the left–right continuum; the qualified majority requirements in the legislature meant that the parliamentary opposition was a sort of 'associated member' of the government, particularly in the creation of the welfare state; presidents monopolized foreign policy decision-making; and presidents were ready to use their powers to keep government in check.

From Mauno Koivisto's presidency it is possible to talk about a fourth phase of executive power. This is the period of parliamentarization, as the semi-presidential features of the Finnish constitution have largely disappeared. During this period, presidents have taken decisions in active co-operation with the government. Moreover, governments have been majority coalitions and they have stayed in office for the whole electoral term. In a word, a stable parliamentary system has been consolidated (Nousianen, 1997).

The main features of this period are that the coalition capability of the parties is high; governments have been strong and stable; the coalition 'elasticity' of the parties has been high—three out of six governments have not been connected coalitions on the left–right continuum; the qualified majority rule has been abolished, meaning that the parliamentary opposition has been weak; the powers of the president have been reduced, which has strengthened the government's role; and in both domestic affairs and Finnish policy towards the EU the prime minister has become the main decision-maker.

## The 1919 Constitution Act

The Finnish semi-presidential system was the result of a number of factors: social development prior to Finnish independence in 1917; the aims of Conservatives to counter the revolutionary pressures of the socialist labour movement; and compromises between Conservative and Liberal politicians concerning the division of power between different state organs.

The 1919 Constitution Act was a compromise between the Conservatives and Liberals. The Liberals won the battle between republicans and monarchists. Finland became a republic. The Conservatives won the battle about the role and powers of the head of state. The president was given large degree of power, both executive and legislative. As a result, presidents were able to counter any revolutionary pressures in parliament.

According to the 1919 Constitution Act, sovereign state power rested with the people. The people were represented by a democratically elected parliament and legislative power was exercised by parliament in conjunction with the president. The president formally presented bills to parliament, promulgated laws, and could enact decrees. The president was elected indirectly for a six-year term by an electoral college of party representatives who themselves were directly elected by the people.

Executive power was divided between the president and the government. The president had supreme executive power. The government, or the council of state, was headed by the prime minister and included a requisite number of ministers.

The need for co-operation between the government and the parliamentary opposition, the Finnish version of political 'cohabitation', was to a great extent based on the guaranteed rights of the minorities. In the original version of the 1919 Constitution, a small minority could block legislation in parliament. According to Section 66 of the Constitution Act, one-third of all deputies (67 MPs) could vote to postpone a law. A postponed law could be considered again in the first session of parliament after subsequent general election and would come into force if it was then supported by a majority of deputies.

The intention of this constitutional arrangement was to prevent radical, socialist reforms being passed by a simple parliamentary majority. In 1916, just a year before the declaration of independence, the Social Democratic party won a majority of seats in the unicameral Finnish parliament, but parliament was dissolved and an early election was called so as to strengthen the power of non-socialist parties.

Since independence, no single party has ever won a majority of seats in the parliament. After the Second World War, when the cleavage between left- and right-wing parties moderated and the coalition capability of parties improved, governments have often had active co-operation from the parliamentary opposition.

## Partial Reforms towards Parliamentarism

The 1919 Constitution was in force for eighty years and was almost unchanged for the first sixty years. In the 1980s and 1990s several reforms were passed, the aim of which was to strengthen the parliamentary features of Finnish political system. The excessive powers of president were criticized as having a detrimental effect on the functioning of the parliamentary system. President Koivisto gave his support for a gradual set of constitutional reforms that connected the powers of the president and the government more closely. As a result, the president's prerogatives were somewhat reduced. As Koivisto put it, he was not afraid that he himself would abuse the prerogatives of president, but it would be wise to prepare oneself for the possibility that some day a worse president might come to power.

These reforms reduced the duality of the executive. They also accentuated the relations between the government and parliament. The most important of these amendments concerned the rights of the minority in parliament. The opportunity for one-third of deputies to postpone legislation was radically weakened, and in the new constitution the possibility for the parliamentary majority to postpone legislation was totally eliminated. This put an end to the 'cohabitation' between majority governments and the parliamentary opposition. The legislative power of the opposition was nullified.

Finally, the method for electing the president was also reformed in early 1990s. Since 1994 presidents have been elected directly by the people. If no candidate wins a majority of votes, there is a second round between the two candidates who gained the most votes at the first round.

## The New Constitution

In late 1990s a completely new constitution was enacted which came into force on 1 March 2000 (Act 731/1999). The new constitution brushed away most of the remaining semi-presidential features of the Finnish political system. The aim was to tie the decision-making powers of the president to the government. Both the president and the government have their own separate duties, mainly as they were in the old constitution. However, now if there is a conflict between president and government, in most cases it is the government which in the last instance makes decisions, although in terms of foreign policy and high-level civil service appointments the president still has the power to conduct his own policy.

The new constitution has changed the power relationship between the president and government in following areas:

- In the old constitution, if it was unclear whether or not an issue should be decided by the president or the government, it was up to the president to decide. In the new constitution, the government has general executive authority and deals with all issues that are not the explicit prerogative of the president or some other state organ (Section 65).
- The new constitution radically restricts the actions of the president in terms of government formation. Parliament elects a prime minister who is then appointed to office by the president. Before the prime minister is elected, the parliamentary party groups negotiate the political programme and the composition of the government. The president appoints all other ministers in accordance with proposals made by the prime minister (Section 61).
- The rules relating to the resignation of the government (Section 64) restate the 1991 constitutional amendments. The president may accept the resignation of the government or a minister in only two cases. The resignation must be either requested by the prime minister or the minister concerned, or parliament must have passed a vote of no-confidence.
- The same point applies to the rules relating to the dissolution of parliament (Section 26). The president may dissolve parliament only in response to a proposal made by the prime minister.
- The opportunity for the president to make changes to government bills has been removed. If the president does not make his/her decision in accordance with the proposal made by the government, the matter is returned to the government for further consideration before being presented to parliament in the form decided by the government (Section 58).
- Parliament may now overturn the president's legislative veto without delay. If the president does not promulgate a law within three months, it is returned to parliament. If parliament readopts the Act without material alterations, it comes into force without the president's confirmation. If parliament does not readopt the act, it shall be deemed to be lapsed (Section 77).
- Previously, unless it was otherwise stated, it was possible for the president to issue decrees relating to the implementation of laws and on matters not regulated by laws. Now the president may issue decrees only if s/he has been

specifically authorized to do so. If there is no specific provision, decrees are issued by the government (Section 80).
* The president no longer has any power of veto relating to state finances (Section 83).
* The new constitution retains the system of dual foreign policy leadership that was established when Finland entered the European Union. According to the new constitution, Finnish foreign policy is directed by the president in co-operation with the government. However, government is responsible for the preparation of decisions to be made in the European Union and decides on the concomitant Finnish measures, unless the decision requires the approval of the parliament. Parliament participates in the preparation of decisions to be made in the EU (Section 93).
* The president is still the commander-in-chief of the armed forces. S/he appoints senior civil servants and may grant a full or partial pardon from a penalty imposed by a court of law (Sections 105 and 128).
* A charge against a member of the government is made in parliament and is treated in a special High Court of Impeachment. The president no longer has the power to make such a charge (Section 114).

### Electoral Rules and the Party System

The key characteristics of the Finnish system, the strength of the president, the weakness of governments and 'cohabitation' between government and parliament, have also been a result of the fragmentation of the party system. In 1906 Finland was the first European nation to adopt a full and equal suffrage in parliamentary elections for both men and women. Since 1906, proportional representation (the d'Hondt system) has been used in general elections and the basic principles of the electoral system have remained the same (Törnudd, 1968).

From the beginning of the twentieth century the left–right cleavage became the most prominent feature of the Finnish party system. Political parties can be situated on the left–right scale according to Figure 5.1 (Nyholm, 1982: 80; Paloheimo, 1984: 56). This ordering of parties has been important in the process of government formation. From the time of Finnish independence to 1987 all majority coalitions were connected coalitions on the left–right scale. The opposition was on either the left or the right or both the left and the right side of the governing coalition. Most minority coalitions, too, were connected coalitions. However, it is an indication of the declining intensity of the left–right cleavage that in 1982–2000 all governments have been majority coalitions and only three out of six have been connected coalitions on the left–right scale.

| Communists/ People's Democrats | Social Democrats | Agrarian/ Centre Party | Liberals and Swedish People's Party | Conservatives |
| --- | --- | --- | --- | --- |

LEFT                                                                                    RIGHT

FIGURE 5.1. The Finnish party system

## THE FREQUENCY OF DIVIDED GOVERNMENT IN FINLAND

An analysis of the features of divided government in Finland must include a study of political coalitions and co-operation between parties on three different levels. First, from 1925 to 1988, when presidents were elected by an electoral college, party bargaining related to the election of the president. Secondly, parties also bargained on the issue of government formation. However, as a result of the minority veto in the legislature parties could still influence legislation even if they were not in office themselves. Thirdly, this meant that there was bargaining in the legislature between government and opposition parties.

### Party Bargaining and the Election of the President

The main changes in Finnish politics have often been made in connection with presidential elections. When President Ståhlberg was elected in 1919, he was supported by the Liberals, the Agrarians, and the Social Democrats. During his presidency, the Liberals and Agrarians held office in every government with the exception of the two caretaker governments. At this time, the cleavage between socialists and the bourgeois (centre and right-wing) parties was so deep that the Social Democrats were unable to enter the government. However, by supporting Ståhlberg the Social Democrats were able to prevent General Mannerheim, the leader of the white army in previous year's civil war, from rising to the presidency.

It would be too simple to say that Ståhlberg simply appointed Liberal and Agrarian politicians to the government because they had supported him at the presidential election. There were deeper ideological reasons that encouraged the Agrarians to support Ståhlberg and that motivated Ståhlberg to include the Agrarians in most governments. Moreover, the Social Democrats could limit the power of the conservatives by supporting the Liberals rather than the Conservatives. Thus, it is possible to talk about a presidential majority. This was a coalition of political parties and their leaders which took most of strategic decisions relating to Finnish politics.

Presidential elections were the most important aspect of this strategic decision-making. If the party composition of the government resembled the presidential coalition, it was not just due to the president's willingness to repay the support he received in the presidential election. It was also the result of strategic decision-making in a semi-presidential regime with a multi-party system. This decision-making took the form of a continuous process of forming élite-negotiated coalitions in a system where the government aimed to isolate opponents from power and the opposition tried to bring the government down.

Both Presidents Lauri Relander (1925–31) and P. E. Svinhufvud (1931–7) were elected with the support of the Conservatives, the Swedish People's party, and the Agrarians. At this time the basic party composition of the governments was oriented towards the centre or centre-right. Both Relander and Svinhufvud unsuccessfully stood for re-election. Relander was too weak to hold back the right-wing extremism of the early 1930s. Thus, in 1931 a stronger leader was needed and Svinhufvud was elected. Svinhufvud's defeat in the 1937 presidential election was the result of the president's refusal to appoint the Social Democrats to government, although support for the party had increased in the 1930s. At this time the Agrarian party was willing to co-operate with the Social Democrats and these two parties together commanded a majority in parliament.

The most important presidential majority in Finnish politics was built in 1937. In the presidential election of this year the Agrarian party and the Social Democratic party made a deal linking the election of the president and the formation of the government. This deal opened up a long period of red–green coalitions between the two parties. For fifty years this was the most common coalition in Finnish governments, a coalition that was often supplemented by the Liberals, the Swedish People's party, and/or the People's Democrats.

When the democratic system or the sovereignty of the nation is threatened, it is common for democratic governments to include all the parties which support the regime (Budge and Keman, 1990). This was the case in Finland during the Second World War. During this time governments were all-party governments. Presidents were elected almost unanimously, but the method of election was exceptional (see Table 5.1).

After the Second World War two different cleavages determined the formation of presidential majorities. In three presidential elections the winning coalition was a block of parties on the left–right continuum. In 1962 Kekkonen was elected with the support of the centre and right-wing parties. In 1968 he was elected with the support of the left-wing parties and centre parties that were in government at the time. In 1982, Koivisto was elected with the support of the left-wing parties. In these cases, there has often been a connection between presidential coalitions and governmental coalitions. After Kekkonen's re-election in 1962, the centre-right presidential majority was also in government for some years. In 1968, when the left-wing parties were

TABLE 5.1. *Presidential elections in Finland, 1919–2000*

| Year | Name | Party | Method of election | Supporting coalition |
|------|------|-------|--------------------|----------------------|
| 1919 | Kaarlo Ståhlberg | L | Parliament | L, A, SD |
| 1925 | Lauri Relander | A | Electoral college | A, C, SPP |
| 1931 | Pehr Svinhufvud | C | Electoral college | A, C, part of SPP |
| 1937 | Kyösti Kallio | A | Electoral college | A, SD, part of L |
| 1940 | Risto Ryti | L | 1937 elect. coll. | Almost all parties |
| 1943 | Risto Ryti | L | 1937 elect. coll. | Almost all parties |
| 1944 | C. Mannerheim | None | Parliament | Almost all parties |
| 1946 | Juho Paasikivi | C | Parliament | Most parties |
| 1950 | Juho Paasikivi | C | Electoral college | C, SD, SPP |
| 1956 | Urho Kekkonen | A | Electoral college | A, PD, part of L |
| 1962 | Urho Kekkonen | A | Electoral college | A, C, L, SPP |
| 1968 | Urho Kekkonen | Ce. | Electoral college | PD, SD, Ce., L, SPP |
| 1974 | Urho Kekkonen | Ce. | Term extended | Most parties |
| 1978 | Urho Kekkonen | Ce. | Electoral college | PD, SD, Ce., SPP, C |
| 1982 | Mauno Koivisto | SD | Electoral college | SD, PD |
| 1988 | Mauno Koivisto | SD | Electoral college | SD, C |
| 1994 | Martti Ahtisaari | SD | Direct election | n/a |
| 2000 | Martti Ahtisaari | SD | Direct election | n/a |

*Sources*: Pietiäinen, 1992; Mylly, 1993; Turtola, 1993; Väyrynen, 1994; Paloheimo, 1994.
*Key*: A: Agrarian; C: Conservatives; Ce.: Centre party (ex-Agrarian); L: Liberals; PD: People's Democrats; SD: Social Democrats; SPP: Swedish People's party.

in office with the Centre party, this so-called 'popular front' also supported Kekkonen's re-election.

In three other presidential elections the Agrarian party and the People's Democrats (communists) formed one coalition, while the Social Democrats and Conservatives formed another. In 1950 and 1988, the winning coalition (for the election of Paasikivi and Koivisto respectively) was based on co-operation between the Social Democrats and the Conservatives. In 1956, the winning coalition (for the election of Kekkonen) was based on co-operation between the People's Democrats and the Agrarians.

When Koivisto was elected in 1982, the left-wing presidential coalition was constructed during Koivisto's premiership in 1979–82. When Koivisto was elected for a second term in 1988, the coalition was once again built on co-operation that had taken place between the various parties in the government, this time between the Social Democrats and the Conservatives. Prime Minister Holkeri's government (1987–91) was the first majority government in which the Agrarian/Centre party was not in office. Thereafter, non-connected government coalitions between Social Democrats and Conservatives have been more frequent than traditional connected coalitions.

The introduction of the direct election of the president in 1994 changed the politics of making presidential majorities. There is no longer as much opportunity for inter-party bargaining. Party élites cannot command citizens as they could the electors in the electoral college. Therefore, it is probable that in the future the connections between presidential coalitions and governmental coalitions will be looser than was previously the case.

## Minority Governments

In the First Republic (1917–39) it was difficult for parties to form coalitions and so minority governments were frequent. During this time fourteen out of twenty-three governments were minority governments (see Table 5.2). In the Second Republic (1944–82) it was easier for parties to form coalitions and minority governments were less common. However, there still were eight minority governments from 1948 to 1982. Since then there have been no minority governments at all.

Most minority governments have been centre-oriented. Five minority governments have been centre-oriented single-party governments and ten have been centre-oriented minority coalitions. These centre-oriented minority governments have been able to work with both left- and right-wing parties in parliament.

Other kinds of minority government have been more unusual. Four minority governments have been centre-right coalitions. Three minority governments have been Social Democratic single-party governments. Social Democratic single-party governments have come into office by winning a general election when the coalition capacity of the centre and right-wing parties has been low.

TABLE 5.2. *Number and types of governments and average days in office*

| Type of government | 1917–39 | 1939–44 | 1944–82 | 1982–2000 | Total no. 1917–2000 |
|---|---|---|---|---|---|
| Single-party minority | 4 | 0 | 4 | 0 | 8 |
| Minority coalition | 10 | 0 | 4 | 0 | 13 |
| Majority coalition | 6 | 0 | 11 | 4 | 21 |
| Qualified majority coal. | 1 | 1 | 9 | 2 | 13 |
| All-party coalition | 0 | 5 | 0 | 0 | 5 |
| Caretaker government | 2 | 0 | 7 | 0 | 9 |
| Total no. of governments | 23 | 6 | 35 | 6 | 70 |
| Average days in office | 365 | 302 | 400 | 1,253 | 444 |

*Note*: In three cases the exit of one party from the government has changed the type of government. These 'b' versions of governments have been counted as separate governments in the table. Qualified majority coalitions are supported by at least 134 members in the parliament (two-thirds of all members). All-party governments are supported by at least 190 members.

## THE CAUSES OF DIVIDED GOVERNMENT IN FINLAND

### *The Division of Power between the President and the Government*

The Constitution and the desire of the president to use the prerogatives vested in the office are not the only factors determining the division of power between president and government. Several factors have also had an effect on the division of executive powers. According to Nousiainen (1985: 22–9) five factors have been relevant.

- The constitution is a general framework. For actors in each of the different political institutions, the Constitution provides some broadly defined space for action. However, it also sets limits that cannot be transgressed.
- The country's political culture and dominant ideologies have also had an effect on the division of power in the political system. After independence (1917) and civil war (1918), it was expected that a strong presidency would bring stability to the system. Since the 1980s, political culture has embraced parliamentarism, although the opinions of the masses have not entirely followed the rapid cultural changes of the political élite.
- The stability, fragmentation, and polarization of the party system have had dramatic effects on the capability of parliamentary party groups to form coalitions and to rule together in governing coalitions. When parliamentary party groups have been capable of forming majority coalitions and ruling together in governing coalitions, the opportunity for presidents to use their powers to the full have been limited. Before the 1960s or the 1970s, stable coalitions were absent from Finnish politics, thus leaving much room and need for an active presidency. This means that when there has been a determined majority coalition in parliament, a conflict between president and government has also manifested itself as a conflict between the president and parliament. Presidents have avoided open conflict with parliament.
- Different political situations have affected both governing styles and the actual division of power. During the Second World War an informal war cabinet discussed and prepared all important strategic political decisions. For forty years after the Second World War, Finnish relations with the Soviet Union were monopolized by the president, as a result of which foreign policy decision-making was both centralized and personalized. When Finland joined the European Union in 1995, the role of the prime minister increased and the role of president declined.
- Personal features of the various presidents, their attitudes and styles of leadership, have affected the relations between president and the government.

The old Finnish constitution made it possible for the presidents to pick up dishes on the constitutional buffet table according to their own taste. Ståhlberg used his powers to institutionalize the functioning of liberal democracy in the period immediately following national independence. In most cases, he left the day-to-day politics to the government. Even in foreign policy, governments had much more to say compared to events during both Paasikivi's and Kekkonen's presidencies. By contrast, Svinhufhud's mission was to tame the authoritarian extreme right-wing movement of the early 1930s and to keep the Social Democrats out of office, whereas Paasikivi's mission was to build a new foreign policy based on friendly relations with the big eastern neighbour. He took the leadership of Finnish foreign policy into his own hands when he was prime minister in 1944–6 and monopolized foreign policy decision-making when he became president in 1946. Foreign policy was too complicated to be understood by ordinary members of the parliament, said Paasikivi. Kekkonen continued Paasikivi's tradition in this respect and over time he also increased his influence over domestic affairs. Koivisto wanted to increase the parliamentary features of Finnish executive. In domestic affairs he, with a few exceptions, supported the government's policies, while in foreign policy he discussed matters with the government before making his decisions.

### *'Cohabitation' between Government and Parliament*

Prior to the 1990s a one-third minority in parliament could effectively block government legislation. Therefore, either parties had to form a coalition commanding a two-thirds majority in parliament, or the government had to co-operate with opposition parties in order to pass legislation. This constitutional requirement, combined with the low capability of the political parties to form stable coalitions, was the basis for the frequency of minority governments in the First Republic and the first decades after the Second World War. When the coalition capacity of the parties was low, it was easier for parties to form minority governments and to bargain with the opposition on an issue-by-issue basis. The same point applies to the minority coalitions that were formed during this period where the ideological distance between governing parties was in most cases very small. Twelve out of fourteen minority coalitions were connected coalitions.

In Finland caretaker governments have been relatively frequent during periods of political deadlock. It is interesting to notice that the reasons for the appointment of caretaker governments were different in the First and Second Republics. There were two caretaker governments in the First Republic. The first (Cajander I, 1922) was appointed as the result of disagreement over foreign policy. The second (Cajander II, 1924) came to office as the result of disagreement over the prohibition of communist activities. In the Second Republic all caretaker governments, seven in total, were in office during periods of economic recession. In fact, between the early 1950s and late 1970s there was only one recession (in the late 1960s) where a political government survived throughout the whole period of economic downturn. In all the other cases the government collapsed. To sum up, we can say that caretaker governments in the First Republic were formed regarding issues relating to the principles of democracy, whereas in the Second Republic they were formed as a result of distributive conflicts.

## THE MANAGEMENT OF DIVIDED GOVERNMENT IN FINLAND

### *Managing the Relations between the President and the Government*

The president only has a small personal staff of about ten civil servants. Thus, the president is almost totally dependent on the government in this regard. In the Finnish executive there are two types of governmental sessions. The first is where the president chairs the meeting and makes his/her decisions on the proposal of the government. The second, the general sessions of the government, are chaired by the prime minister and are the occasions when governmental decisions are made. Overall, presidents have gone against the government only very rarely. It is important to appreciate that presidents have had an influence on the preparatory phases of the decision-making process. As a result, the power of the president cannot simply be measured by counting the number of occasions when the president has opposed the opinion of the government. Instead, informal discussions between president and government have often had affected the preparation of the issue in question and governments have amended their proposals to take account of the will of the president.

### *Making and Breaking Governments*

Under the old constitution the process of government formation was the most powerful means for presidents to steer the political system. The Constitution merely stated that president appoints native citizens known for their honesty and ability to serve as members of the government, and that members of the government must enjoy the confidence of parliament. The old constitution said nothing about the interplay between the president, parliament, and political parties. This meant that, right from the start, it became the convention that the president listened to the opinions of both the speaker of the parliament as well as the parliamentary party groups, and, thus, was well aware of the available alternatives. On the one hand, parties typically avoided making detailed proposals in the initial stages of the process so as to sustain their coalition capability to the very end of the negotiations. On the other hand, though, this strategy left a great deal of room for manœuvre for the president. (Jansson, 1993: 206–21; Arter, 1987: 89–96).

Usually presidents have had a relatively free hand in selecting a government *formateur*. On occasions, they gave orders as to the suitable party composition of the government, and the *formateurs* generally followed these orders. Presidents have also had their say on the nomination of ministers. Typically, the minister of foreign affairs was personally selected by the president or at least the president had a veto over the proposed nomination.

Now that the capacity of parties to form stable majority coalitions has improved, presidents have much less say about the party composition of the government. Since the 1980s, the leader of the largest party in parliament after the general election has been asked to form the new government. The formation of Holkeri's 1987 government is the only exception to this rule.

In addition, the old constitution said nothing about president's ability to dismiss the government. On five occasions governments resigned because of a disagreements with the president (see Table 5.3). In three of these five cases the president also dissolved the parliament and called a general election.

By the 1970s the president's prerogatives with regard to the appointment of the government, the power to give orders relating to the party composition of the government, the ability to dismiss the government by dissolving parliament, and the president's role in the appointment of ministers combined to make the Finnish president an almost omnipotent head of the state. Indeed, presidential power in Finland during this time was clearly greater than that of US president. In a democratic presidential regime, there is always a system of checks and balances between the legislature and the executive. However, in Finnish politics, parliamentary party groups deferred to the president. A united and determined parliament could have beaten the president at any time.

The strong position of the president in the 1970s was followed by a counter-blow in the 1980s. The belief that parliament should play a greater role in political life encouraged parties to reform the Constitution and the president

TABLE 5.3. *Reasons for government resignation in Finland, 1917–2000*

|  | 1917–39 | 1939–44 | 1944–82 | 1982–2000 | 1917–2000 |
|---|---|---|---|---|---|
| *Parliamentary reasons* | | | | | |
| General election | 1 | 0 | 5 | 5 | 11 |
| Lack of support | 7 | 0 | 0 | 0 | 7 |
| Vote of no-confidence | 3 | 0 | 1 | 0 | 4 |
| Enlargement of coalition | 0 | 0 | 1 | 0 | 1 |
| *Government reasons* | | | | | |
| PM becomes president | 3 | 1 | 3 | 0 | 7 |
| Resignation of PM | 0 | 1 | 1 | 0 | 2 |
| Disagreements in govt. | 1 | 1 | 8 | 0 | 10 |
| *Presidential reasons* | | | | | |
| Disagreements with pres. | 3 | 0 | 2 | 0 | 5 |
| Presidential election | 0 | 1 | 2 | 0 | 3 |
| Foreign policy reasons | 2 | 2 | 3 | 0 | 7 |
| *Caretaker governments* | 2 | 0 | 7 | 0 | 9 |
| Totals | 22 | 6 | 33 | 5 | 66 |

to support these reforms. Amendments to the Constitution passed in 1991 made it compulsory for the president to consult the parliamentary party groups before a new government is appointed and placed strict conditions on the president's ability to dismiss the government (see above).

## The Dissolution of Parliament

In a parliamentary system when there is a disagreement between the government and parliament the government may appeal directly to the people and dissolve the parliament. In Finland when there has been a disagreement between the president and government the dissolution of parliament has been a way in which the president has tried to assert his authority over the government.

The president has dissolved parliament seven times. Disagreements between the government and president provoked Ståhlberg to dissolve parliament on one occasion and Kekkonen twice. Paasikivi ordered an early election in 1954 when a parliamentary government had broken down, while Kekkonen dissolved parliament and dismissed the incumbent minority government when he sought approval for his own actions in the so-called 'note crisis' of 1962. In two cases only, has parliament been dissolved on the initiative of the government. In 1929 Mantere's government disagreed with parliament on the issue of the salaries of civil servants. In 1930 Svinhufvud's government wanted to speed up legislation prohibiting revolutionary activities and dissolved parliament so as to circumvent the procedures for postponing legislation.

## Legislation

In Finland, the president presents about 200–300 government bills to parliament each year. Most of these bills are part of government's policy programme. In most cases, the president's role is purely formal. Every now and then, though, there are times when the president wants to influence the issue concerned. On these occasions, presidents may have informal discussions with the ministers before the bill is presented in the presidential session of the government. They may also go to the media to publicize their cause.

The occasions when presidents have changed a government bill or have refused to present a bill to parliament are rare. So too are the occasions when presidents have refused to ratify laws passed in the parliament. However, most presidents have used these prerogatives (Jyränki, 1981). In the new constitution, though, the role of president in legislation is totally parliamentarized. If the president and the government disagree on a bill, the government has the last word. If the president uses his/her powers to postpone legislation, parliament may immediately overturn president's veto. Moreover, the president may issue decrees only in the areas where the constitution explicitly gives the president this power (see above).

*Foreign Policy Leadership*

Styles of decision-making in foreign policy have varied over the four periods identified in this chapter. During the drafting of the old constitution the manner in which foreign policy would be conducted was not thoroughly discussed. Section 33 of the old constitution was taken from the Swedish model of Gustavian, ruler-centred leadership, which had already provided the model for Finnish home rule in Russian empire. President Ståhlberg kept the final say on foreign policy matters and personally chose the minister of foreign affairs. Ståhlberg also began the tradition that ministers of foreign affairs are trustees of the president, assuming the practice whereby the president either made foreign policy decisions in the presidential sessions of the government on the basis of proposals made by the minister of foreign affairs, or a least relied on co-operation with the minister of foreign affairs (Kalela, 1993).

The exceptional conditions during the Second World War led to a concentration of decision-making and shifted foreign policy-making outside the realm of normal public political debate. Since 1940, foreign policy has been a key issue in presidential elections and all presidents have had experience in international affairs at the time of their election.

After this time, Paasikivi concentrated all important foreign policy decisions in his own hands, while Kekkonen continued the same style but went even further. He often by-passed the minister of foreign affairs and issued orders directly to the senior civil servants. In Fenno-Soviet relations Kekkonen held personal summits with the leaders of the Soviet Union. Similarly, on the Russian side contacts were often organized by the international department of the Communist Party of Soviet Union, instead of the Ministry for Foreign Affairs. The term 'personal relations' had a special meaning during Kekkonen's presidency and were used to justify his control over foreign affairs.

This situation was one of the main reasons why President Koivisto changed the nature of foreign policy-making. As prime minister, in 1968–70 and 1979–81, Koivisto sometimes found that he was not informed on issues when he should have been. He believed that the president should lead foreign policy in tandem with the government. Thus, when Finland entered the European Union Koivisto gave his support to a new division of labour in Finnish foreign policy-making, whereby the president was responsible for foreign policy issues in the EU and the government was responsible for everything else. As a result, at EU summits Finland has a 'tradition of two plates'. The president participates alongside the prime minister when issues concerning foreign and security policy are on the agenda.

*Managing 'Cohabitation' between the Government and Parliament*

'Cohabitation' between government and parliament has been managed in various different ways. Moreover, the style of management has varied both from one type of government to another and from one time period to another. Caretaker governments have taken responsibility for routine business only. They have not prepared large policy programmes. The number of bills presented to parliament during caretaker governments has been low. Most minority governments have been centre-oriented and have sought the support of both left-wing and right-wing parties in parliament. Some minority governments have experienced a situation of 'permanent cohabitation' with parties not represented in the government. Others have looked for support on an issue-by-issue basis. That said, all minority governments have had to modify their policies according to the parliamentary situation. Thus, for minority governments, 'cohabitation' has been like being on a bog and jumping from one tussock to another. There is always the chance that you might land in a hole.

In the Second Republic a new kind of 'cohabitation' emerged between majority governments and the parliamentary opposition. Especially from the late 1960s onwards, red–green majority governments began to build the welfare state. Because legislation could be delayed governments needed at least the passive support of the Conservative party which wanted to keep taxes to a moderate level. As a result of this situation the Finnish welfare state was built much more slowly than in Sweden, Norway, and Denmark. At the same time, though, when the Conservatives were in government they did not demand any radical cuts in the public welfare system. Therefore, governmental co-operation between the Conservatives and the Social Democrats has been just as possible as co-operation between the Conservatives and the Centre party or between the Social Democrats and the Centre party. After each general election two of these three big parties have generally made a deal which has left the third one in the political wilderness. Now, the parliamentary opposition has almost no power at all. Thus, the sole purpose of the largest party in opposition is to find its way back to government after the next general election.

## CONCLUSION

Since the introduction of the new constitution presidential power has varied less than was previously the case. As Dag Anckar has put it, there are just small morsels left for the president on the constitutional buffet table. Therefore, the era of strong presidential leadership is over. From this point, presidents are simply heads of state in a parliamentary system in which their powers are limited (Anckar, 1999).

Several factors contributed to the parliamentarization of Finnish political system. The coalition capability of political parties is much better than it was before. There are no longer any unstable minority governments. When governments are stable, when they command a majority in parliament and when the result of the general election clearly affects the party composition of the government, there is no longer either much need or much room for the president to intervene on a day-to-day basis. Moreover, nowadays the distinction between foreign and domestic policy is like a line drawn on water. It is difficult, if not impossible, to continue the division of labour that developed under the Second Republic, where foreign policy was the prerogative of president and domestic affairs were mainly the business of government. Indeed, this point is particularly true for Finland's relations with the EU. At the time of accession the country had to decide whether the president or the government should lead Finnish policy-making at this level. The responsibility was given to government. In addition, the collapse of the Soviet Union further reduced the highly personalized tradition in the management of Fenno-Soviet relations.

These point noted, there are also trends towards the personalization of politics (Hague *et al.* 1998: 208–9). There is a growing need for co-ordination as governance becomes more complex. Heads of states are increasingly involved in international co-operation and summit politics. Heads of state, either prime ministers or presidents, are more and more in the spotlight of the media. In parliamentary systems these trends strengthen the role of prime minister as the *de facto* head of the state. In Finland, these trends have increased the role of prime minister too, but the system of divided executive may still give rise to a kind of rivalry between president and prime minister in regard to their role in international summit politics. Moreover, Finnish political culture has not been totally parliamentarized and there seems to be a clear division between the political élite and the masses. During the last twenty years, the élite culture has almost totally parliamentarized, but the mass culture has not. There are large groups who have high expectations about the active role of president as a personal leader. With decisions being increasingly made at the international level and with parliamentary decision-making dealing more and more with technical matters, the masses begin to desire strong leaders who can show the way ahead. This is particularly true when presidents are elected directly by the people (Anckar, 1984: 201–13). In the last twenty years the electoral turnout at parliamentary elections has been falling, but at presidential elections it has remained at a high level. Indeed, at the 2000 presidential election turnout was 77 per cent in the first round and 80 per cent in the second round. By contrast, at the 1999 general election turnout was only 68 per cent. Moreover, in an opinion poll taken at the time parliament was examining the new constitution only 21 per cent of people thought that president had too much power, and 16 per cent would have liked to strengthen the powers of the president (EVA, 1999).

In this context, popular expectations about the active role of the president may give rise to tensions in the executive system. Parliament and most of the political élite are willing to work according to the principles of parliamentarism. Presidential pressures among the electorate may, however, encourage presidents to use their powers more actively than the parliamentary élite would like. Decisions in foreign policy are still made by the president. This keeps open the possibility that even under the new constitution Finnish presidents may still have more power than is typical in a normal parliamentary executive.

# 6

# 'Cohabitation': Divided Government French-Style

## *Robert Elgie*

In a political sense the term 'cohabitation' was first employed in France in the mid-1970s (Cohendet, 1993: 11–13; Massot, 1997: 14–16). However, it only entered popular usage in the early 1980s (see, for example, Balladur, in *Le Monde*, 16 Sept. 1983). Since its first appearance the concept has been defined in various different ways (Duverger, 1986; Massot, 1997: 16; Parodi, 1997: 300). Whatever the precise wording of the definition, though, in France 'cohabitation', or split-executive government, occurs in the context of a system in which both the president and the prime minister are significant political actors and is brought about when the president is faced with an opposition majority in the National Assembly and thus is obliged to appoint a prime minister who has the support of that majority. It describes the situation where one part of the executive is pitted against at least one house of the legislature and, as a result, where one part of the executive is opposed to the other. In this context, some writers have argued that the particularities of 'cohabitation' mean that it is almost unique to France (Parodi, 1997: 300; Pierce, 1991: 270–1). Other writers have argued that there are similarities between 'cohabitation' in France and the politics of both minority government in parliamentary regimes (Greilsammer, 1989) and divided government in presidential regimes (Shugart, 1995). In fact, 'cohabitation' is best understood in this latter sense as a country-specific manifestation of a more general political phenomenon.

This chapter examines the politics of 'cohabitation', or divided government French-style. It begins by setting out the basic powers of the protagonists in the Fifth Republic's dual executive. It then looks at the frequency, causes, and management of 'cohabitation' in France. Overall, it is argued that 'cohabitation' has been characterized by constant competition between the president and prime minister. However, there are well-established procedures which have minimized the overall extent of the conflict within the executive and which have ensured the continuity of the system.

## THE DUAL EXECUTIVE IN THE FIFTH FRENCH REPUBLIC

France is a semi-presidential regime, or a regime in which a popularly elected fixed-term president exists alongside a prime minister and cabinet responsible to parliament (Elgie, 1999: 13). The basic characteristic of such a regime is the dual executive. Within the executive there are two sources of popular legitimacy. The president has a direct link emanating from the people. The prime minister has an indirect link mediated through the legislature. In some semi-presidential regimes the president is merely a political spectator, or popularly elected figurehead. In these cases, the prime minister is the uncontested leader of the executive. This is true in Austria, Bulgaria, Iceland, Ireland, and Slovenia. By contrast, in other countries the head of state is a major political actor who is at least as powerful as the prime minister if not more so. This is the situation in France. Here, while the Constitution appears to place the prime minister at centre of the decision-making process, in practice the president has often been able to dominate the system. This section provides an introduction to the study of the French dual executive by setting out the basic constitutional and political powers of the president and prime minister.

The 1958 Constitution sets out a list of prime ministerial powers, presidential powers and powers which are shared between the two institutions.[1] The prime minister is the key policy-making actor within the executive. For example, Article 21 states that the prime minister leads the government, while Article 20 indicates that the government determines and conducts the nation's policies. Thus, the prime minister is installed at the head of a government charged with the overall responsibility for policy-making in the country. In addition, the Constitution also endows the prime minister with the power to issue decrees (*règlements*) which have the force of law and which do not require the president's countersignature. This power flows from the fact that the French parliament may only pass laws in a limited number of areas. Outside these areas, therefore, the prime minister has the power to act as a sort of substitute legislature. Finally, the prime minister is responsible for the government's dealings with parliament more generally. The Constitution includes a raft of measures which were designed to privilege the position of the government in relation to parliament (see below). The prime minister is the beneficiary of these measures. All told, therefore, the prime minister is constitutionally responsible for the whole range of government business on a day-to-day basis.

By contrast, the president enjoys only a restricted set of constitutional powers. The most important of these powers include the appointment of the prime

[1] This interpretation of the constitutional powers of the president and prime minister follows the schema set out by Massot (1997: 83–133). However, so well-entrenched is the study of public law in France that there are alternative interpretations (see e.g. Duverger, 1986).

minister; the ability to dissolve the National Assembly, although not more than once in any twelve-month period; the freedom to resign and hence to provoke a presidential election at which the president may stand again; the power to ask the Constitutional Council to scrutinize a piece of legislation; the right to appoint three of the nine members of the Council itself, albeit ordinarily at certain predetermined times; and the power to assume emergency powers but only when there is a serious and immediate threat to the system. Overall, there is no doubt that these powers are very significant. However, with the main exception of the right to send a bill to the Constitutional Council, they are either one-off powers or ones that can only be exercised at discrete intervals. Thus, they ensure that the president is integral to the political game, but as an independent and autonomous actor of only either the first instance or the last resort.

In addition to the discretionary powers of the president and prime minister, there are two sets of shared constitutional powers. The first set comprises three policy areas in which the president, the prime minister, and government ministers have certain responsibilities. So, the 1958 Constitution establishes the president as the head of the armed forces and as the guarantor of national independence and the integrity of the national territory.[2] It also states that the president negotiates and ratifies treaties and is then responsible for ensuring that treaties are respected. Finally, it indicates that the president guarantees the independence of the judiciary and heads the Higher Council of the Magistrature, the body which oversees the judiciary. At the same time, however, the Constitution also states that the prime minister is responsible for national defence. It implies that the government is involved in the process of drawing up treaties. Moreover, the Minister of Justice is designated as the vice-president of the Higher Council of the Magistrature. Thus, over and above the actual distribution of power conditioned by the political circumstances of the day, there is at least some legal-constitutional justification for the day-to-day involvement of both the president, the prime minister, and other members of the government in these three policy areas.

The second set of shared powers covers three more general types of situation. The first constitutes the cases where the decision-making initiative lies with the prime minister but where the president must formally approve the decision in question. For example, the prime minister proposes the names of government ministers to the president who then appoints them. The second involves decisions which are taken by the president but which then have to be countersigned by the prime minister and/or by other members of the government. This is the case, for example, for many administrative and state-sector appointments. The third consists of the instances where prime ministerial

---

[2] There are also various laws and decrees which reinforce the role of the president in this domain (see Howorth, 1993).

decisions have to be discussed in the Council of Ministers. This category includes all government bills which have to be approved by the government collectively before they can go to parliament. In these cases, the president, as the chair of the Council of Ministers, is at least party to the decision-making process. Altogether, the net effect of this second set of shared powers is to tie in many of the president's decisions with the approval, or at least the acknowledgement, of the prime minister and vice versa.

The Constitution, therefore, provides both the president and the prime minister with a range of powers, both discretionary and shared. At bottom, it would appear to establish the prime minister as the person who is formally in charge of the day-to-day running of the country. In practice, however, the president has been the main political actor. The prime minister has been a central, but none the less subordinate figure within the executive.[3]

The president benefits from the expectation that the head of state should be the primary source of political leadership in the Fifth Republic. This expectation was established in the period immediately following the foundation of the new regime in 1958 during the presidency of Charles de Gaulle (1958–69). The first president of the Fifth Republic exploited his considerable personal authority to focus political attention on the office. He was personally responsible for certain policy areas, such as defence policy and the resolution of the Algerian crisis. He also gave the impression that he had the power of initiative and veto in all other areas as well. He was the main representative of France on the world stage and claimed to speak on behalf of the French people as a whole, both at home and abroad. In short, he installed a vision of an active presidency in the minds of the political class and the population alike.

This vision of the presidency has been perpetuated by de Gaulle's successors, albeit with more mixed results. The basis of presidential authority is now primarily derived from the 1962 reform which introduced the direct election of the president. Since this time, presidential elections have been the keystone of the regime. They have provided the opportunity for candidates to propose a manifesto for reform. They have also obliged candidates to construct a wide-ranging coalition of forces in support of this manifesto, as the rules of the contest mean that the successful candidate must win more than 50 per cent of the votes cast. Partly as a result, to date at least presidential elections have been won by long-standing party leaders, or at least senior figures from the established political class. Thus, successful candidates have come to office supported by a 'presidential majority', on the basis of a plan for government, with considerable experience of the political process and in the knowledge

---

[3] Just as there are alternative interpretations of the constitutional relationship between the president and the prime minister in the Fifth Republic, so there are also conflicting interpretations of the political relationship between the two (see Elgie and Griggs, 2000: ch. 2).

that they cannot be dismissed from office for a fixed period of time. Prior to the constitutional reform in September 2000 the president's term of office was seven years. From the time of the next presidential election, which is scheduled for 2002, the term of office will be five years.

This mixture of presidential powers has been a potent cocktail. The presidency has emerged as the site of political leadership and the manifestation of popular authority. Against this background, the prime minister is usually seen as little more than the person who is responsible for marshalling the presidential majority in parliament and for implementing the president's legislative agenda. This is not to imply, though, that the head of government is a cipher. On the contrary, the prime minister is the cornerstone of the governmental system, overseeing the work of government ministers, piloting the policy-making process, and intervening in the process when and where necessary. The prime minister also heads an extensive network of administrative resources and technical services, placing the office at the very centre of the core executive. Thus, while there is no doubt the prime minister has been politically subordinate to the president for most of the Fifth Republic, there is also no doubt that on these occasions the prime minister has still been the second most influential figure within state system as a whole.

In France, therefore, 'cohabitation' takes place against an established background of constitutional and political powers. The prime minister is the key constitutional figure, but the president has been the principal political actor. As will be seen, however, 'cohabitation' questions the basic political rules of the game and focuses attention on the intricacies of the constitutional framework within which the two main elements of the French dual executive have to operate.

### THE FREQUENCY OF DIVIDED GOVERNMENT IN FRANCE

Since 1958 France has experienced periods of both unified and divided government. Moreover, in terms of the latter it has experienced both minority government and split-executive government, or 'cohabitation' (see Figure 6.1).[4] Unified government predominated during the first thirty years of the Fifth Republic. More recently, though, divided government has become the norm. (For an overview, see Duverger, 1990: 529–607.)

For the most part, the Fifth Republic has been characterized by unified government. During this time the parliamentary majority has supported the president. Consequently, the president has also been able to appoint a supportive prime minister. This is not to say, of course, that there have not been

---

[4] In this chapter, it is assumed for sake of argument that the upper house of the French legislature, the Senate, is not a working house. That is to say, its powers are insufficient to hinder the work of a government to which it is opposed politically.

| | |
|---|---|
| 1. The president and government are from the same party or coalition and are supported by a majority in the National Assembly (unified government) | 1962–86, 1995–97 |
| 2. The president and government are from the same party or coalition but fail to command an absolute majority in the National Assembly (minority government) | 1959–62, 1988–93 |
| 3. The majority in the National Assembly is opposed to the president, meaning that the president and prime minister are also opposed ('cohabitation') | 1986–88, 1993–95, 1997– |

FIGURE 6.1. Government/parliament relations in France, 1959–2000

tensions between the president and the prime minister, between the president and the parliamentary majority and between the prime minister and the parliamentary majority. Indeed, for much of the time from 1974 to 1976 the relations between President Giscard d'Estaing and Prime Minister Chirac were extremely poor, which was at least partly a result of the fact that they represented different coalition parties. Similarly, from 1969 to 1972 there were difficulties between President Pompidou and Prime Minister Chaban-Delmas, even though this time they were both drawn from the same party. It is simply that, whatever the political circumstances of the day, the president's supporters were represented in the government and the government commanded a parliamentary majority. There was unified government in the arithmetical sense.

By contrast, the Fifth Republic has twice experienced a period of minority government. The first period corresponds to the earliest years of the regime when the party system was fluid.[5] The second period occurred immediately after President Mitterrand's re-election in 1988. On both occasions the president, prime minister, and government were drawn from the same party or coalition of parties. However, these parties failed to enjoy an absolute majority of seats in parliament. They were, thus, in a minority situation in the National Assembly. This is not to imply, though, these governments were either unstable or politically impotent. On the contrary, governments remained in power and passed a considerable amount of legislation by using their constitutional powers to the full and by doing deals with independent deputies and sympathizers from opposition parties.[6] Thus, in France this particular form of divided government is not necessarily associated with stalemate or gridlock.

[5] Duverger (1986: 22–5) states that this was a period of 'cohabitation'. While it was undoubtedly a period of divided government, as understood in Ch. 1 of this book, it was not an example of 'cohabitation' in the sense there was no split-executive government.
[6] For a comprehensive study of the 1988–92 period, see Zarka (1992).

In addition, on three occasions there has been split-executive government or 'cohabitation'.[7] In contrast to the US, divided government French-style has never occurred at the beginning of the president's term of office.[8] Instead, to date at least, in France 'cohabitation' has always occurred part way through the president's term. So, in 1986, five years into the president's then seven-year term, the right-wing coalition won a National Assembly majority. This obliged the socialist president, François Mitterrand, to appoint a political opponent as prime minister. He chose the leader of the Gaullist party, Jacques Chirac. This period of 'cohabitation' ended in 1995 when Mitterrand was re-elected as president and immediately dissolved the National Assembly, resulting in the election of a minority socialist administration. In 1993 the same scenario occurred again when the right won a large parliamentary majority. This time Mitterrand appointed another leading Gaullist, Édouard Balladur, as prime minister. This period of 'cohabitation' ended in 1995 when Jacques Chirac was elected as president. Finally, in 1997, only two years into his presidency, Chirac dissolved the National Assembly. Rather than the return of another right-wing majority as he had hoped, a five-party, left-wing so-called 'plural majority' coalition was elected. As a result, Chirac appointed the leader of the Socialist party, Lionel Jospin, as prime minister. All other things being equal, this third period of 'cohabitation' will continue at least until 2002 when the next set of National Assembly and presidential elections are both scheduled to take place.

It is apparent, therefore, that taken as a whole the Fifth Republic has experienced more years of unified government than divided government. From 1959 to 2000 inclusive there was a total of twenty-six years of unified government and fifteen years of divided government, embracing eight years of minority government and seven years of 'cohabitation'. However, in recent times divided government has become the norm. From 1986 to 2000 inclusive there were only two years of unified government, whereas there were twelve years of divided government, comprising five years of minority government and all seven years of 'cohabitation'. Moreover, during this latter period 'cohabitation' was the most regular pattern of government. From 1986 to 1997 inclusive there were five alternations in power. These resulted in one period of unified government, one period of minority government, and three periods of 'cohabitation'. All told, therefore, divided government has represented the most common form of government in France in the last few years. In this context, the rest of this chapter focuses on the politics of 'cohabitation'.

[7] Speculation that this type of government may come about was present prior to the 1967, 1973, and, most notably, the 1978 legislative elections. On all three occasions the incumbent government was re-elected and a period of unified government was returned.

[8] In 1981 and 1988 the newly elected president was faced with an opposition majority and so immediately dissolved the National Assembly, returning a supportive administration on both occasions.

## THE CAUSES OF 'COHABITATION' IN FRANCE

There is little or no literature which deals systematically with the causes of 'cohabitation' in France. Consequently, it is only possible to extrapolate from some of the more general studies of French politics in order to account for the reasons why it occurs. Against this background, it will be argued, first, that the institutional structure of the system has created the potential for 'cohabitation' to occur and, secondly, that increasing levels of electoral volatility and intentional voting may be cited as the most likely behavioural reasons as to why this potential has been realized. However, it will also be argued that evidence regarding intentional voting remains sketchy.

### *Institutions*

The institutional framework of the Fifth Republic provides the setting within which 'cohabitation' can easily occur. In this context the effect of the electoral cycle and the mechanics of the electoral system are particularly salient.

One of the main proponents of the institutionalist approach to French politics is Jean-Luc Parodi. He was the person who first identified the theoretical cycle of presidential and legislative elections in France (Parodi, 1981). Writing prior to the September 2000 reform, he observed that because that the president was elected for a seven-year term and because the National Assembly was elected for a five-year term and assuming that both sets of elections were initially held simultaneously or at least quasi-simultaneously (as was the case in 1981),[9] what emerged was an electoral cycle which, all other things being equal, repeated itself every thirty-five years (see Figure 6.2).

| P | 1981 | | 1988 | | 1995 | | | 2002 | | 2009 | | 2016 |
|---|------|------|------|------|------|------|---|------|---|------|------|------|
| L | 1981 | 1986 | | 1991 | | 1996 | 2001 | | 2006 | | 2011 | 2016 |
| Y | N/A | 5 | 2 | 3 | 4 | 1 | 5 | 1 | 4 | 3 | 2 | 5 |

*Key*: P = presidential election, L = legislative election, Y = number of years between elections.
*Source*: Adapted from Parodi, 1981: 48.

FIGURE 6.2. The cycle of presidential and legislative elections in France prior to the September 2000 constitutional reform

[9] In France, presidential and legislative elections have never taken place at the same time. Indeed, under the current rules they cannot do so because the gap between the first and second rounds of presidential and legislative elections is two weeks and one week

The rhythm of this complex electoral cycle meant that there was plenty of opportunity for 'cohabitation' to occur. One reason was because 'mid-term' elections could occur well into the president's mandate. Assuming that presidential and legislative elections were held simultaneously, then the first decisive electoral test came after a full five years. This was plenty of time for resentment towards the president and/or government to have built up and for a desire for change to be firmly established. Thus, the public was able to go to the polls with the feeling that it finally had the freedom to sanction an unpopular president or government. This picture corresponds neatly to the circumstances in which the elections that brought about the first two periods of 'cohabitation' were held.

Paradoxically, a further reason why 'cohabitation' could occur so frequently in this context was because 'mid-term' elections could also take place quite early on in the president's term of office. Assuming that presidential and legislative elections were not held simultaneously, then the president could face a crucial test of support after just one or two years in office. This could be too short a period for reforms proposed during the presidential election to have had an impact on the system, or it could simply coincide with a temporary slump in the popularity of the president and/or government but one which was then immediately subject to the judgement of the electorate.

In these ways, then, the rhythm of the electoral cycle in France helped to create the potential for 'cohabitation' to occur. Indeed, this was one of the main reasons why the president's term of office was reduced to just five years in September 2000. All other things being equal, there is no longer the opportunity for mid-term elections to be held and so 'cohabitation', it is thought, will be less likely to occur. Even after the reform, though, it should be noted that the electoral cycle still has the potential to create the conditions for 'cohabitation'. If the president resigns, dies in office, or dissolves the Assembly prematurely, then presidential and legislative elections will no longer be synchronized. In this case, the cycle of quasi-simultaneous elections will only be restored if the president dissolves the National Assembly and brings the two elections back into line. However, if he or she does not, then mid-term elections will still occur.

As well as the mechanics of the electoral cycle, the potential for 'cohabitation' was, and remains, a function of the type of electoral system which is used for legislative elections. With the exception of the 1986 legislative election, throughout the Fifth Republic National Assembly elections have been fought on the basis of the two-ballot majority system. This system favours small

respectively. However, quasi-simultaneous presidential and legislative elections have only taken place on three occasions: 1958, 1981, and 1988. On these occasions the two sets of elections were separated by little more than a month. Even then, in 1958 the president was not directly elected. Thus, to date, there has been little opportunity for the French to engage in US-style split-ticket voting, even if they were so inclined.

parties and/or frivolous candidates at the first ballot, but big parties or at least big alliances of parties at the second ballot. In so doing, though, it helps to create artificially large parliamentary majorities (Machin, 1993). In 1986 the right was sufficiently popular to be able to gain a majority in the National Assembly despite the fact that this was the only parliamentary election to be held so far on the basis of a proportional (PR) system. In 1993 the Socialist party was so unpopular that the right would still have gained a majority if the election had been fought under a PR system. In 1997, however, the two-ballot majority system was crucial to the onset of 'cohabitation'. It helped to manufacture a left-wing parliamentary majority which would not have been forthcoming had a PR system been in place. Thus, whereas in parliamentary regimes proportional electoral systems can be identified as an institutional source of divided government by encouraging minority administrations, in France the electoral system can be as a similar type of source but this time because it helps to foster majority administrations and, hence, split-executive government.

## *Electoral Volatility*

Whatever the institutional framework of the Fifth Republic, in France 'cohabitation' has not been caused by split-ticket voting. That is to say, it has not come about because of the return of opposing majorities at simultaneous or at least quasi-simultaneous elections. However, there is evidence that the French electorate is becoming more volatile and the presence of increasing electoral volatility may be proposed as one of the main causes of 'cohabitation'.

The traditional explanation of French voting behaviour indicated that there were three main determinants to the vote: left/right self-placement, social class, and religion (see, for example, Capdevielle *et al.*, 1981). These three factors worked together to produce two relatively stable electoral subsystems. So, those who placed themselves on the left tended to be over-represented among certain social categories, such as manual workers, intermediate professions, and employees, and included a disproportionately large proportion of non-practising Catholics or people without any religious affiliation. By contrast, those who placed themselves on the right were equally over-represented in other social categories, such upper managers, the liberal professions, and heads of industry and commerce, and were much more likely to be practising Catholics. The logic of this model implied that the electorate was relatively stable. The factors which structured the vote were well established, long-standing, and culturally embedded. Moreover, for much of the 1960s and early 1970s the relative weight of these subsystems meant that the right was in a majority.

This explanation of French voting behaviour began to evolve in the mid-1970s and early 1980s. At this time, it was argued that France was undergoing a period of social change. Moreover, this change was said to favour the left (see Lancelot, 1986). There was an increase in salaried workers and a rise in 'cultural liberalism', reflecting at least in part an increase in deconfessionalization. In this way, the stage was set for the left to be sociologically majoritarian and win power, which of course it finally did in 1981.

However, elections in the mid-1980s and 1990s fundamentally challenged the study of French voting behaviour. In particular, the 1986 and 1988 elections suggested that the electorate was much more volatile than the traditional model indicated. As a result, commentators suggested that a significant percentage of the population was now susceptible to short-term electoral factors, positing amongst other things an increase in the salience of issue-voting, a greater degree of popular sensitivity to the conduct of electoral campaigns and a growing tendency for people to vote on the basis of their immediate personal economic and social circumstances rather than their long-term party-political allegiances (Habert, 1990). In sum, the outcome of French politics was more unpredictable.

This overview of French electoral studies feeds into the debate about the causes of divided government. The long period of unified government from 1962 to 1986 matches the time when it was argued that 'heavy' socio-cultural variables structured the vote and provided first the right and then the left with a majority. In this context, the conjunction of presidential and legislative majorities during this time merely reflected the majoritarian status of the right and left in the country as a whole. By contrast, the increasing prevalence of divided government from 1986 onwards corresponds to the period when French voters began to be more volatile and less likely to support the same party from one election to the next. In this context, therefore, it might be argued that the increasing incidence of 'cohabitation' is merely a reflection of the changing social structure of the country and the rise of short-term factors as the main determinant of the vote for a considerable percentage of the electorate.

### Intentional Voting

The literature on 'cohabitation' frequently indicates that the public fully approves of this pattern of government. This observation provides at least the foundation for an argument that voters want the country to experience a period of 'cohabitation' and vote accordingly. However, to date there is little or no substantive evidence to back up this thesis.

There is no doubt that in some respects at least 'cohabitation' is popular. One of the main observations about the first period of 'cohabitation' was that the popularity of both the president and the prime minister remained relatively high throughout. In particular, the onset of 'cohabitation' saw a dramatic turn around in the satisfaction ratings for the president (Zarka, 1992:

150). The second period of 'cohabitation' appears to have been equally popular. For example, in April 1993 66 per cent of people felt that 'cohabitation' was working well (Duhamel, 1993: 293). Finally, the third period of 'cohabitation' merely seems to have confirmed this general trend. So, for example, in November 1999 one poll showed that 78 per cent of people wanted 'cohabitation' to continue until 2002 (*Le Monde*, 13 Nov. 1999). In addition, 70 per cent thought that the president's behaviour was helping 'cohabitation' to function well, while 66 per cent thought the same about the prime minister.

The popularity of 'cohabitation' raises the question of whether or not the French intentionally vote in such a way as to bring it about. Prior to the first period of 'cohabitation' there was a distinct sense in which people were anxious about how the system would function. For example, in February 1986 more people thought that 'cohabitation' was a bad thing for France than a good thing (Duverger, 1987: 52). This judgement, though, was soon reversed when it was demonstrated that the institutions could work efficiently. By contrast, prior to the second period of 'cohabitation' there was much less of a feeling that the country was heading into the institutional unknown. This, it might be argued, made people more willing to vote for parties opposed to the president in the knowledge that the system would still function effectively. The same logic can be applied at least in theory to the third period of 'cohabitation' as well. Indeed, if it applies in this case it is all the more important given the closeness of the result in 1997.

The problem with this argument is that there is little hard evidence to substantiate it. For example, studies of the 1993 election indicate that voters supported the right as a protest against the left and in particular the scandals that had engulfed the Socialist party and the government's poor management of the economy (Perrineau and Ysmal, 1993). There is no evidence that they supported the right primarily because they wanted to experience a period of 'cohabitation' for its own sake. Similarly, although one analysis of the 1995 election does at least note that the voters were not afraid to reject President Chirac's call to return the outgoing majority to power (Duhamel, 1998: 24), this is not to say that voters actively sought a period of 'cohabitation'. They simply had to live with it in order to sanction Chirac and the outgoing administration.

More fundamentally, there is also evidence to suggest that support for 'cohabitation' is not quite as widespread as the above figures suggest. In 1986, the reason why 'cohabitation' was seen to be popular and why Mitterrand's poll rating soared was precisely because the president was only able to influence policy at the margins (Parodi, 1988: 170–1). Right-wing voters approved of the left-wing president because the right-wing government was still able to govern. Thus, what the polls actually demonstrated was not so much that voters liked 'cohabitation', but that they were willing to put up with it for so long as their basic political preferences were still being met.

Overall, therefore, it appears as if the institutional framework of the Fifth Republic created the potential for 'cohabitation', but that it was the increasing volatility of the French electorate, rather than intentional voting, that best explains why 'cohabitation' only began to manifest itself in the period from the mid-1980s onwards. The question remaining unanswered is whether the September 2000 reform, which changed the institutional architecture of the Fifth Republic, has reduced the potential for 'cohabitation' to any significant degree. After all, if the electorate is sufficiently volatile, then there is no reason why it might not start to return opposing majorities even at quasi-simultaneous elections.

## THE MANAGEMENT OF 'COHABITATION' IN FRANCE

'Cohabitation' has challenged the very foundations of the French dual executive. It has done so by installing the prime minister as the main political actor in the policy-making process and by greatly restricting, although not totally effacing, the role of the president. In so doing, it has established a system characterized by both conflict and compromise. The two main actors try to maximize their own influence over the political process, but they are also obliged to co-operate with each other, partly because the constitution forces them to do so and partly because co-operation has worked to the mutual advantage of both.

### *The Constitution, the Whole Constitution, Nothing but the Constitution* [10]

During 'cohabitation' prime ministers have been primarily responsible for policy-making within the executive. In particular, they have dominated virtually all aspects of domestic decision-making, while they have also had some influence over foreign policy as well. By contrast, the president's role has been much more limited. Presidents have only managed to delay certain domestic policy reforms, although they have retained a degree of control in certain areas, most notably defence policy.

Prime ministers have exercised policy leadership during 'cohabitation'. For example, they have decided which elements of the government's programme should be introduced and in what order. So, in 1993, one of Balladur's main priorities was to improve the economy. To this end, he quickly promoted a government-sponsored savings scheme (*l'emprunt Balladur*), which was a considerable success and which was used to reduce the budget deficit and increase spending in key areas. Similarly, in 1997 Jospin moved swiftly to

[10] This is a quotation by François Mitterrand from the beginning of the first period of 'cohabitation' in Apr. 1986.

tackle the problem of unemployment by introducing an ambitious state-directed job creation scheme to reduce youth unemployment. At the same time, 'cohabitation' prime ministers have also been responsible for key policy arbitrations at the most sensitive stages of the policy-making process. So, in 1986 the government decided to privatize one of the country's state-controlled television channels. Following a fierce debate between rival ministers, it was finally Chirac who personally decided that TF1 was the most appropriate channel to be sold off (Elgie, 1993). Equally, on more than one occasion after 1997 Jospin was obliged to choose between the competing demands of his socially minded minister for employment and solidarity, Martine Aubry, and his more business-friendly minister for the economy, finance and industry, Dominique Strauss-Kahn, at least until the latter's resignation in November 1999.

In these ways, there is no doubt that during 'cohabitation' power shifts from the president to the prime minister. This is particularly true for domestic policy initiatives. However, there is a reorientation of policy-making responsibilities in the field of defence and foreign-policy affairs as well. For example, in 1986 Chirac established a 'diplomatic cell' within his set of policy advisers, to provide him with the information with which to influence foreign-policy decisions. In 1993 Balladur was instrumental in determining France's position during the GATT world trade negotiations. He also proposed a European Stability Pact which was designed to establish the terms of the relationship between EU member states and candidates for membership in Central and Eastern Europe. Finally, in 1997 Jospin came to power ready (at least ostensibly) to upset the preparations for European Economic and Monetary Union if employment and social concerns were not addressed more clearly. All told, therefore, during 'cohabitation' prime ministers have finally been in a position to lead the government and to determine and conduct at least almost all aspects of the nation's policies.

In contrast to the activism of 'cohabitation' prime ministers, presidents have been relatively powerless, particularly in terms of domestic policy. Here, they have been able only to delay the introduction of certain reforms. For example, in 1986 President Mitterrand refused to allow the government to legislate by decree (*ordonnance*), which blocked some of the more controversial aspects of the government's reform programme for a few weeks or months. Similarly, in 1993 Mitterrand refused to allow the bill on the financing of private schools to be debated in a special session of parliament. This meant that the bill which would have been introduced in June of that year had to put back until the autumn. In turn, during the third period of 'cohabitation', President Chirac effectively vetoed the government's proposed constitutional amendment regarding the Higher Council of the Magistrature. Thus, in terms of domestic policy presidents have been able to establish themselves as the main opposition to the prime minister and the government, but only very rarely have they been able to shape the policy-making process in any meaningful way.

In terms of defence and foreign policy, presidents have enjoyed somewhat greater latitude. So, in 1986 President Mitterrand successfully insisted that France's short-range nuclear arms were not 'tactical', battlefield weapons, but were part of a wider, 'strategic' whole (Howorth, 1993: 158). Also in 1986 defence was the only budget to be decided in a meeting chaired by the president. All the others were decided by the prime minister and the finance minister in the absence of the president and his advisers (Elgie, 1993). Similarly, throughout the whole of the second period of 'cohabitation' Mitterrand managed to maintain France's moratorium on nuclear weapons testing, despite the opposition of the prime minister. Moreover, during this time Mitterrand also used his position as head of state to insist that he was the main representative of France at G7 meetings. As a result, Prime Minister Balladur refused to attend at all rather than be seen as subordinate to the president in this respect (Balladur, 1995: 81–3). Thus, during 'cohabitation' the president does maintain a degree of influence in a limited range of areas. However, even in these areas the extent of the president's influence is much less than is usually the case.

In these ways, 'cohabitation' marks the revenge of the prime ministership. The established pattern of the Fifth Republic's policy-making process is challenged. The prime minister becomes the main decision-maker with the dual executive. By contrast, the president is sidelined, maintaining a degree of influence only in the realm of 'high' politics and falling back on his so-called 'fonction tribunicienne' (Parodi, 1997: 303) as the symbol of opposition to the government of the day and the manifestation of the long-term continuity of the state.

## *Conflict . . .*

The fact that during 'cohabitation' power shifts from the president to the prime minister should not be taken to mean that the former merely acquiesces to the latter. On the contrary, 'cohabitation' is characterized by a period of ongoing conflict between the two main actors within the executive. To date some of the main ways in which this conflict has manifested itself include a degree of gridlock, the increased use of extraordinary constitutional, administrative, and political procedures, and the ongoing battle for public opinion.

In France 'cohabitation' can lead to gridlock in certain areas. Balladur writes that in some instances 'cohabitation paralyses the power to act, preventing movement and innovation'. The likelihood of gridlock is strongest in the areas where the president and prime minister can both legitimately claim to have policy-making powers, namely foreign and defence policy-making and European initiatives. Here, there are strong incentives for prime ministers to intervene so as to maximize their profile as a leading player on the world stage. At the same time, though, there are equally strong incentives for presidents to intervene so as to maintain their own leadership image and influence policy. To date, these conflicting interests have not resulted in a complete breakdown of policy-making structures in these areas. However, they have led to the postponement of particular initiatives, or, more accurately, to the continuation of certain foreign and defence policies which were established prior to the onset of 'cohabitation' and about which there is disagreement between the president and prime minister as to how they should be changed. Thus, while gridlock is confined to a small number of areas, it can still stifle policy innovation in those domains.

More generally, 'cohabitation' encourages the use of extraordinary constitutional, administrative, and political procedures. For the prime minister these measures are usually employed so as either to accelerate the legislative process or to minimize the likelihood of gridlock. For the president they are used to delay the political process and to make life as difficult as possible for the prime minister.

The prime minister has used the full set of constitutional powers at the government's disposal so as to speed up the legislative process. The use of these powers is not confined to 'cohabitation'. Indeed, they were employed extensively during the period of minority government after 1988 and on occasions they have been applied quite liberally during periods of unified government as well (Keeler, 1993). However, there is no doubt that the exercise of these powers was one of the principal features of the first two periods of 'cohabitation' at least.[11] For example, in 1986–88 Prime Minister Chirac declared a bill to be urgent on sixty occasions; he used the 'blocked vote' procedure sixty-eight times so as to weed out unwanted parliamentary amendments; he declared a bill to be a matter of confidence eight times, which allows bills to pass unless the government is voted out of office altogether (Article 49–3); and he also resorted to trying to legislate by decree (*ordonnance*) on a number of occasions, albeit unsuccessfully. Similarly, in 1993–5 Balladur declared a bill to be urgent forty-one times and he used the 'blocked vote' thirty-seven times[12] (all figures from Bigaut, 1995: 6). In 1986 one of the main reasons why Chirac used these powers was because he only enjoyed a very slim parliamentary majority. In addition, on both occasions prime ministers have been faced with a very time-limited electoral framework. In contrast to Jospin, Chirac and

[11] In 1997 the government was faced with a period of 'cohabitation' which was scheduled to last five years. Thus, there was less need for it to accelerate the legislative process and force bills through parliament. Moreover, had the prime minister tried to do so, then he would have run the risk of alienating his coalition partners. As a result, the government's exceptional powers were not a main feature of the period 1997–9.

[12] It should be noted, though, that Balladur employed Article 49–3 only once and he refrained completely from trying to legislate by decree.

Balladur came to power knowing that there would be a presidential election within two years. Thus, they both needed to move swiftly and so they used everything within their power to pass legislation.

In addition to accelerating the legislative process, prime ministers have resorted to other relatively unusual procedures so as to freeze the president out of the decision-making process and minimize the likelihood of gridlock or at least presidential criticism. For example, during the first period of 'cohabitation' Chirac resurrected the so-called Cabinet Council (*Conseil de Cabinet*). These are government meetings which, unlike the Council of Ministers, are held in the absence of the president (Duverger, 1987: 32).[13] The practice of holding Cabinet Councils fell out of favour after the first couple of years of the Fifth Republic. However, Chirac felt that they were a useful device in that they allowed the government to discuss policy collectively without any danger of presidential interference. Balladur continued this practice and similar meetings (*séminaires*) have also been held quite frequently during the third period of 'cohabitation'.

In contrast to the prime minister, presidents have resorted to exceptional constitutional and political measures so as to slow down the decision-making process (see above). For example, prior to 1986 there was a fierce debate between some of the country's most respected constitutional lawyers as to whether or not the president had the right to refuse sign a bill allowing the government to legislate by *ordonnance*. In the end, though, President Mitterrand simply refused to do so, thus setting a precedent for the future.

In addition, presidents have also used unusual political procedures with a view to maximizing their influence over the policy process. Here, for example, one of the innovations of the third period of 'cohabitation' has concerned the president's relationship with the Senate (Verdier, 1998). The Senate has an in-built right-wing majority. As a result, during the first two periods of 'cohabitation' the government could rely on its support. However, during the third period the Senate has opposed the government. Mindful of this situation, in 1998 President Chirac and his advisers discretely lobbied to have his preferred candidate elected as president of the Senate so as to increase his purchase over the upper house. Although the Senate has relatively few powers, it is able to delay the legislative process and in certain areas, such as constitutional reform, its assent is required in order to bring about change. Thus, while the upper house has not simply followed presidential instructions since 1997 and even though the second chamber is clearly subordinate to the first, the president has benefited from the 'indéfectible soutien' (Verdier, 1998: 81), or unwavering support, of the Senate in the battle with the government.

The final manifestation of conflict between the president and the prime minister concerns the battle for public opinion. During 'cohabitation' the

---

[13] By contrast, the president chairs the weekly meeting of the Council of Ministers.

opposition is present not just in parliament, but in one part of the executive as well. One result of this situation is that the president has often used his position as chair of the Council of Ministers to distance himself from government policy. So, for example, in 1986–8 the president frequently spoke out against the government during the course of these meetings. Moreover, he did so in a large number of policy areas, ranging from the proposed introduction of private-sector prisons to a meeting between the culture minister and the head of the Angolan guerrilla movement. Similarly, in 1993–5, even though the president was somewhat less confrontational than he had been previously, he still used his presence in the Council of Ministers to criticize the government on a number of occasions, such as the reform of the Bank of France and the list of companies which the government intended to privatize.[14]

Over and above criticisms in the very formal atmosphere of the Council of Ministers, the president and prime minister utilize other forms of political communication to express their opposition to each other. For example, both protagonists carefully choreograph their public engagements. So, in September 1999 President Chirac visited the agricultural show organized by the National Centre for Young Farmers. A day later Prime Minister Jospin made a similar visit. During his visit the president tried to establish himself as the natural spokesperson for the rural community, implicitly criticizing the government's policy in so doing. During his visit the prime minister reminded people that the government, not the president, was responsible for agricultural policy and claimed that he too was in touch with farmers' needs.

Whereas this sort of tit-for-tat criticism is an everyday part of 'cohabitation', on rare occasions the antagonism between the two actors has become almost unbearable. For example, in July 1986, when President Mitterrand first refused to sign the bill allowing the government to legislate by decree, there was a debate within the government as to whether or not the prime minister should resign in protest.[15] In the end he stayed, but the relationship between the two actors was sorely tested. Similar problems have also occurred during the third period of 'cohabitation'. Here, while Jospin never really contemplated resigning, there were at least two occasions when the prime minister's relations with the president really soured. In May 1998 the justice minister implied that the president might be charged if there was evidence that he was involved in the scandal that had engulfed the Paris town council.[16] The president immediately retaliated by instructing his advisers to examine the prime minister's background, implying that he too may have committed a fault. Similarly, in November 1999 when the president appeared to suggest that the prime minister was involved in the events that led to the

[14] A full list of the president's criticisms during the first two periods of 'cohabitation' can be found in Bigaut (1995: 13).

[15] See the account in Favier and Martin-Roland (1991: 512–22).

[16] Prior to his election as president, Chirac had been mayor of Paris.

resignation of the finance minister, Dominique Strauss-Kahn, Jospin replied by referring once again to the scandals in Paris (*Le Monde*, 5 Nov. 1999). On both occasions, 'cohabitation' survived but in other circumstances there may well have been a different outcome.

### . . . *and Compromise*

Even though 'cohabitation' is characterized by conflict, it is also marked by compromise[17] between the Élysée Palace and Matignon. Both the president and the prime minister know that they have to work with each other in certain respects, but they also realise that cooperation can work to the mutual advantage of both.

During 'cohabitation' contact between the president and the prime minister is very limited but carefully regulated (Colombani and Lhomeau, 1986: 157; Favier and Martin-Roland, 1991: 486). For example, whereas during periods of unified government and minority government presidential advisers have routinely attended government policy-making meetings, during 'cohabitation', with the exception of certain defence and foreign policy meetings, they have not. Instead, the president and prime minister meet each other face to face only once a week immediately prior to the meeting of the Council of Ministers. The only other regular contact takes place on a daily basis between the president's most senior adviser, the General Secretary of the Élysée, and the head of the prime minister's personal staff, the *directeur de cabinet*, and the most senior civil servant in the system, the General Secretary of the Government.

The relative absence of contact during 'cohabitation' suits both sides. It emphasizes that they are political opponents. It allows the president to be distanced from potentially unpopular government policies, while it also allows the prime minister to claim full credit for such policies if they are successful. At the same time, though, the existence of regular channels of communication means that common tasks can still be carried out and that mutually inconvenient mistakes can be avoided. Thus, while there are strong incentives for the president and prime minister to oppose each other during 'cohabitation' (see above), there are also incentives for them to co-operate. To date at least, both actors have calculated that they have more to lose by ending 'cohabitation' suddenly and acrimoniously than by continuing an admittedly uncomfortable relationship.

In general terms the discussions and negotiations between the president and prime minister take various forms. For example, Balladur (1995: 79–81) has confided that out of courtesy the president informed him whenever he was

---

[17] *Conflict and Compromise* is the title of the classic text on the French Fourth Republic by Philip Williams (1972). Prior to 1986 some people were opposed to 'cohabitation' because they argued that it would lead to a return to the instability of the Fourth Republic.

about to make an announcement concerning foreign, defence, and European policy and vice versa. In addition, there is every reason to believe that presidents have informed the prime minister in advance on the occasions when they have criticized government policy in meetings of the Council of Ministers. Indeed, the preparation of the Council of Ministers is undoubtedly marked by very close collaboration between the two main protagonists and their representatives (Fournier, 1987: 65–7). Finally, while it is difficult to prove, there are also indications that presidential and prime ministerial advisers have played a key role in pacifying the relationship between the two actors on the few occasions when the very existence of 'cohabitation' has been threatened.

More specifically, perhaps the best example of the institutionalized co-operation that occurs between the president and prime minister during 'cohabitation' concerns public-sector appointments. This is a highly political matter. Throughout the Fifth Republic there has been a tendency for incoming governments to appoint known sympathizers to key posts in both the civil service and the state sector more generally. Indeed, so pervasive has been this practice that newly elected governments have sometimes been accused of engaging in a witch-hunt, dismissing people appointed by the previous administration and installing their own favourites. During 'cohabitation' this issue has been particularly sensitive because prime ministers have wanted to dismiss appointments made by the president's party. However, because many of these appointments need the formal approval of both the president and prime minister, both actors have been obliged to negotiate and deal with each other.

In practice, a considerable proportion of public-sector appointments during 'cohabitation' has been made according to the principle of 'donnant-donnant' (Bigaut, 1995: 9), or one-for-me and one-for-you. So, for example, one writer states that in 1986 Mitterrand obtained Chirac's agreement that twelve of the twenty-four heads of nationalized industries could remain in post (Duverger, 1987: 24). Similarly, the president and prime minister have each appointed one of France's two European commissioners when vacancies have arisen during 'cohabitation'. Moreover, on various occasions there has been agreement that people whom the prime minister wants to move should remain in office until a sufficiently important replacement post becomes available. For instance, in May 1986 Mitterrand refused to allow the appointment of the government's proposed new ambassador to Tunisia to be discussed in the Council of Ministers. As a result, the appointment was delayed until the outgoing ambassador was found a suitable alternative posting (Zarka, 1992: 125). This is not to say, of course, that there have not been occasions when the president and prime minister have disagreed. For example, Balladur discloses (1995: 80) that in about a dozen cases, mostly concerning judicial appointments, the president questioned the prime minister's preferred nomination. Moreover, Favier and Martin-Roland (1991: 573–8) recount in great detail the sometimes acrimonious and certainly tortuous discussions surrounding the appointment of a number of senior police officials in 1986. But negotiations do occur so as to keep the appointment's process functioning to the general satisfaction of both the president and the prime minister.


## CONCLUSION

In the 1980s and 1990s 'cohabitation' became a regular part of the French system of government. The French themselves came to accept it as a normal state of affairs and their political leaders established a set of routines to deal with the problems that it provoked. Many people, though, remained fundamentally opposed to 'cohabitation' and the problems that they considered to be associated with it. Some saw it as a suboptimal institutional arrangement which needed to be addressed for the sake of better policy performance. Others viewed it as a perversion of de Gaulle's vision of the Fifth Republic and argued that it needed to be eliminated altogether for the sake of the long-term stability of the regime. This was the background in which the September 2000 constitutional reform was adopted. Rather than creating a fully fledged presidential or parliamentary regime, the reform merely addressed one institutional issue, the length of the president's mandate. The hope of the reformers was that after 2002 'cohabitation' will become a thing of the past. In this way, the authority of the president will be strengthened and the decision-making process will become more efficient. Such hopes are likely to be dashed. This is because the president's authority has been undermined by more than just 'cohabitation'. The decision-making environment of the Fifth Republic has come under stress from a wide variety of social, economic, and political factors (Elgie and Wright, 1996). Moreover, the institutional potential for 'cohabitation' remains in place. If the volatility of the French electorate continues to increase, then 'cohabitation' may still occur, if not in 2002 then perhaps in the not-too-distant future.

# 7

# Divided Government in Poland

## *Ania Krok-Paszkowska*

Poland has a semi-presidential regime in which 'a popularly-elected fixed-term president exists alongside a prime minister and cabinet who are responsible to parliament' (Elgie, 1999: 13). The form of divided government is one in which a party (or parties) opposed to the president has (have) a majority in the key house (Sejm), leading to the appointment of a prime minister who is also opposed to the president. However, as Elgie points out in Chapter 1, the concept of divided government can be used in different ways. In the US literature, which is by far the most prolific source of studies on divided government, the concept is understood in either a purely arithmetical sense, that is, reflecting the distribution of power between the executive and legislative branches of government, or in a behavioural sense, that is, a function of divisive political behaviour. The latter reflects a situation where relations are conflictual whatever the political (partisan) make-up of the different branches of government. Although this case-study will be based upon a purely arithmetical definition of divided government, it is important to understand the specific context in which divided government in Poland has functioned.

For most of the period under consideration, 1989–99, irrespective of whether the president and/or prime minister enjoyed majority support in the legislature, the relationship between parliament, government, and president has been marked by ongoing competence struggles. This was largely due to the nature of the power-sharing deal worked out between the communist and Solidarity élites in the context of the 1989 roundtable negotiations and the sequence of events which followed. The direct election of a president in late 1990 before fully competitive parliamentary elections had been held and before any decisions had been taken as to the future competencies of the presidency laid the ground for a potentially dangerous constitutional conflict. When a fully democratic parliament was elected in autumn 1991, presidential prerogatives based on agreements reached in the roundtable negotiations, that is, created under constraining circumstances, were even more open to question. As existing and newly emerging political actors gained control over one or another institution, they tried to consolidate their power bases. In part, this stemmed from a fundamental difference of opinion between president and parliament as to which institution should form the core of the democratic system: a presidency with wide executive powers, with the president heading the executive and the government answerable to both the president and the parliament, or parliamentary government based on a broader representation of interests. In part, it was also based on personality clashes and an excessive personalization of politics. This sequence of events encouraged institutional rivalry and helped to prolong the constitution-making process until 1997. This context should be kept in mind in any analysis of divided government in Poland.

This chapter is divided into three sections: the first will deal with the frequency of divided government, the second will analyse the causes of divided government, and the third section will explore how divided government has been managed.

## THE FREQUENCY AND FORM OF DIVIDED GOVERNMENT IN POLAND

Divided government is defined on the basis of either the president or the prime minister failing to enjoy majority support in at least one working house of the legislature. Since the first fully competitive parliamentary elections in 1991, some form of divided government has been the rule rather than the exception in Poland. Throughout most of this period, constitutional uncertainty and a lack of clearly delineated powers have been a persistent feature of the institutional landscape.

Initially, under the 1989 roundtable agreements, the communists were able to impose certain conditions which they hoped would enable them to control the transition to democracy. The opposition accepted a strong presidency[1] as part of a broader package which included free elections to an upper chamber (Senate), a guaranteed 65 per cent seats for the communists and their allies in the more powerful lower chamber (Sejm), and the legalization of Solidarity trade union. The unexpected electoral success of Solidarity, which won all but one of the Senate seats and all contested seats (35 per cent) in the Sejm, undermined the scenario of gradual and controlled transition. However, in keeping with the spirit of the roundtable agreements, the legislature duly elected the communist candidate, General Jaruzelski, as president. At the same time two former satellite parties, the United Peasant Party (ZSL) and the Democratic

---

[1] The powers of the president to be elected by a communist-controlled legislature included a legislative veto and full control over foreign policy, the military, and internal security. The president had sole right to nominate the prime minister, as well as the right to dissolve parliament if its decisions impinged upon his ability to carry out his constitutional prerogatives.

Party (SD) broke with the Polish United Workers' Party (PZPR) and joined in a Solidarity-dominated government led by Tadeusz Mazowiecki. This left the president in opposition to a majority in both houses of parliament, and when the PZPR dissolved itself in January 1990 the president lost any formal support he may have had in the Sejm. The transition formula, which was to have guaranteed a communist-dominated executive supported by a large majority in the legislature while allowing for a small opposition during a four-year transitional period, turned into post-communist Poland's first experience of a divided executive.

Direct presidential elections took place in November/December 1990, almost one year before the first fully competitive parliamentary elections were held. The first round failed to provide an outright winner, but Lech Walesa won convincingly in a second round run-off.[2] Walesa's legitimacy, stemming from direct free elections and his authority resulting from his past record as leader of Solidarity, made for a president who intended to exercise his powers to the full. Walesa nominated Jan Krzysztof Bielecki to lead what was in effect a caretaker government (January–November 1991) filling the gap between Mazowiecki's resignation as prime minister following his failed presidential bid and the holding of the first free parliamentary elections.

Following parliamentary elections on 27 October 1991 both president and parliament were able to claim full electoral legitimacy. The parliament which emerged after the elections was characterized by a large number of internally divided, undisciplined, and unstable parties and political groups. Indeed, during the term of the first freely elected Sejm (1991–3) it proved impossible to put together a government supported by a majority in parliament: both prime ministers, Olszewski and Suchocka, presided over formal minority coalitions. At the start of the parliamentary term, in the face of a majority in the Sejm unwilling to support his candidate for prime minister, Walesa was forced to nominate the Sejm's preferred candidate, Jan Olszewski. Although both Walesa and Olszewski came from the broadly termed Solidarity camp, it had by this time broken up into mutually antagonistic factions. The Olszewski cabinet lasted just over six months (December 1991–June 1992) before succumbing to a vote of no-confidence which was largely instigated by the president.

Walesa's candidate for prime minister, Waldemar Pawlak, was approved by the Sejm but proved unable to form a government acceptable to a majority in the Sejm. Under the so-called Little Constitution[3] in force at that time, it was then up to the Sejm to propose a new candidate. It chose Hanna Suchocka to lead what was to have been a coalition of eight parties. However,

---

[2] In the first round Walesa received 40% of the vote; in the second round he won 74.3% of the vote.

[3] The failure to reach agreement on a full new constitution led to the passing of the interim Constitutional Act of 17 October 1992.

one of the parties left the coalition negotiations even before the government was sworn in, leaving a minority coalition which commanded only 200 of the 460 seats in the Sejm. The Suchocka government (July 1992–May 1993) was, thus, forced to rely on the informal support of the Solidarity faction in the Sejm. The government survived for eighteen months before it was removed by a simple vote of no-confidence. The concurrent failure of the Sejm to name a candidate prime minister (constructive vote of no-confidence) allowed the president to dissolve parliament and call early elections.[4]

Elections, under a new, less proportional electoral law, were held in September 1993. From then until the end of the presidential term in November 1995, the executive was divided. President Walesa was confronted with a large parliamentary majority, only four seats short of the two-thirds majority needed for constitutional reform. The majority was formed by two post-communist parties: the Alliance of the Democratic Left (SLD) and the Polish Peasant Party (PSL). The two parties formed a coalition government, headed by Waldemar Pawlak, the leader of the weaker party, the PSL. However the government did not last the parliamentary term and again the president was largely instrumental in bringing about its fall. In February 1995 the president called for the cabinet to be restructured and headed by a new prime minister. Although Walesa had no formal powers to dismiss the government, he threatened to find a way to dissolve parliament. This played into the hands of the SLD which had become increasingly unhappy with Pawlak's style of leadership. On 1 March 1995 the Sejm passed a constructive vote of no confidence in the government designating Josef Oleksy (SLD) as prime minister-elect. Again this was an example of divided government, with Oleksy heading an SLD/PSL coalition opposed to the president. Oleksy was forced to resign on 25 January 1996 following allegations of KGB spying.[5] By this time, however, a new president had been elected.

Aleksander Kwasniewski, who was leader of Social Democracy for the Republic of Poland (SdRP) as well as the chairman of the SLD parliamentary club, resigned as SdRP party leader and handed in his party membership when he was elected president in November 1995. Nevertheless, he continues to be closely associated with the SLD by friends and foes alike. His election thus served to more clearly define the fault lines between coalition and opposition in parliament. The new Cimoszewicz government (January 1996–September

---

[4] Under the Little Constitution the president had the right to dissolve parliament in the following cases: (*a*) if the Sejm had passed a simple vote of no-confidence in the council of ministers; (*b*) if the budget was not passed by the Sejm within three months of the submission of a draft budget; and (*c*) if no government capable of receiving the confidence of the Sejm had been formed following a complex five-step procedure in which the president and the Sejm took turns to nominate their candidate for prime minister.

[5] The allegations were made in the Sejm by the minister of internal affairs, Andrzej Milczanowski, on the basis of evidence supplied by the Interior Ministry's secret service department.

1997) which continued the SLD/PSL coalition was an example of unified government with the president and prime minister from the same political camp. It represented a period of co-operation between the president and prime minister, backed by a large parliamentary majority, although the intra-coalitional relationship was not always smooth.

Parliamentary elections in September 1997 resulted in a victory for Solidarity Electoral Action (AWS), which won 33.8 per cent of the vote, beating SLD which won 27.1 per cent. A government was formed by the AWS together with the Freedom Union (UW) and headed by Jerzy Buzek. The second half of the Kwasniewski presidency has once again been a period of 'cohabitation' or divided government.

## THE CAUSES OF DIVIDED GOVERNMENT IN POLAND

The literature on the causes of divided government brings us to two general types of explanation, those linked to elections and voting behaviour and those along structural/institutional lines. Most of the literature is based on experiences in the United States and as such is not always directly applicable to semi-presidential systems. Moreover, the period since transition to democracy in Poland is still relatively short (ten years). Although there already have been a number of elections both parliamentary (1989, 1991, 1993, 1997) and presidential (1990, 1995), electoral laws have been frequently changed and adapted. Administrative reforms carried out in 1998 mean that further changes will need to be made to electoral districts before parliamentary elections in 2001. Lack of continuity in electoral provisions has been mirrored by the absence of a stable and established party system. With each new round of elections, presidential, local, and parliamentary, new political groups were formed disorienting the electorate by their sheer number and lack of identifiable programmes. The lack of stability made it difficult for parties to function as effective instruments of the democratic process (Millard, 1994).

It is also important to understand that the party system itself is built on a division that has functioned on the political scene since the 1989 elections and that is still largely shaped by Solidarity—broadly defined—and the former communist establishment (Wasilewski, 1994; Slodkowska, 1997; Majcherek, 1997). This makes for a conflictual political culture which overlays a basic consensus about the desirability of rule of law and a market economy. The fact that many supporters of the post-communist formations, the so-called 'Lewica' (the left), have also been able to take advantage of the socioeconomic transition, while support for Solidarity has traditionally come from workers in declining state industries, has acted to muddy conventional distinctions between 'left' and 'right'. The dichotomy between the two camps is based on history and on an ideological, value-based rhetoric which has little to do with interest articulation and which, despite the existence of multi-dimensional cleavages, still manages to persist.[6] This state of affairs has evident repercussions for coalition formation in that it has tended to limit the field of potential partners for winning parties and has left coalition governments internally divided on quite substantial policy areas such as privatization and decentralization.

The fundamental cause of divided government in Poland has, thus, been systemic change, bolstered by the timing of elections and electoral formulas. Structural/institutional explanations rather than voting behaviour appear to be a more promising preliminary line of enquiry in explaining the causes of divided government in Poland in 1989–99.

## Structural/Institutional Explanations

Divided government, as it emerged from the power-sharing transitional formula, preceded free parliamentary elections and most party formation. However, it was the holding of direct presidential elections well before fully competitive parliamentary elections that had the most impact on the pattern of political competition in Poland. At first glance, the most obvious cause of divided government in Poland is the fact that presidential and parliamentary elections have never been held concurrently. The president is elected for a five-year term, while a parliamentary term lasts for four years. Although this means that presidential and parliamentary elections will be held in the same year once every twenty years, it will not be until 2005 that we will be able to see what effect, if any, concurrent elections may have on voting behaviour.

In the literature, the likelihood of divided government is held to be greater if executive and legislative elections are not held concurrently (Shugart, 1995). This provides voters with the opportunity to sanction decision-makers. In the case of presidential elections, voters can elect a president associated with a party in opposition; in the case of parliamentary elections, a party opposed to the president may win a legislative majority. This line of reasoning presupposes, however, that the president is backed by a political party and that reasonably stable parties with clear programmatic profiles have emerged. Neither premise is particularly convincing for either the presidential elections in 1990 nor the parliamentary elections in 1991, although elections since then have been more party-dominated. Moreover, although the winner of the 1995 presidential elections does have a party-political background and clearer programmatic profiles have emerged in successive parliamentary elections, governments have consisted of coalitions made up of at least two parties.

---

[6] On dimensions cutting across the Polish party system, see Wesolowski (1996), Markowski (1997), Toka (1997). See also Powers and Cox (1997) on the relative importance of non-economic and economic issues in determining voting behaviour.

Political practice has shown not only divisions between the coalition and the opposition, but internally divided cabinets and unreliable parliamentary majorities. A clear-cut dichotomy between coalition and opposition does not always exist, making it difficult to analyse voting behaviour.

Presidential elections in 1990 were held before any of the newly emerging parties had been exposed to electoral competition. The early period of democratization had been marked by little or no institutional effort to strengthen or even promote the formation of political parties. Although most presidential candidates were supported by a political party, the success in the first round of an entirely unknown *émigré* businessman, Stanislaw Tyminski, points to a disoriented electorate open to populist rhetoric. The winner in the second round, Lech Walesa, chose not to form a strong presidential party, preferring instead to present himself as the unquestioned leader of Solidarity. By this time, however, the broad Solidarity movement had acrimoniously fallen apart and he was challenged by parliamentary leaders who had formerly been his allies. The so-called 'war at the top' was not only based on different approaches to political and economic reform.[7] It was also a battle about the respective powers and responsibilities of the president, the parliament, and the prime minister and cabinet, that is, the institutional set-up itself. Quite apart from the ambition and powerful personality of Walesa, which would have made conflict rather than consensus the order of the day, the context of unfinished constitutional business (a temporary constitution) and political élites engaged in the process of building parties (intense competition) make structural explanations of divided government more compelling at this stage than electoral explanations.

Divided government during the 1991–3 Sejm came about because of the fragmented nature of the parliament and personal animosities between president and prime minister (and other cabinet members) rather than the differing formal political affliations of president and prime minister. A relatively pure form of proportional representation (PR) combined with an unstructured party system resulted in a legislature composed of twenty-nine parties which went on to form eighteen parliamentary clubs (caucuses). By March 1993 not one of the clubs was left with the same number of members it had started off with and the Sejm was made up of eleven clubs, six 'circles' (a group of less than fifteen but more than three members), and fifteen independents. This fragmentation meant that much time and energy were spent in forming workable governing coalitions in a parliament in which at least five parties were needed to form a majority coalition.

In such a situation, a new electoral law was passed, aiming at rationalizing the party system and laying the ground for governments based on stable

---

[7] Former Solidarity prime minister and presidential contender, Tadeusz Mazowiecki, favoured a more gradualist approach while Lech Walesa and the Centre Alliance (PC) argued for an acceleration of change and more radical reform.

parliamentary majorities. The 1993 electoral law reflects the 1991 law in structure, but the mathematical formula used to translate votes into seats, the
national list, the thresholds, and low average district magnitudes contribute
to results that are more disproportional than those usually associated with a
list PR system. The first elections held under the new law in 1993 produced
highly disproportionate results owing to a large percentage of wasted votes,
that is, votes cast for parties that failed to cross the electoral thresholds of 5
per cent for single parties and 8 per cent for coalitions. This reflected the failure of small parties emerging from the Solidarity movement either to recognize the full implications of reductive measures of the electoral system or to
assess realistically their electoral strength. The results of the 1997 elections, in
which two broad electoral alliances, Solidarity Electoral Action (AWS) and
the Alliance of the Democratic Left (SLD), won 33.8 per cent and 27.1 per
cent of the votes respectively, indicated that the implications of the new electoral rules had been more clearly understood and adapted to by both parties
and voters.[8]

Although electoral engineering has had an effect upon electoral behaviour
and strategies, it has had only limited impact on the party system itself. There
has been little incentive for small parties to abandon their individual existence. Large electoral alliances based on the post-communist/post-Solidarity
division are likely to contest parliamentary elections for the foreseeable
future, given that only a few parties can risk contesting elections on their own.
Under the 1997 Constitution, however, social organizations are precluded
from registering electoral lists. For the next parliamentary elections the two
largest electoral alliances represented in parliament, AWS and SLD, will have
to change their status as social organizations. The SLD turned itself into a
single party in April 1999. The situation to the right of the political spectrum
is more fluid. Although an attempt to create an overarching party, the Social
Movement of Solidarity Electoral Action (RS AWS), has been reasonably
successful in attracting non-party members of the AWS coalition, many of
the individual parties that contested elections on the AWS electoral list, such
as the Christian National Union (ZChN) and Conservative Peasant Party
(SL-K), are unwilling to give up their independent existence.

Paradoxically the 1995 presidential elections both reinforced the post-
communist/post-Solidarity divide and provided voters with the opportunity
to sanction decision-makers by crossing that very divide. Although presidential and parliamentary elections are not held concurrently, they are very much
interconnected. Presidential elections are held under a majority run-off system which encourages the leaders of even small parliamentary parties as well

---

[8] A much smaller percentage of votes was cast for parties which failed to cross electoral
thresholds in 1997 (12%) than in 1993 (34%). In 1997 almost three-quarters of the votes cast
went to the three largest electoral lists; in 1993 the three largest winners had received less
than half the votes.

as independents to enter the presidential race. Parties have seen presidential elections as a way of profiling themselves. For parties which were not represented in parliament, fielding a candidate in the 1995 presidential elections was a chance to gain media coverage and support from outside the party. In 1990, sixteen candidates declared their intention to run, although only six became formal candidates. In 1995, thirteen candidates stood for election, in the hope of coming second and upsetting the front-runner in the run-off or gaining leverage with the two leading candidates to make deals between the rounds. However, despite this system which is held to encourage fragmentation (see Mainwaring and Shugart, 1997*a*), the continuing salience of the post-Solidarity/post-communist divide tends to reinforce bipolar rather than multipolar structures. Despite a PR electoral system for the parliament which makes the likelihood of single-party government rather small, the second round of presidential elections provides voters with a clear choice of whether to vote in a unified or divided executive.

As in other post-communist democracies, the painful effects of restructuring the economy, privatization, and welfare reforms have meant that governing parties are unlikely to win two consecutive terms in office. There has also been intense competition between coalition partners and a tendency to put party-political affiliation above competence and ability in allocating ministerial posts, which has led to frequent cabinet dismissals, reshuffles, and scandals. With public confidence low, incumbents, if they survive the full parliamentary term, are more than likely to be voted out in the next elections. Since presidential elections are less frequent than parliamentary elections, the chances of 'cohabitation' for at least part of either term are pretty high.

### Electoral Explanations

Given the background of changes to the electoral system, fluid party structures, and indeed, changes in the powers of the presidency, it has been difficult for voters to engage in strategic voting or systematically choose or reject divided government on the basis of, for instance, achieving more balanced marcro-economic policies. Voting behaviour, as well as coalition-forming, has been more a function of a newly emerging democracy trying to come to terms with its authoritarian past. On the one hand, there is a gulf between post-communist and post-Solidarity formations which is proving very difficult to bridge. Although informal co-operation and consensus-building does take place, it is as yet unthinkable for a post-communist party and a post-Solidarity party to form a coalition government together. On the other hand, experience of one-party rule and the lack of separation of powers means that great care was taken to provide for a balance and division of powers in the Constitution. There has been a wariness of putting too much power in the hands of one person or party. In an opinion poll carried out shortly after the 1995 presidential elections, 63 per cent of respondents thought that it was bad for the country to have a president who came from a party, the SLD, with the largest representation in the Sejm and which dominated in government (*Rzeczpospolita*, 28 Nov. 1995). This was despite the fact that the SLD by itself did not even have a legislative majority: it held 37 per cent of Sejm seats.

Yet there is also evidence from the 1995 and 1997 elections that voters are willing to bridge the communist/Solidarity divide if one side is too dominant and/or too radical in either parliament or the presidency. In this respect, Fiorina's (1996) 'balancing' theory stands up rather well, with the electorate tending to vote for more moderate, centrist, and less confrontational candidates in next elections if behaviour and policy is seen as having been too extreme. In Poland, given the intense party competition and intra-coalitional squabbles, voters and most politicians want to see a president who is a moderating and stabilizing participant on the political scene. Walesa's elastic interpretations of his constitutional prerogatives and his confrontational style were not popular with a large part of the electorate. His presidency also demonstrated how divided government can produce institutional conflict and even gridlock. The 1995 presidential elections showed that moderate voters, whether left-of-centre or right-of-centre are willing to vote for a candidate from the opposite camp if that candidate is seen as being more professional, centrist, and more willing to act as arbiter. Kwasniewski in his electoral campaign was more conciliatory than Walesa, placing an emphasis on future reforms rather than past antagonisms and stressing the need for co-operation rather than conflict between president and parliament (*Polityka*, 11 Nov. 1995). The fact that the president's main competencies are in foreign and defence policy (and even here they are rather limited), on which moderate post-communists and moderate post-Solidarity parties are in broad agreement, may have made it easier for voters to engage in split-ticket voting. In future elections, Solidarity-linked candidates espousing strongly nationalist and religious policies may also push more centrist voters to vote for a post-communist candidate who is not associated too strongly with the former regime and is not violently anticlerical. With time, as increasing numbers of the electorate have no direct experience of the former regime, historical divisions may become just that: memories that have little effect on voting behaviour.

The more settled and cohesive nature of the SLD also makes it easier for the left to come up with a single presidential candidate. Parties of the right are more fragmented and dispersed, even those within the AWS bloc, and this makes it more difficult for them to agree on a single candidate. Intense rivalry between leaders within the AWS bloc as well as significant ideological differences between the AWS and its potential coalition partners makes it difficult for individuals to resist the temptation to compete in a wide field of first-round candidates. In such circumstances, an SLD candidate will always get past the first round and can then try to pull in centrist votes in the second round. The president's limited powers, but his/her ability to exert influence even when majorities are divided through his/her powers of legislative initiative and suspensive veto of electorally unpopular bills, make split-ticket voting a rational choice for voters unsatisfied with the performance of parties they had voted for in parliamentary elections. Moreover, limited powers also allow a politically astute president to champion popular causes without carrying the blame for any failed policies.

However, electoral explanations of another kind may be put forward to hypothesize why divided government may become less frequent than has been the case to date. As well as being a more cohesive party, the electoral cycle has allowed the SLD to profit from reforms instigated by Solidarity-led governments. SLD-led coalitions have continued the reforms without taking significant initiatives to introduce new ones. The most far-reaching and painful reforms, such as Leszek Balcerowicz's 'shock therapy' in 1989/90 and recent reforms of local administration as well as the pension, healthcare, and education systems, were all carried out by Solidarity-led governments. Such reforms hit the state sector badly, affecting coal miners, steelworkers, nurses and doctors—all traditional Solidarity strongholds. Such stringent reform programmes also cause huge tensions within coalition governments. Under the government led by Prime Minister Jerzy Buzek, which came to power after the 1997 elections, ministers have been charged with incompetence, ministers and their deputies representing different coalition parties have found it difficult to work together, and there have been frequent resignations and reshuffles. Government performance has come under criticism not only from the opposition SLD, but almost as frequently, and often more sharply, from the parties making up the government. Co-operation between the more reformist UW and parts of the AWS with trade-union links comes at a high price. The disruption and hardship caused by reforms in the short term, as well as chaotic and deteriorating relations between coalition partners, do not go down well with voters. They are likely to sanction decision-makers by voting in a SLD-dominated coalition in the next elections. The AWS/UW coalition came apart in June 1999, leaving the AWS to head a minority government. Moreover, the AWS failed to turn itself into a single party and presidential elections in October 2000 were easily won at the first ballot by the incumbent, Aleksander Kwasniewski. This victory may pave the way for a lengthy period of unified government after parliamentary elections in autumn 2001. The frequently alternating pattern we have seen so far may be overturned.

## THE MANAGEMENT OF DIVIDED GOVERNMENT IN POLAND

Divided government in Poland has at times been very confrontational. At its worst it has led to brinkmanship stopping just short of major constitutional crisis. It has involved such creative interpretations of presidential powers that both governing and opposition parties have united in the defence of parliament as an institution, bringing the conflict from the level of party-political rivalry to institutional confrontation. At other times, relations between the president and a parliamentary majority opposed to him have been reasonably consensual. The president has helped to ease through government policies on which broad agreement can be reached, while the parliamentary executive has recognized that consultation rather than confrontation with a popular president may be in their best interest.

There are, as Cox and Kernell (1991) have argued, several options for managing divided government in a presidential regime. One option is to take a unilateral approach: the executive and legislative branch of government decide to pursue their own ends without taking each other into account. Another is for the two branches of government to reach some sort of accommodation with one another, with each side trying to get the best deal through negotiating tactics involving delay, bluff, and brinkmanship. Finally, leaders of one or the other branch can 'go public' and present their policy preferences directly to the public with the aim of strengthening their bargaining position with the other branch. In Poland's semi-presidential regime all three strategies can be discerned, despite the fact that government is answerable to parliament and the president has only limited policy-making powers. However, as will be seen below, not only have presidents and prime ministers 'gone it alone', reached accommodation, or 'gone public' when faced with divided government, but both have also tried to build ad hoc coalitions to win support. Moreover, Poland has also had two experiences of minority government, in one case opposed and in the other supported by the president.

Divided government at an early stage, before the foundations of the system had been consolidated, led to great difficulty in resolving disputes between president and prime minister. It is, however, difficult to speak of a clear case of divided majorities between Walesa and governments accountable to the 1991–3 Sejm. Parliamentary parties were still too unstructured and fluid and political affiliations too fragile for a clear pattern to emerge. President Walesa failed to build a centrist coalition based around the then largest party, the Democratic Union (UW) led by former Prime Minister Mazowiecki, and was forced to accept the Sejm's preferred candidate, Jan Olszewski, as prime minister. Although both Walesa and Olszewski shared a Solidarity background, the Olszewski cabinet quickly clashed with the president. Olszewski wanted to enhance his powers *vis-à-vis* the president, especially with respect to who should control the armed forces and co-ordinate security and defence policies.

Olszewski pushed through his favoured candidate as defence minister, with the result that there was ongoing conflict between minister of defence, Jan Parys and Walesa's national security office. The prime minister was also a fierce critic of the Balcerowicz economic austerity programme which was backed by Walesa. In a bid to slow down the pace of reform Olszewski tried to convince the Sejm to grant him special powers to rule by decree. His attempt at 'going it alone' was thwarted by a lack of parliamentary support for his policies and a more general reluctance to grant the executive powers which parliament would be unable to control. The breakdown in relations between prime minister and president came to a head in May 1992, when as part of a bungled effort to outmanœuvre the president, interior minister Antoni Macierewicz produced files alleging that the president had secretly collaborated with the former security services.[9] This was the last straw for a parliamentary opposition (both Solidarity and post-communist) that had become increasingly concerned by Olszewski's political manipulation. After only six months in office, the government fell following a no-confidence vote. The motion of no-confidence was backed up by a letter from the president to the speaker of the Sejm calling for immediate dismissal of the government. In political terms the president's 'loss of confidence' in the government provided an important signal showing his support for an *ad hoc* parliamentary majority to pass such a motion.

Relations between president and prime minister under the Suchocka cabinet (July 1992–May 1993) were more consensual. This was an example not of a divided executive, but of a 'formal' minority government. The seven parties making up the coalition had a common Solidarity heritage, but were divided on practically everything else. The fragile nature of the coalition meant that it had to adopt a pragmatic, issue-by-issue approach in order to survive. The lack of stable legislative support for the government also allowed the president to flex his muscles in relation to the Sejm, as well as reminding the government of the danger of 'going it alone'. For example, a few days before the budget was to be debated in the Sejm, the president told the prime minister, on television, that he would dissolve parliament if it did not pass the budget.[10] This was support with a sting in its tail. Moreover, with increasing doubts on the part of governing parties whether they could muster enough support to pass the budget, bargaining and bluffing strategies were employed to try to increase support. Liberal members of the government urged the prime minister to present the opposition PSL with an ultimatum: either they vote for the

---

[9] The files, many of which may have been forged by the communist secret police, involved over sixty leading politicians and government officials, including Walesa himself, the Sejm speaker, as well as certain members of the government.

[10] Article 21(4) of the Little Constitution provided that 'if the budget has not been passed within a period of three months following the submission of a draft fulfilling the requirements of budgetary law, the president may dissolve the Sejm'.

budget, or top civil servants with PSL party affiliation could lose their jobs. The threat was not carried out and all but two PSL members voted against the budget. Former Prime Minister Olszewski, now in opposition, suggested that his party would support the budget in return for government support for his party's bill on lustration (vetting) which was specifically aimed at the president and his ministers. Not all the coalition parties could agree to this so Olszewski's party also voted against the budget (with two abstentions). In the end, the budget was passed with the support of independents, the German minority, and the parliamentary club of the Solidarity trade union which, while not formally part of the coalition, usually provided soft support for the government. Three months later, though, the motion of no-confidence in the Suchocka government was actually instigated by Solidarity. It had grown increasingly unhappy with the fiscal and monetary policies pursued by the government's liberal reformers. The ploy to force the government to concede wage increases for striking public-sector employees backfired when the motion of no-confidence was accepted by the margin of one vote. The president's decision not to accept the prime minister's resignation but to dissolve parliament and call early elections was taken unilaterally thus allowing him to present the parliamentary executive with a *fait accompli*.

The management of divided government in 1993–5 took place in a different context. For the first time the president was faced with a coalition government which was supported by a large and stable majority. The two parties making up the government were both organizationally stronger and more experienced in parliamentary work than the new parties which had formed the Solidarity governments from 1991 to 1993. The senior coalition partner, the SLD, was dominated by Social Democracy for the Republic of Poland (SdRP), a repackaged successor to the communist party which had changed its name and image in order to gain legitimacy in the new political order. Although it unequivocally accepted the democratic rules of the game, it drew upon members and organizational structures of the communist regime. The junior coalition partner, the PSL, was more acceptable to the president. Although its organizational structures are based upon those of the United Peasant Party (ZSL), a former ally of the ruling party, it had merged with the remnants of the pre-communist peasant movement and parts of Rural Solidarity. It effectively used the symbols and traditions of its pre-war predecessor to present a new image.

Aware of the sensitivities aroused by the coming to power of formations with roots in the former regime, the SLD/PSL government tried to achieve good relations with the president by accepting that the ministers of foreign affairs, defence, and internal affairs would be picked by Walesa. These three 'presidential' ministers formed an integral part of the SLD/PSL government, but at the same time stood outside it as none of the three ministers were connected to the coalition parties and owed their allegiance primarily to the president. This in itself was a difficult set-up for any government to manage. The scope for confrontation was increased by a president intent on strengthening his constitutional position by creating political custom which would tilt the balance of power in his favour. With only a temporary constitution in place, the goal was to push through a more presidential form of government. The president was thus following his own constitutional agenda. To weaken the government, he consistently favoured one governing party, the PSL, over the other, the SLD. Through weekly meetings with Prime Minister Pawlak of the PSL, the president tried to impose his policy preferences without consultation with the other coalition partner, thus driving a wedge between the coalition parties. The president also made full use of his legislative powers—his right to submit bills, his right of legislative veto, and his right to send bills to the Constitutional Tribunal to achieve his aims. However, yet again it was the ambiguity of constitutional provisions relating to the respective prerogatives of president and cabinet with respect to the armed forces that triggered a near-breakdown in relations between the coalition and president. Following a disagreement between the army chief of staff and the minister of defence, in which the president took the side of the former, Pawlak was persuaded to fire the defence minister. The prime minister concurred, but refused to accept Walesa's candidate for the post. Pawlak's removal of the minister of defence was strongly criticized, by his coalition partner SLD and the opposition, as weakening civilian control of the army. In October 1994 a cross-party resolution passed by a huge majority accused the president of destabilizing the constitutional order by involving himself in the dispute between the army chief-of-staff and the minister of defence. This did not deter the president from continuing to 'go it alone', this time concentrating his fire on the government's fiscal policies and the budget. The president's veto of the 1995 tax bill was overridden by the Sejm, after which the president tried to delay it further by submitting the bill to the Constitutional Tribunal. The passage of the tax bill had repercussions for the passage of the state budget. Citing the inability of the parliament to pass the budget within three months of the submission of the draft budget—a delay caused by the president's legal manœuvres—Walesa again threatened to dissolve parliament. This was countered by the Sejm's statement, supported by 92 per cent of the deputies present at the vote, that it would undertake impeachment proceedings were the president to act upon his threat. Walesa then suggested that a change in prime minister might persuade him to remove his objections to the budget. He had already stated in an interview that 'the situation had outgrown the prime minister' and 'the possibility of his having a vacation should be created' (*Polityka*, 14 January 1995: 3). Then, in televised proceedings, Walesa met in the Sejm with the speakers and parliamentary party leaders. He accused the Pawlak government of incompetence, party nepotism, and slowing down reforms. At this point, the president's interests coincided with those of the SLD, unhappy with Pawlak's style of leadership and his disloyalty to the coalition. The next day the coalition parties proposed Jozef Oleksy (SLD), speaker of the Sejm, as candidate prime minister.

The Oleksy cabinet was endorsed by the Sejm on 3 March 1995. Again the three so-called presidential ministries went to candidates chosen by Walesa. The president, with no formal support in parliament apart from sixteen deputies in the Non-Party Reform Bloc (BBWR),[11] had managed to bring about a change in government and keep control of the three critical ministries. However, although Walesa's unilateral approach enabled him to achieve the improbable, it was extremely unpopular with the public. Early in 1995, just after his stand-off with the Pawlak government, his popularity plummeted, with approval ratings fluctuating between 7 per cent and 13 per cent of those who declared they would vote in the forthcoming presidential elections (Jasiewicz, 1996).

Yet in November 1995 Walesa lost to Aleksander Kwasniewski by a very narrow margin.[12] The election of Kwasniewski ushered in a period of unified government (December 1995–September 1997), during which relations between president and prime minister were good. Halfway through Kwasniewski's term of office, however, elections were won by Solidarity Electoral Action (AWS). Another period of divided government ensued and it was not made any easier by the enactment of a new constitution. The 1997 Constitution removed some of the ambiguities of the Little Constitution, as well as slightly weakening the position of the president relative to the legislative branch of government (Van der Meer Krok-Paszkowska, 1999).

Under a new constitution precedent and interpretation are very important in forming political custom. The new government was faced with an incumbent president who was used to informal consultation and co-operation with the government, both within and outside his constitutional spheres of influence. Although formally non-party, the president was nevertheless clearly associated with the SLD. Initially the Solidarity-led government of Jerzy Buzek took a rather confrontational stance towards the president. It started by announcing that the president or his representatives would not be welcome at regular meetings of the council of ministers. The cabinet based its stance on a rather convoluted interpretation of Article 141–1 of the 1997 Constitution. This provides that, on matters of particular importance to the state, the president may summon and preside over a cabinet council made up of members of the council of ministers. Under the Little Constitution in such matters the

[11] In the run-up to the 1993 parliamentary elections, Walesa created a presidential alliance, the BBWR, which he hoped would be able to gain at least 20% of seats in the next parliament, thus giving him a substantial parliamentary base. However, Walesa distanced himself from the group when it became clear that the alliance would not become the powerful political force he had anticipated.

[12] In the second-round run-off Kwasniewski won 51.7% against 48.3% for Walesa.

president had presided over the full council of ministers. The new government argued that, since the new body of cabinet council was not the same as the council of ministers, it could not have the same competence as a decision-making body. Its task should therefore be restricted to discussing and deliberating. Although this provision relates only to exceptional circumstances, the government insisted that it also had more general repercussions for the role of the president in executive decision-making. The idea was to isolate the president and increase the power of the prime minister. Although the formal constitution puts the initiative in the hands of the prime minister (that is, the prime minister decides whether to invite the president to cabinet meetings), had the 1997 Constitution come into force under conditions of unified government, the presence of the president (or a representative of the president) in cabinet meetings would have become a matter of course—forming political custom. In practice, the cabinet council has been convened only a few times (twice by the end of 1998) and is a largely without function.

The reaction of the president was also to go it alone and show that he was not entirely powerless. This he did by exercising his right to veto legislation and showing that he could use it effectively.[13] The president also used the media to outline his policies and score political points. In the run-up to local elections in 1998 he accused ministers of failing to deliver on promises to pass a new law governing local authority financing before elections were held. Indeed, there is a tendency on both sides to air personal and ideological differences in public. However, the president has also been quite successful in presenting himself as an arbiter of conflicts. He has not engaged in the type of institutional brinkmanship displayed by President Walesa. His political instinct has been to favour constructive dialogue above one-upmanship as a way of achieving his aims. Despite his links with the opposition SLD, he has at times gone his own way and helped to ease reform policies through government, signing bills despite the opposition's call for a veto. By supporting the reforms and not undermining government attempts at introducing electorally unpopular changes, he can reap the benefit of being seen to back reforms, while not carrying the responsibility for their implementation. If the reforms fail, it is the government's fault. If they succeed, the president shares in their success. At the same time, through a judicious use of his veto, and taking advantage of intra-coalition disputes on administrative reform, he

---

[13] Early in the new parliamentary term, the president successfully vetoed bills on changes to valourization of pensions and on rules governing sex education in schools. In July 1998 he also vetoed the act on the administrative division of the country. Since the coalition parties themselves were divided on how many new voivodships (provinces) there should be, the veto was not overturned. By forcing a renegotiation of the administrative division, the president managed to bring about a division closest to that favoured by the opposition SLD, namely sixteen voivodships. However, a presidential veto of a vetting bill (regulating the selective opening of secret service files from the communist era) was defeated by the AWS/UW coalition with the support of the opposition PSL.

has been able to achieve an administrative division of the country which was closest to the SLD's wishes.

Since mid-1997, largely coinciding with the period of divided government, Kwasniewski's approval ratings have consistently reached well over 60 per cent, at times rising to over 70 per cent. Prime Minister Buzek has seen his approval ratings steadily fall from 59 per cent in late 1997 to 49 per cent in July 1999. At times approval has fallen to 35 per cent.[14] It should be pointed out, however, that these lower scores are due mainly to his perceived inability to manage problems within the coalition itself rather than with respect to his relations with the president.

## CONCLUSION

Poland's experience of divided government has shown that there is little option but to 'bargain within the beltway' if gridlock and institutional conflict are to be avoided. Given the experience of the past ten years, there is an awareness that divided government engenders the necessity to work together in certain areas and that some form of co-operation is certainly a lesser evil than all-out conflict between president and prime minister. Political practice has shown that on foreign affairs and especially defence, president and prime minister accentuate party-political differences at their peril. Two governments were indirectly toppled by conflicts about defence. As a result there is a real awareness of the dangers of conflict in these fields and the need to build up political traditions encouraging more co-operative forms of cohabitation.[15] Although a prime minister with a large and stable majority could be tempted to 'go it alone' by outvoting presidential legislative initiatives and overturning vetoes, the political reality is that governments have to date been made up of several parties, and they have not always been able to rely on the loyalty of parties making up the coalition. Indeed, it is the lack of cohesion within the legislative branch of government which has allowed presidents to exercise more influence than might be expected from their constitutional prerogatives alone. Indeed, even under divided government, a prime minister may find the support of the president to be essential in getting through difficult but necessary reforms. In this respect, the challenges facing governments in post-communist democracies are far greater than in more established democracies with long-standing market economies.

---

[14] Pentor surveys in *Wprost*, 49 (7 Dec. 1997); Centrum Badania Opinii Spolecznej (Centre for Public Opinion Research), Dec. 1999, http://www.cbos.pl/SPLSKOM.POL/1999; *Wprost*, 29 (18 July 1999).

[15] With this aim in mind, a seminar was held in the Sejm on 29 Jan. 1998 where French and Polish experiences of cohabitation were discussed.

The prospects for constructive rather than destructive 'cohabitation' have also been improved by a more stable constitutional order. Despite repeated threats by parties not represented in the 1993–7 parliament which prepared and passed the new constitution, to extensively amend it once they came to power, there have been no serious attempts to re-open the constitutional debate. Although there has been the inevitable jockeying for position between president and prime minister under the new constitution, no major constitutional crises have arisen since it came into effect. The Constitution appears to provide for a workable balance of powers between president and prime minister even under conditions of divided government.

# 8

# Divided Governance: The Case of Denmark

## *John Fitzmaurice*

Naturally, the opposition should have influence . . .
(Poul Schlüter, prime minister, 1982–93)

Can the concept of divided government have any meaning in a parliamentary system like that in Denmark? Clearly, it is not present in its purest form, found in systems with a formal system of separation of powers or with some collegiate or proportional type of executive. The best known and clearest example is that of the United States. Here, the system is underpinned by a clear ideology of separation of powers that is clearly established in the Constitution itself. Executive and legislative branches have a distinct and independent existence. Congress cannot remove the president and the president cannot dissolve Congress. Each has its own clear and distinct function. Each too has its own electoral basis, independent of the other. The Congress does not elect the president. The people can and do elect a president and House of Representatives of differing political colour at the same time, as they did in 1996. The US is then the extreme, or control case. A less clear European example can be found in Switzerland. Here, the Federal Council (executive) is elected by Parliament, but on a proportional basis and is in long-standing practice immovable until the next elections. As a result, the Federal Council does not need or have a fixed parliamentary basis and must construct legislative majorities from issue to issue. Defeat in legislative votes cannot affect the life of the executive. Here political practice has created and effective separation of powers not dissimilar to the American model, though within what is still a parliamentary system.

In a parliamentary system like that of Denmark, there clearly cannot be a formal separation of powers on the American model, though there can be an some approximation to that situation, as there is in Switzerland. In Denmark, as we shall see, the executive (government) is in a permanent state of formal dependence on the Folketing (parliament), though it may, as we shall see, *in*

This chapter was written with research assistance from Christian Gronbech Jensen.

*practice*, achieve a degree of independence from Parliament. The Folketing can at any time decide to remove a government that stretches that independence too far for the majority of the Folketing. At the same time, the Folketing may itself achieve a degree of independence from the *de facto* control of the executive that would be unthinkable in some other parliamentary systems, such Britain. The concept of divided government must therefore be applied to the political practice observed in Denmark, rather than to the formal constitutional position. One might consider that where the government does not automatically or at least usually control a fixed and stable operational legislative majority, then there is prima-facie evidence of divided government. This is certainly the case in Denmark, as we shall see. Indeed, it is one of the central and almost instinctive characteristics of the Danish political system, as the quotation from Poul Schlüter at the head of the chapter demonstrates.

The questions that we need to examine are, therefore, how far do the government and the Folketing actually develop a degree of independent existence? How far does the government develop a stable and independent basis for action, irrespective of whether or not it commands formal stable majority support? How far can the Folketing operate as an independent actor, building variable geometry majorities, with or without the intervention of the government? How far do political actors and parties regard executive and legislative power as distinct political goods to be sought in their own right? However we answer these questions, divided government in a parliamentary system will never do more than approximate to the separation of powers model, but as we shall seek to demonstrate, the Danish system goes some considerable way in that direction, with varying degrees of intensity over time and across different issues. A form of divided government emerged strongly in the mid-1980s, only to recede somewhat in more recent years, as we shall see.

## SETTING THE SCENE: THE DANISH POLITICAL SYSTEM

Denmark is a constitutional monarchy (Fitzmaurice, 1981). Executive power is in the hands of a government appointed by the Crown, but responsible to the single chamber Folketing. The 179-member Folketing is elected by proportional representation for a maximum term of four years, though early elections are often held. The average term of the Folketing has been close to three years. 175 members are elected in metropolitan Denmark and there are four so-called North Atlantic seats (two from the Faeroe islands and two from Greenland). The threshold is very low, at 2 per cent. There have therefore always been a fairly large number of parties, except during the 1950s when the party system remained stable. It is relatively easy for new parties to enter the Folketing. In the 1950s there were the four 'old' parties (the Social Democrats, Radikale Venstre, Venstre, and the Conservatives) and the Communists,

Justice Party, and the Independents. The third branch of government, the judiciary, is independent and has no tradition of intervention in the political domain. It has not invalidated laws passed by the Folketing and does not act as an arbitrator between institutions, as is the case in some systems, especially federal systems.

It is at this point perhaps worth looking briefly at the Danish party spectrum (Fitzmaurice, 1981: 96–123), so as to situate the various players in what follows. From the 1960s, a section of the political spectrum to the left of the Social Democrats has been inhabited by up to three political parties (the Socialist People's party, the Left Socialists/Unity List and the Communist party) that developed out of the old communist tradition and the 1960s libertarian/new left traditions. The Socialist People's party is a more traditional left party that has matured and moderated its economic, European and security policy positions over time. The Unity List is made up of various small green and libertarian socialist groupings, as well as some remnants of the old Communist party.

The Social Democrats have been the largest party since the 1920s, always with over one-third of the vote, but never more than about 45 per cent. The Social Democrats have played a dominant role in Danish politics since then, being in government for the majority of the time, though always having to govern in a Folketing with a 'bourgeois' (non-socialist) majority. It is a modern, mainstream, pro-European, pro-NATO, social democratic party, committed to the mixed economy and the welfare state. It effectively occupies a centrist position in the spectrum, with potential allies to its left and in the centre, giving it considerable strategic flexibility in a fragmented Folketing.

There is now a definable centre in Danish politics, made up of several parties, principally Radikale Venstre, the Christian People's party, and the Centre Democrats. Radikale Venstre is the historical and archetypal swing party, although in line with its traditions it is more inclined to work with the Social Democrats. Centre parties are moderate, pragmatic, non-ideological parties, seeking to maximize influence and participation in government. They are able to work with the Social Democrats or with the centre-right parties and have shared office with both at various times. Indeed, in 1993 they moved seamlessly from one alliance to the other without an election. Their centre position clearly enhances their strategic options. The down-side is their relative lack of clear identity and core voters, making them electorally vulnerable.

The Conservatives and Venstre are the historic 'responsible' centre-right parties. There is now very little policy difference between them. The old dichotomy between the urban and suburban Conservatives and rural Venstre has lost its importance. Differences are now more matters of style, leadership personality, and, indeed, despite the indispensable co-operation between them, there has been a strong competition between them for primacy on the centre-right and hence the post of prime minister in a 'bourgeois' government.

In the 1980s Venstre seemed to place itself more aggressively to the right and seek to benefit from the then prevailing 'Thatcherite' *zeitgeist*, though given the need for centrist allies this could never be taken too far.

Since 1973, there has been a new populist player to the right of the spectrum, represented at first by the Progress party. Now it has been joined by the Danish People's party, a splinter party that at times seems more pragmatic in its approach and more open to co-operation with other parties, though still espousing the same basic issues. They have both taken up populist themes such as taxation, bureaucracy, welfare fraud, opposition to progressive culture and more recently immigration. With a solid 10 per cent of the vote between them, they represent an obstacle to the formation and effective functioning of centre-right governments.

## THE FREQUENCY OF DIVIDED GOVERNMENT IN DENMARK

Minority government is certainly not a new or recent phenomenon in Denmark. It occurred in the 1920s, disappeared during the long period of majority Social Democrat–Radikale Venstre government in the 1930s only to reappear in 1945–57 and then again after 1964. Indeed, since 1964, majority coalitions have been rare, occurring only between 1968 and 1971, in 1978–9, and from 1993 to 1996. These minority governments have been neither more inherently unstable nor ineffective than majority governments.

Looking in more detail at the period since 1945, one can identify three types of government in Denmark. Majority coalitions are rare. There have been six since 1945, covering 150 months (total time 636 months) These were the Social Democrats+Radikale Venstre (one case); the Social Democrats+Radikale Venstre+the Justice party (one case); Venstre+the Conservatives+Radikale Venstre (two cases); the Social Democrats+Venstre (one case); and the Social Democrats+Radikale Venstre+the Centre Democrats+the Christian People's party (one case). The most frequent type of government is the one-party minority government. There have been eleven since 1945, mostly Social Democratic, but with two Venstre one-party cabinets, covering in all 260 months. There have been no new cases since 1982. Since then, all except one government have been minority coalitions. There have been seven of these, covering in all 196 months. These were either the Social Democrats+Radikale Venstre, the Social Democrats+Radikale Venstre+the Centre Democrats, Venstre+the Conservatives+the Centre Democrats+the Christian People's party, or Venstre+the Conservatives+Radikale Venstre. There was also a minority coalition in 1950–3 (Venstre and Conservative). The Social Democrats have been by far the longest in government (393 months), followed by the Radicals with 249 months (figures from Goul Andersen, 1995: 170–2). Thus, divided government is not an aberration, but rather the norm.

It is clearly important to make a conceptual distinction between minority government and divided government. By definition, during periods of majority government there cannot be divided government. There may still, in accordance with Danish traditions, be significant co-operation between the government and some opposition parties, especially but not exclusively in foreign and European affairs. Minority government may or may not mean divided government in the sense that we have defined it. There will be gradations between situations such as that prevailing during the Schlüter governments between 1982 and 1989, where there was divided government or in 1966–8 and in 1971 when there were 'virtual' Social Democrats–Socialist People's party coalitions in place. Minority government is therefore a necessary, but not sufficient condition for divided government. The increased frequency of minority and divided governments since 1973 has gone far to make these the expected norm, which clearly conditions the behaviour of parties and political leaders.

## THE CAUSES OF DIVIDED GOVERNMENT IN DENMARK

The primary cause of divided government is the frequency and long-term expectation of minority government. That, in turn, results from the configuration of the Folketing and its permanent fragmentation. Denmark has never had large parties (Pedersen, 1988). It has always had one fairly large party (the Social Democrats) and two other major parties (Venstre and the Conservatives) and a number (between three and seven) of small parties. That situation has been accentuated and has indeed stabilized since the 1973 election, which, as we shall see, radically and probably irreversibly increased the fragmentation of the Folketing.

In the period between the mid-1920s when the modern party system was laid down and that election, there was a core four-party system, with minor and marginalized parties of the far-left or far-right appearing from time to time. The only significant change in that model was the gradual emergence of the Socialist People's party into the mainstream, forming part of the government's parliamentary basis for the first time in 1966.

There are of course deeper sociological causes of this increased fragmentation that have been well covered in an extensive literature on the subject (see Goul Andersen, 1995: 170–2), but which go beyond our scope here. For our purpose here, it suffices to underline two points. First, the low electoral threshold of only 2 per cent of the votes cast has permitted and indeed encouraged new entrants into the political arena and can enable them to survive once there. The configuration of the Folketing into two closely balanced blocs has given even quite small parties considerable leverage and reduced incentives to mergers. Fragmentation hides the fact that the broad balance between the blocs has remained stable, though fragmentation within them has increased.

TABLE 8.1. *Danish governments since 1945*

| Government | Date | Party support | Status |
| --- | --- | --- | --- |
| Buhl (S) | 1945 | all | Minority |
| Kristensen (V) | 1945–7 | V | Minority |
| Hedtoft (S) | 1947–50 | S | Minority |
| Eriksen (V) | 1950–3 | V, K | Minority coalition |
| Hedtoft II (S) | 1953–5 | S | Minority |
| Hansen I (S) | 1955–7 | S | Minority |
| Hansen II (S) | 1957–60 | S, R, DR | Majority |
| Kampman I (S) | 1960 | S, R, DR | Majority |
| Kampman II (S) | 1960–2 | S, R | Majority |
| Krag I (S) | 1962–4 | S, R | Majority |
| Krag II (S) | 1964–6 | S | Minority |
| Krag III (S) | 1966–8 | S (SF) | Minority |
| Baunsgaard (R) | 1968–71 | R, K, V | Majority |
| Krag IV (S) | 1971–2 | S (SF) | Minority |
| Jorgensen I (S) | 1972–3 | S (SF) | Minority |
| Hartling (V) | 1973–5 | V | Minority |
| Jorgensen II (S) | 1975–8 | S | Minority |
| Jorgensen III (S) | 1978–9 | S, V | Majority |
| Jorgensen IV (S) | 1979–82 | S | Minority |
| Schlüter I (K) | 1982–7 | K, V, CD, KrF | Minority coalition |
| Schlüter II (K) | 1987–8 | K, V, CD, KrF | Minority coalition |
| Schlüter IIII (K) | 1988–90 | K, V, R | Minority coalition |
| Schlüter IV (K) | 1990–3 | V, K | Minority coalition |
| Rasmussen I (S) | 1993–4 | S, R, CD, KrF | Majority |
| Rasmussen II (S) | 1994–6 | S, R, CD | Minority coalition |
| Rasmussen III (S) | 1996- | S, R | Minority coalition |

*Left*: Enhedslisten (Unity List) EL; Venstre Socialisterne (Left Socialists) VS; Danmarks Kommunistiske Parti (Communist party) DKP; Socialistisk Folkeparti (Socialist People's party) SF; Socialdemokratiet (Social Democratic party) S
*Centre*: Radikale Venstre (Radikale Venstre) RV or R; Centrum Demokraterne (Centre Democrats) CD; Kristelig Folkeparti (Christian People's party) KRF; Danmarks Retsforbund (Justice or Single Tax party) DR
*Traditional Right*: Venstre (Agrarian Liberals) V; Konservative Folkeparti (Conservative party) K or KF
*Populist Right*: Dansk Folkeparti (Danish People's party) DFP; Fremskridtsparti (Progress party) FRP

Influence can be exercised within each party's 'own' bloc. Small can be beautiful in the Danish party spectrum.

The Danish party system underwent such a dramatic and permanent change after the 1973 election that it is probably accurate to speak of an 'old' party system before 1973 and a 'new' party system after that date. The key players in the old and relatively stable party system dating essentially from around the First World War were the four traditional parties: Social Democrats, Radikale Venstre, Venstre, and the Conservatives. Other parties came and went. Apart from the temporary success of the Communists in the immediate aftermath of the Second World War and the Justice party in the early 1950s, none achieved any significant or long-term representation and none played more than a marginal role in parliamentary politics. A virtual two-bloc system emerged within in the constellation of the old parties: the Social Democrats+Radikale Venstre and the Conservatives+Venstre. In 1960, the Socialist People's party entered the Folketing as a permanent force to the left of the Social Democrats, redefining the blocs, which now became the Social Democrats+the Socialist People's Party and Venstre+the Conservatives+Radikale Venstre. Co-operation between the Social Democrats and the Socialist People's Party caused Radikale Venstre to move away from the previous almost semi-permanent alliance with the Social Democrats that had dominated Danish politics since the 1920s and pushed it towards membership of the centre-right.

The 1973 election saw serious fragmentation of the Folketing (Pedersen, 1988). The four 'old' parties plus the Socialist People's Party all lost relative ground that they have not as yet fully recovered. No single party can now expect to come even close to a majority alone. Majority government has become rare and short-lived and must be expected to remain so. A much greater number of smaller parties has become a permanent feature of the political landscape and other parties have entered or re-entered the Folketing and disappeared again. Minority coalitions of three or four parties have, as a result, become quite frequent. The complexity of parliamentary politics has increased. Yet, there is still a visible, if different and fuzzier, two-bloc pattern, with a better defined centre than there was earlier, that now holds the balance between the cores of the two blocs, made up of the Social Democrats and the left-wing or Venstre and the Conservatives. The Progress party and the Danish People's party are maverick and unreliable parties that belong to the outer-right part of the spectrum. Their votes can and do count in determining the relative weight of the two blocs, but any deeper and more formal co-operation with them has proved difficult and politically risky. The Danish People's Party at least appears likely to remain a long-term feature of the landscape, posing a problem for the centre-right.

The most important point to underline is that divided government has become a norm. It is a natural and routine dimension of Danish political culture, based on managing two expectations held both by voters and political leaders. First, everyone expects that the present fragmentation of the Folketing will continue. No one expects majority government to become the norm. Secondly, it is a clear expectation that seats in parliament should work in terms of influencing policy output. This is expected by voters and accepted by politicians. Taken together, these two expectations make forms of divided government an appropriate strategic response by the political system, as it tries to operate within the parameters of these central expectations. This response then reinforces the expectations. If all seats can be used to influence policy within a divided government model, there is no reason to look for larger parties. Small parties can be perfectly functional.

## How Governments are Formed

### Constitutional and customary procedures

Neither the Constitution nor Danish parliamentary tradition requires a new government, on its formation, to demonstrate that it enjoys firm positive majority support, nor to obtain a positive vote of confidence in the Folketing. To be appointed, a government needs only to demonstrate to the satisfaction of the monarch that there is no majority against it and therefore that it will not be defeated as soon as it presents itself before the Folketing, even if it might have difficulty in passing legislation or even maintaining itself in office for more than a very short period of time. This is the Danish principle of negative parliamentarianism (Goul Andersen, 1995: 168; Germer, 1995: 30–3). This limited condition could sometimes be met by several possible prime ministerial candidates. However, mostly the situation will be relatively clear and not require the monarch to exercise any discretion.

The practice that has evolved is that after an election, or the resignation of a government without an election, a so-called Royal Round Table (*Dronningrunde*) is held. Delegations from each party represented in the Folketing (usually the party chair and their parliamentary floor leader) are called in to see the queen in order of size. Each is asked whom they wish to be prime minister (literally, whom they wish to 'point to', *pege paa* as prime minister). To be nominated, a candidate must muster indications of support from parties representing the magic ninety seats on the floor of the Folketing, that is a majority of the 179 seats. In an exceptional situation no person might achieve that. Then, the monarch might decide to appoint someone who, though not having clear indications amounting to ninety votes, at least seemed likely not to be defeated on a no-confidence motion in the Folketing immediately it reconvened. Sometimes, the position may be complicated by the unclear, or even deliberately temporizing, responses given by some of the parties, which may offer views such as their preference for a broad-based government across the centre or who may express negative rather than positive preferences, indicating what they will not support, rather than what they will support. This may drag out the process or require the monarch to exercise some discretion in interpreting the real meaning of the positions of such parties.

In the Danish tradition, the fact that a party 'indicates' a candidate in a *Dronningrunde* does not mean any wider commitment to join any coalition or to provide support from outside on a fixed or even ad hoc basis. Nor does it mean support for any future legislative measures. It may mean any of these or none. It is no more than a commitment not to support a no-confidence motion against such a prime minister when she/he first appears before the

Folketing, no more, no less. It gives the monarch the necessary assurance that she is not violating the parliamentary principle by appointing a government that will be immediately defeated in the Folketing. Under this Danish negative parliamentary tradition, a government only needs to be sure that there will not be a majority against it. In fact, the procedure of the *Dronningrunde* as usually applied, by requiring positive indications by parties representing ninety seats on the floor of the Folketing, actually gives a slightly stronger assurance than this bare minimum, condition, in so far as it might actually be possible for a government that could not achieve positive indications representing ninety votes nevertheless to survive in the Folketing, either through abstentions by some parties, or simply because there might well be a tacit agreement that no one would in fact table a no-confidence motion, thereby signifying generalized though implicit toleration of the new government (on procedures see Damgaard, 1990: 18–20).

It follows that the solidity and stability of a government's parliamentary base may vary very widely, from the strongest possible base of a majority coalition, through various forms of more or less firm agreements with a set group of parties, through to mere toleration of a government, with limited support being given for its measures on a case-by-case basis. Where the parliamentary basis is willing to do no more than protect a government from censure, it may well have to mobilize widely differing, variable-geometry legislative majorities to pass its programme. Such governments may have to accept that they will lose votes in the Folketing and even that measures will be passed that they have actively opposed. This need not to lead to resignation. Governments and the parties in the Folketing are perfectly used to this complex game and are quite comfortable with this precarious and complex method of policy-making, with fluid lines between government and opposition. Prime Minister Schlüter (head of the so-called Four-Leafed Clover minority government) argued, for example, that it was quite normal and reasonable that the opposition should be allowed to exercise some influence, provided that it did not affect the core priority areas of government policy, which for his government were economic reform. In other areas, he took defeat in the Folketing calmly.[1]

Thus, one can distinguish two distinct types of majority-building: one fixed for government formation—that is, the parliamentary basis of the government—and one for policy-making. Typically, after an election, two blocs of near equal size will emerge: the Social Democrats+the far-left and Venstre+the Conservatives. Government formation will depend on which bloc can mobilize enough support from the centre, in addition to their natural constituencies, to take it over the key ninety-vote level. Sometimes, the balance between the two blocs can be very close, of the order of one or two seats

---

[1] In an interview with the author on 5 May, 1999.

as at present. That is enough to determine the formation of government. A government with such a narrow parliamentary basis can nevertheless survive a full four-year period. Once it is formed, the opposition parties will not place it under permanent siege, as would happen in Britain to a government with such a narrow majority. It should be added that there are no by-elections that can alter the parliamentary arithmetic in the course of the legislature.

### 1998: An Illustrative Case-Study

The 1998 election offered an extreme, but instructive case. The outgoing government camp was made up of two parties in a minority coalition (the Social Democrats+Radikale Venstre) and two other leftist parties that made up the government's parliamentary basis (the Socialist People's party+the Unity List). In the 1994–8 legislature, there were four opposition parties (the Centre Democrats, the Conservatives, Venstre, and the Progress party). After the 1998 election, they were joined by a new old party, the Christian People's party in the centre and the new Danish People's party on the right. The 1998 election result was as narrow as it could possibly be. It was decided by a small swing to the centre-left candidate close to the Social Democrats in one of the two Faeroese seats. With that gain, the government camp just reached the magic figure of ninety seats, enabling it to continue in office. No one expects a change of government in the short term. The Venstre and Conservative leaders resigned. However, had the six bourgeois (centre-right) parties gained the magic ninety seats, there is no doubt that they would have sought to form a government, probably a minority Venstre+Conservatives government and would have been able to do so. It is also likely that such a government, despite its very narrow majority and its very broad political base, would indeed survive. In both cases, the parties outside the coalition would protect the government from a motion of censure from the other side of the House, but little more, so no motions of censure would actually be tabled.

In either scenario, the behaviour of the non-coalition support parties would be based on a least worst case for them. They would try to protect their electoral base and maximize influence in the subsequent ongoing policy-making coalition formation. It would be difficult for the Socialist People's party and the Unity List to refuse to give a preference to a Social Democrat-led government, rather than a Venstre-led government. Equally, were the six right-wing parties to have a majority, it would be difficult for the parties on the right, the Progress party and the Danish People's party, not to give their preference to a Venstre-led government. For the parties of the centre (the Centre Democrats and the Christian People's party) the situation is less clear. They have both supported the Social Democrats and Venstre-led governments. However, they had already declared a preference for a Venstre-led government before the 1998 election. Beyond this imperative, support parties will try to derive policy influence from their position. However, their potential to do so should not be exaggerated. Effectively the Socialist People's party and the Unity List, on the one hand, and the Progress party and the Danish People's party, on the other hand, have nowhere else to go, which could reduce their influence. Of course, the Socialist People's party and the Unity List would have no influence on a Venstre government at all and the Progress party and the Danish People's party would have no influence on a Social Democrat-led government. Their respective preferences would represent, as a minimum, a least-worst outcome for them. This does not mean that other parties outside the government's parliamentary basis may not have more influence on policy-making. Indeed, it is quite likely that they will. The Socialist People's party and the Unity List frequently complain that the Social Democrats prefer to co-operate with the centre and even the centre-right, excluding them from influence, relying only on them where all else fails. When the centre-right was in power, the same complaints came from the Progress party about its co-operation with the Social Democrats, who of course lay outside the government's parliamentary basis

## THE MANAGEMENT OF DIVIDED GOVERNMENT IN DENMARK

In analysing the management of divided government, it is important to bear in mind the distinction between the formation of government majorities and pol-icy-making majorities that I have already underlined. The rules of policy majority formation are somewhat different. Here, majorities form, dissolve, and reform on a largely case-by-case basis. Governments may not seek to rely exclusively nor even mainly on their parliamentary basis for policy-making majorities. Indeed, the Social Democrats, for example, would not wish to be forced to rely exclusively on the far-left parties, though on some crunch votes it may have to do so and crucially knows that as a bottom line, it can do so if all other options fail. It would far rather work with the centrist parties. Equally, all other players in the game know this too. A Venstre-led govern-ment would for its part not wish to rely on the right-wing Progress party and the Danish People's party. Indeed, were it to make policy concessions to these parties, it would create severe tensions with the centrist part of the govern-ment's parliamentary basis. It would rather work with the Social Democrats and Radikale Venstre. Lines of demarcation between government and oppo-sition become fuzzy. Here, the centre parties can maximize their influence. The moment it became clear that the Social Democrat-led camp would win the 1998 election, however narrowly, the two centrist parties in particular began almost without blushing, to back-track from their opposition positions and offer their co-operation to the government, as an alternative to reliance on the Socialist People's party and the Unity List, and the government gratefully accepted this offer. It even declared that it would work with Venstre and the Conservatives. All this was stated, almost as a matter of course, as it were quasi-automatically, during election night itself. That illustrates the extremely pragmatic nature of Danish politics and the culture of putting votes to work rather than making grandstanding ideological pronouncements. In the period since the election, the government has shown the strength of its position in the centre by working with broad majorities, but also by adopting a budgetary package involving expenditure cuts and tax relief for lower income families, with the exclusive support of the Socialist People's party and the Unity List. Had the boot been on the other foot, the new Venstre-led coalition would have sought co-operation above all with the Social Democrats. As the largest party in the Folketing and occupying a centrist position in the spectrum, even in opposition the Social Democrats would have been a major player.

This tendency for policy-making to operate within a limited part of the party spectrum, involving essentially the four 'old' parties (the Social Democrats, Radikale Venstre, the Conservatives, and Venstre) and the two new centrist parties (the Centre Democrats and the Christian People's party), with the Socialist People's party coming close within recent years to entering this 'magic circle', is underpinned not only by a pragmatic consensual political culture, but also by needs of continuity in economic policy and foreign policy. Reliable majority support for NATO and EU membership was only to be found within this part of the political spectrum. For example, it is generally agreed that the EEC issue was an important motive for the bourgeois parties not to seek to bring about the defeat of the Social Democrat minority government in the 1971–3 period, until Danish EC membership was well launched. They rightly thought that a Social Democrat government would be more effective in mobilizing public support for EC membership. During the cold war, Social Democrat-led governments needed centrist support for its pro-NATO and EU policies that it could not find in its natural parliamentary basis to its left. Had a Venstre-led government emerged from the 1998 election, it would have needed the support of the Social Democrats for its EU policy and above all to win the referendum on the Amsterdam Treaty. There tends to be spill-over from these foreign policy alliances into co-operation on domestic policy, such as the Finance Bill. Furthermore, package dealing may force a bourgeois government to pay a domestic price for Social Democratic support on EU issues for example.

How has such a system operated in the periods between government formations when the independence of the parliamentary branch is at its height, because the life of the government is mostly not in question, whatever parliament may decide on policy-making matters? It is not infrequent for Danish governments to lose votes in the Folketing.[2] This is a normal, almost routine

---

[2] The following section draws on figures and analysis in Damgaard (1990: 26–30).

occurrence that does not need to have any further political consequences for
the life of the government, as it would in Britain. The government can simply
accept the defeat as gracefully as it can and move on. It does need to consider
its position and certainly need not consider the issue to be a matter of confidence unless the circumstances are exceptional. Rejection of the Finance Bill at
its final reading would probably, though even here not inevitably, lead to the
resignation of the government or to an election being called (Rasmussen,
1985). On the two occasions where this has happened in modern times (1929
and 1983), an election was called. The rejection of other key bills might also
cause the government to consider its position, though such a situation is very
rare. Most defeats, whether they take the form of direct rejection of a bill, radical amendment, being forced to abandon a measure, or adoption of a measure against the wishes of the government—and all these can and do
occur—are simply accepted and lived with by the government. Schlüter has,
though, indicated that he would, in the 1982–8 period, when such defeats
were frequent, have as it were 'drawn a line in the sand' when it came to the
government's programme of economic and labour-market reforms. Defeat
here would have meant resignation and an appeal to the voters.[3] It may,
though, use its position as the executive to undertake some form of damage
limitation, such as slowing or hindering implementation of a measure
adopted against its advice, by not publishing implementing circulars or not
proposing the necessary appropriations.

The number of such defeats has varied over time, though there has been a
tendency evident since 1973 for them to increase. In the 1971–3 legislature,
where there was a Social Democrat minority government supported by the
Socialist People's Party, the percentage of such defeats on final votes was very
small, being a mere 0.2 per cent. It was again low during the Social Democrat
minority governments of the mid to late-1970s and early 1980s and the near-
majority Social Democrats+Venstre government, though still higher than
before 1973. The 'small' one-party Venstre government that held office
between 1973 and 1975 lost 3.2 per cent of all final votes. The various 'bourgeois' governments of the 1980s lost a much higher percentage of final votes,
rising to 8 per cent for the Four-Leafed Clover cabinets from 1982 to 1988.
The 1990–3 Venstre, Conservative coalition lost 6 per cent of final votes and
even the broader-based Venstre, Conservative, Radikale Venstre government
of 1988–9 lost 4.6 per cent of final votes. The percentage has fallen again during the majority and near-majority Social Democrat-led coalitions after 1993
and is now under 3 per cent.

As these figures indicate, the Four-Leafed Clover coalition lost one in
twelve votes. Thirty-three bills were adopted against its wishes, eleven in the
1985–6 session alone. These were in non-economic domestic policy areas,

---

[3] In an interview with the author on 5 May 1999.

such as green issues, housing, social policy, legal reforms, and local government taxation. In these areas, Radikale Venstre, which supported the government's rigorous macro-economic policy, voted with left opposition, as it did on foreign and security policy issues, as we shall see. By 1991, the level of defeats had declined as the key economic reforms were in place, conflict over security policy had disappeared, and Radikale Venstre had held office in 1988–9, but they had still not totally disappeared. In 1991, there was only one important defeat, with the Folketing majority imposing $CO_2$ taxation.

## Domestic Policy Alternative Majorities

During this period, government defeats were not merely occasional and the result of temporary *ad hoc* voting coalitions, as always happens from time to time, but followed a clear pattern.[4] The government lost control of foreign and European policy and domestic policy outside its priority area of economic reform, where it could rely on Radikale Venstre support. Elsewhere it could not rely on Radikale Venstre support. There were in effect two coherent majority groupings in the Folketing: the economic policy majority (the Conservatives+Venstre+the Centre Democrats+the Christian People's party+Radikale Venstre and sometimes the Progress party) and an 'alternative' majority variously called the alternative foreign and security policy majority or the green majority, composed of the Left Socialists+the Socialist People's Party+the Social Democrats+Radikale Venstre. In addition to setting the agenda on foreign and security policy issues, to which I shall return, and to a lesser extent on EU issues, this alternative majority was active in a range of non-economic domestic policy areas such green issues, energy policy, law reform, housing policy, and social policy. It will be noted that Radikale Venstre was the swing party, involved in both majority groupings. In another sense, the running was made by the Social Democrats: especially on foreign policy they were in a key position to determine how much of the agenda of the left they wished to implement, in the light of their own strategic interests as a potential future government party. In another variant a different alternative 'social policy majority' emerged on some issues after Radikale Venstre entered the government briefly in 1988–9 involving the Socialist People's party+the Social Democrats+the Centre Democrats+the Christian People's party. While during this period there were operative and more or less stable alternative majorities on some issues, co-operation between its various components remained informal and was never in any sense institutionalized. Indeed, at least two of its components (Radikale Venstre and even the Social Democrats) never broke off relations with the government.[5]

[4] On the various alternative majorities, see Goul Andersen (1995: 172–3).
[5] Ritt Bjerregaard, at that time Social Democrat group leader in the Folketing, in an interview with the author.

Faced with these alternative majorities, the government opted to avoid direct confrontation, which might have overstrained its relations with Radikale Venstre and provoke a breach that would have led to the demise of the government and with it much of its reform agenda. Provided it avoided an open break with Radikale Venstre, it knew that it was safe from a censure motion. In those areas of policy that it could not control, it chose to adopt a low profile and use its prerogatives as the executive to moderate, wherever possible, the impact of the decisions imposed on it by the alternative majority. Thus, it did not use the ultimate weapon of refusing to present bills approved by the Folketing to the queen for the Royal Assent. Under Article 22 of the Constitution, a bill must receive the Royal Assent within 30 days of its adoption. Only then does it receive the force of law. All Acts of the queen require the counter-signature of a minister, including her assent to bills. The legal literature is clear and unanimous in the view that the government is under no legal obligation to send a bill for the Royal Assent (Gerner, 1995: 74; Zahle, 1997: 271–5). It could have simply not presented such bills to the queen for her assent and informed the Folketing accordingly. Interestingly, Schlüter, prime minister in the 1982–92 period when such defeats were frequent, regarded such a course of action as inconceivable whatever the formal legal position. It seems not to have entered his head to act in that manner.[6] Clearly, the logical response of the Folketing would then be to adopt a motion of no-confidence in the government. In the circumstances of the mid-1980s, and not least due to the attitude of Radikale Venstre, it is by no means certain that this would have happened. Clearly, the government preferred not to run that risk and to tolerate such laws.[7]

This created a complex situation in which power was shared and in which there were different 'power centres' from issue to issue. The Folketing and its political groups became autonomous actors in those areas in which the government could not control the agenda The alternative majority was itself obliged to create forms of strategic co-ordination. It had to set its priorities, test how far it could go, and co-ordinate action between its various components Its bills, amendments, and motions had to be prepared and co-ordinated. This co-ordination process represented an alternative power centre in those areas in which the government could not exert control and remained passive. There was thus a degree of power-sharing between the different majority groupings. In those areas, the opposition was the government and the government was the opposition. It also demonstrates that a form of divided government *à la danoise* can exist and work efficiently over a period of time.

---

[6] Interview with the author on 5 May 1999.
[7] Poul Schlüter, in an interview with the author, May 1999.

### The Alternative Foreign and Security Policy Majority

A unique example of alternative majorities occurred during the early to mid-1980s, when, as we have seen, variable-geometry 'domestic policy majorities' and 'foreign policy majorities' emerged for a period of several years.[8] During that period, the government broadly controlled at least the economic policy side of domestic policy decision-making, but an alternative parliamentary majority ran foreign policy.

In the early 1980s, at the height of the cold war, as all across Europe, Social Democratic parties lost power. The long-term foreign-policy consensus that had existed since the establishment of NATO began to break down over the stationing of Cruise and Pershing–2 missiles in several NATO countries (although not Denmark) under the NATO twin-track decision of December 1979. Many Social Democrats, including the Danish party, had supported the initial twin-track decision, but opposed actual deployment of the missiles when the time came.

It was in this broader context that the Danish Social Democrats lost power in 1982, essentially on issues of economic policy. The centre ground was ready to bring about a change in economic policy in alliance with the 'bourgeois parties' (Venstre+the Conservatives), in order to control inflation and public spending so as to increase the competitiveness of the Danish economy. The centre of gravity of parliamentary opinion moved to the right on economic matters, but at the same time moved to the left on foreign-policy matters. As usual in Danish politics, Radikale Venstre was the key swing party. This party is a centrist party on economic and social issues. Historically, it was pacifist and neutralist. It had always supported disarmament. It had opposed NATO in 1949 and had not thereafter taken part in government until 1957, reconciling itself reluctantly to the by then well-established Danish low-profile membership of NATO In the era of détente, NATO issues were not for all practical purposes controversial for Radikale Venstre and posed no difficulty when it was in government with the 'bourgeois' parties for the first time in 1968–71. However, even external support for a pro-NATO foreign policy of a bourgeois coalition was always going to be more problematical for Radikale Venstre in a period of heightened East–West tension. The party could not agree to support the new centre-right minority coalition on issues related to NATO's twin-track decision. Obviously, the small parties of the far-left, the Socialist People's Party and the Left Socialists, would also oppose NATO policy. This placed the ball very squarely in the court of the Social Democrats. The Social Democrats were a traditional 'NATO party' and had, in government in 1979, signed the twin-track decision. It was their shift that became

---

[8] See Fitzmaurice (1987: 112–36) for an analysis of the alternative foreign and security policy majority in the 1980s.

crucial. Without them there could be no alternative security policy majority; with them there was. It seemed, though, at this period that this issue could serve as the basis of a broad mobilization against the centre-right.

In the period between 1982 and the May 1988 election, the alternative security policy majority made the running. It determined policy through a series of no less than twenty-three motions through which it imposed obligations and restrictions on a reluctant government. It was a progressive and iterative process. The Social Democrats at least did not wish to carry the process too far from the traditional principles of Danish NATO membership and here was at least in principle on common ground with the government. The government for its part mostly sought to avoid too direct confrontation with the alternative majority, which after all included the Radikale Venstre that was part of its economic policy-making majority. It could not afford to force the Radikale Venstre to choose. It often abstained rather than voting against the motions, whilst criticizing them, indicating difficulties in implementing them, and then doing the bare minimum to do so. It managed to avoid a motion of no-confidence, though it skated close to the wind.

In the period between October 1982 and May 1984, a series of motions gradually moved towards an ever more critical stance on the NATO twin-track decision, calling for extensions of the time limit on the negotiating track, for a positive western negotiating position, opposing deployment, blocking the Danish contribution towards INF infrastructure. At this stage, the government underlined that they understood these motions as remaining within the twin-track decision, which Denmark had signed under a Social Democrat government and as such could be 'tolerated' by the government. As the alternative majority clearly remaining in the driving seat, it began to try to stake out not just a negative policy, but also a positive alternative, with the Social Democrats and the Socialist People's party in particular circling round each other. The Socialist People's party was obviously keen to develop common ground that could serve as a basis for a future Social Democrat+Socialist People's party coalition government, neutralizing the defence and security issue that had earlier prevented such co-operation. The 3 May 1984 motion became the comprehensive statement of the alternative majority's standpoint. It resulted from complex negotiations between the parties involved. It set out a series of objectives which the government should work for, including a nuclear-free Denmark (no nuclear weapons on Danish soil at any time) and more broadly a Scandinavian nuclear-free zone guaranteed by the US and the USSR. The motion was still considered compatible with NATO obligations, as it involved no unilateral actions. This was the government's line in the sand that was not crossed, despite numerous later tighter variations on the theme of the 3 May motion, until May 1998. Then, a motion was adopted that required examining whether ships entering Danish waters complied with the nuclear-free requirement. This was considered by the government to cross the line of NATO compatibility and provoked an election. There was no basis for a change of government, but Radikale Venstre were brought into the core Venstre+the Conservatives coalition, while the Centre Democrats and the Christian People's party left. The altern- ative majority was split. In any case, the issue was losing its saliency as the cold war wound down.

## EU Policy-Making

The making of Danish EU policy exemplifies the need for and commitment to forms of co-operative parliamentarianism. It is, as it were, a *lex specialis* in this important area. The mechanisms established by the Folketing since 1973, by which it exercises not only control over the positions taken by Danish ministers in the EU Council, but also direct input into the policy-making process, illustrate the blurring of both the executive/parliamentary and government/opposition distinction that is so characteristic of the Danish political system. The Folketing has delegated its participation in European policy-making to its Europe Committee (formerly Market Committee) and within that committee policy is determined by a co-operation between a small group of broadly pro-European parties that will always include both the Social Democrats and Venstre, irrespective of whether they are in govern- ment or opposition.

Since Denmark joined the EC in 1973, a procedure for mandating ministers before they go to attend meetings of the Council has been established. Under this procedure, the Europe Committee acts as the agent of the Folketing. It is a high-powered committee, whose members are specialists in the complexities of EU issues, but who can also commit their parties. The committee meets in private and does not report back to the Folketing. All Commission proposals are sent to the committee with a Danish government memorandum, setting out the observations of the government on the proposal. The committee meets weekly, usually on Fridays, to review and finally decide on all items scheduled for discussion in Council in the following week. The minister responsible for each item sets out the proposed negotiating mandate. He or she can only proceed if there is not a majority against the proposed line in the committee. The minister does not need a positive majority in favour. The mandate may not be arrived at on a take-it-or-leave-it basis, but may involve some negotiation within the committee, probably following some more infor- mal prior contacts between some of the parties. The chair sums up, noting that there is a mandate without a majority against. He or she does so not on the basis of counting heads in the committee on a one-person-one-vote basis, but on the basis of the strength of the parties on the floor of the Folketing, counting each party as a bloc. Should it be necessary to amend the mandate in the course of the negotiations in Council, there are provisions to call the full committee or an inner contact group into session at very short notice, even at night, during weekends, or in the parliamentary recess. The committee has become integrated into the policy-making process. It is, as it were, the final decision point in a process that begins within the executive branch. It is partner of the executive in EU policy-making, as the government will virtually always need to find support from at least one other party in the committee (Fitzmaurice, 1981: 134–45; Fich, 1993: 59–67).

### Executive Power in Divided Government

These examples from the Schlüter period illustrate at its most extreme the general truth that control of executive power in Denmark does not always necessarily also mean control of the legislative process. Executive power may of course be considered as a separate political good in its own right, worth seeking irrespective of how far it also, in a given situation, brings with it control of the legislative process. Executive power and legislative power could be considered as distinct political goods, each with an intrinsic value that parties might seek in their own right. As we have seen, in the post-1982 period, the parties of the centre-right regarded it as essential to remain in control of the government, even if their control of the legislative process was imperfect. This strategic choice was made to enable them to carry through a coherent and rigorous policy of economic reform, designed to restore the balance-of-payments situation and improve the competitiveness of the Danish economy, principally through measures to control inflation, limit public spending, and increase the flexibility of the labour market. In the 1970s, the Social Democrats returned to power as soon after their catastrophic defeat in 1973 as they decently could. They did so in part because there were pressures from within the party and especially from their affiliated bodies such as the trade unions which understood the value of holding office, even where the government would be weak in legislative terms. Long and stable tenure of office enables a party to permeate the bureaucracy with its influence and control important executive decisions. No one was better placed to understand this than the Social Democrats.

Executive power confers important advantages on its holders. It is a weapon in maintaining party discipline. It gives power over appointments; over granting subsidies; the use of discretionary powers over state aids; competition policy; over implementation (or non-)implementation of legislation; the preparation of the Finance Bill; taking initiatives such as setting up Royal Commissions; and the determination of Denmark's position in the EU Council of Ministers. Even if the government has a weak position in the legislative arena, it can still exercise a not inconsiderable influence on legislation. It always remains difficult to legislate around the government. It is automatically a player in the legislative game, even if it cannot control the process fully.

Other players look to it take an active role. Other parties will at least try to bring the government on board, even if they end up by ignoring it, if only because to do so will improve the chances of ensuring effective and rapid implementation of legislation after it has been passed.

It is in this sense that the notion of divided government can be applied to political systems like Denmark which are parliamentary systems with a 'mixture' rather than separation of powers. Clearly, the independence and the existence of parliament as an autonomous actor is not as great as in a system with a formal separation of powers, but in Denmark it has on occasions been considerable.

## CONCLUSIONS: DIVIDED GOVERNMENT, A DANISH WAY OF LIFE?

The foregoing analysis shows that, as a result of a combination of specific characteristics of the Danish political system, such as the fragmentation of the Folketing especially since 1973, the resulting tendency towards weak minority governments and even minority coalitions and a co-operative, pragmatic political culture, forms of power-sharing, cohabitation, or divided government have developed in Denmark. Lines of demarcation between the government and the opposition have been fluid and there have been periods in which there have been alternative majorities in play. Legislative and executive power have been seen as to some extent separate and even able to be traded off.

These forms of divided government have not arisen out of any formal institutional provisions, indeed on the contrary, as Denmark is clearly a parliamentary system, nor have they arisen out of any prior preference or philosophical predilection. They have arisen in the first instance out of the cards that the electorate deals to the political leaders. However, the frequency of such fragmented and balanced outcomes suggests that the electorate does have an inherent and perhaps even subconscious desire to maintain such checks and balances. In any event, it is part of the Danish political culture that parties should put their votes to work to influence policy. Voters expect this of their politicians and punish those who do not maximize their influence. Parties must operate effectively within the parameters given to them by the electorate and seek to maximize their influence on policy-making, either through exercising executive or legislative influence or a combination of both. Tendencies towards divided government can, therefore, wax and wane over time, losing force in periods of majority government and regaining it in periods of greater fragmentation, but they never totally disappear.

Indeed, the quotation at the head of this chapter from former Prime Minister Schlüter suggests that the various forms of divided government that have been identified are not temporary accidents, grudgingly tolerated until the preferable norm can be reasserted, but rather they represent a permanent and almost instinctive dimension of the Danish political culture that is seen by the electorate, if not always by the political class, as a normal and indeed desirable state that enhances rather than reduces both democracy and efficiency of governance.

# 9

# Divided Government in Germany:
# The Case of the Bundesrat

## *Roland Sturm*

In the 1970s German governments, led by the Social Democratic party (SPD), complained bitterly about the obstruction of a Bundesrat majority which in their opinion forced them to give up their legislative proposals or to modify them almost beyond recognition. It sounded like a not-so-distant echo of this time when in the 1990s the Federal Chancellor, Helmut Kohl, scolded the mean tricks of the opposition which, as he saw it, was using its influence in the Bundesrat to delay and to block major initiatives of his Christian Democrat (CDU)/Liberal (FDP) coalition government on issues such as pension and tax reform. In the German political system, so it seems, the *de facto* upper house of the legislature, the Bundesrat, can provide a power-base for the opposition. Thus, if divided government is understood to mean the situation where different political parties control different branches of government, then Germany has indeed experienced divided government at certain periods of time. In this way, Tsebelis's (1995) observation is correct: the Bundesrat can become a 'veto player' in the democratic decision-making process. However, when comparing German institutional arrangements and the kind of party-political use that is made of them with other countries, it is important to keep certain historical and constitutional perspectives in mind.

The Bundesrat has no party-political tradition (Lehmbruch, 1998). It has its origin in historical efforts to bring together the representatives of a great number of independent German states. In 1871, when a German Reich was finally created, the Bundesrat embodied the new Reich. The meetings of the members of the federation gave legitimacy to the Reich and provided leadership. The chairman of the Bundesrat was the Chancellor of the Reich appointed by the Kaiser. After 1918 in the Weimar Republic the new Reichsrat was much less powerful and was no longer an efficient voice of the main subnational units of government in Germany, the Länder. Hitler's dictatorship, which followed the destruction of the Weimar Republic, dissolved the Länder and centralized power in Berlin.

After the Second World War the Allied Powers helped to rebuild the Länder as a first step towards a new German democracy. Länder representatives decided on the federal constitution. There was widespread support for a new and again efficient voice of the Länder in federal politics. This was to be the task of the new Bundesrat. A vertical division of powers between the federal and the Land level was regarded as a necessary prerequisite for avoiding the kind of centralism associated with the Nazi period and for safeguarding German democracy. At the same time, no attention was paid to the role of parties in the Bundesrat. It was assumed that the Bundesrat should combine three virtues, none of which was in any way party-political: (*a*) the ability to act as the *sanior pars*, the thoughtful and wise institution, in the legislative process; (*b*) the ability to bring administrative know-how into the legislative process, because most the federal legislation is implemented by the Länder; and (*c*) the capacity to act as the voice of the Länder population at the federal level of decision-making.

These ideas are reflected in the constitutional set-up. Article 50 of the German Constitution, the Basic Law, defines the Bundesrat not as the second chamber of the federal parliament, but as one of the five supreme federal institutions in the country. In a strict constitutional sense, therefore, an opposition majority in the Bundesrat does not correspond to the parliamentary model of divided government (see Chapter 1 above) if this is taken to mean the situation where the national government fails to command a majority in at least one working house of parliament.

The special character of the Bundesrat also manifests itself in its procedures. Decisions taken in the Bundesrat are predetermined by decisions taken by Land governments. Each of the Land representatives in the Bundesrat— unlike deputies in the federal parliament, the Bundestag—do not have a free vote. Instead, they are obliged to cast a block vote. Moreover, when so doing, they must follow the instructions of their Land government. In terms of party politics in the Bundesrat this means that: (*a*) the Bundesrat is not the type of political arena in which new political ideas develop as a result of the party competition, lines of conflict between the parties are drawn on the Land level; (*b*) the composition of the Bundesrat does not reflect the relative strength of the parties on the Land level, but only the party political make-up of Land governments; and (*c*) the fact that Land governments are in most cases coalition governments forces the two or three parties in power at the Land level to agree on how its representatives should vote, because its block of votes cannot be divided up along party-political or other lines.

From the point of view of parliamentary practice and because of commonly held expectations about the ground rules of party-political competition, this may sound as if the organization of the Bundesrat is not particularly democratic. This is, however, a misleading perspective. The Bundesrat does not try to imitate a parliament. Instead, it justifies its voting rules on the basis of the idea that Land governments are each expected to speak with one voice for their respective areas.

Thus, divided government in Germany is more than an arithmetical phenomenon. It is also a strategic option. This means that opposing majorities in the Bundesrat and the Bundestag are a necessary precondition for the phenomenon to occur. However, they are not a sufficient condition. It would be wrong to expect party-political confrontation in the Bundestag to be automatically repeated in the Bundesrat. Länder governments cannot permanently ignore Land interests. If, on certain issues, Länder follow their own interests and vote with the government, this may have the consequence of reducing the opposition's arithmetical majority in the Bundesrat. Divided government is only politically relevant if Land governments see no problem in accepting the party line or if they consider that there is more to be gained from party-political confrontation at the federal level than from acting as advocates of their Land's interests. Thus, there has to be sufficient support among the Länder governed by the opposition to use the opposition majority in the Bundesrat as a way of restarting the political battles that the opposition has already lost in the Bundestag.

## THE FREQUENCY AND FORM OF DIVIDED GOVERNMENT IN GERMANY

For a decision to be passed in the Bundesrat an absolute majority of votes is needed (Basic Law, Article 52(3)). Since 1949, when the Federal Republic of Germany was founded, such a majority has been present for only a relatively short period of time (see Table 9.1). Thus, divided government in the arithmetical sense (an absolute opposition majority in the Bundesrat) occurred in only one-third of the years from 1949 to 1999. This situation was most problematic for the SPD/Liberal government of the 1970s and early 1980s, led first by Willy Brandt (who was confronted with an opposition majority in the Bundesrat in 1972–4) and then by Helmut Schmidt (1974–82). In this context, it is all the more surprising that Schmidt is regarded as the most effective of all German Chancellors, the one who was able to lead most productively. This reminds us that it is necessary to take a closer look at the realities of divided government before judging its effects. Thereafter, Helmut Kohl and his CDU/FDP coalition faced the threat of total obstruction by the Bundesrat only in 1990 and again in 1998. In 1991 the addition of five new Länder to the Bundesrat after German unification broke this deadlock for the Kohl government and in 1998 Helmut Kohl lost the general election.

An interesting observation is that where there was an absolute majority for either the opposition or the government in the 1970s and 1980s the category 'others' (that is, Länder with coalitions which included both government and

TABLE 9.1. *The strength of government and opposition parties in the Bundesrat, 1949–1999*

| Year[a] | Government support | Opposition support | Others[b] | Total[c] |
|---|---|---|---|---|
| 1949 | 8 | 4 | 31 | 43 |
| 1950 | 17 | 5 | 21 | 43 |
| 1951 | 16 | 9 | 18 | 43 |
| 1952 | 13 | 9 | 16 | 38 |
| 1953 | 13 | 9 | 16 | 38 |
| 1954 | 16 | 9 | 13 | 38 |
| 1955 | 21 (M)[d] | 4 | 13 | 38 |
| 1956 | 16 | 4 | 18 | 38 |
| 1957 | 21 (M) | 4 | 16 | 41 |
| 1958 | 5 | 7 | 29 | 41 |
| 1959 | 5 | 15 | 21 | 41 |
| 1960 | 5 | 15 | 21 | 41 |
| 1961 | 5 | 15 | 21 | 41 |
| 1962 | 26 (M) | 4 | 11 | 41 |
| 1963 | 26 (M) | 4 | 11 | 41 |
| 1964 | 26 (M) | 4 | 11 | 41 |
| 1965 | 26 (M) | 4 | 11 | 41 |
| 1966 | 26 (M) | 7 | 8 | 41 |
| 1967 | 22 (M) | 0 | 19 | 41 |
| 1968 | 22 (M) | 0 | 19 | 41 |
| 1969 | 22 (M) | 0 | 19 | 41 |
| 1970 | 20 | 16 | 5 | 41 |
| 1971 | 20 | 16 | 5 | 41 |
| 1972 | 20 | 21 (M) | 0 | 41 |
| 1973 | 20 | 21 (M) | 0 | 41 |
| 1974 | 20 | 21 (M) | 0 | 41 |
| 1975 | 20 | 21 (M) | 0 | 41 |
| 1976 | 15 | 26 (M) | 0 | 41 |
| 1977 | 15 | 26 (M) | 0 | 41 |
| 1978 | 15 | 26 (M) | 0 | 41 |
| 1979 | 15 | 26 (M) | 0 | 41 |
| 1980 | 15 | 26 (M) | 0 | 41 |
| 1981 | 15 | 26 (M) | 0 | 41 |
| 1982 | 15 | 26 (M) | 0 | 41 |
| 1983 | 26 (M) | 15 | 0 | 41 |
| 1984 | 26 (M) | 15 | 0 | 41 |
| 1985 | 23 (M) | 18 | 0 | 41 |
| 1986 | 23 (M) | 18 | 0 | 41 |
| 1987 | 27 (M) | 14 | 0 | 41 |
| 1988 | 23 (M) | 18 | 0 | 41 |
| 1989 | 23 (M) | 18 | 0 | 41 |
| 1990 | 18 | 23 (M) | 0 | 41 |
| 1991 | 27 | 26 | 15 | 68 |
| 1992 | 21 | 26 | 21 | 68 |
| 1993 | 21 | 26 | 21 | 68 |
| 1994 | 10 | 34 | 24 | 68 |
| 1995 | 10 | 34 | 24 | 68 |
| 1996 | 16 | 34 | 18 | 68 |

| Year[a] | Government support | Opposition support | Others[b] | Total[c] |
|---------|--------------------|--------------------|-----------|----------|
| 1997    | 16                 | 34                 | 18        | 68       |
| 1998    | 16                 | 38 (M)             | 15        | 69       |
| 1999    | 23                 | 28                 | 18        | 69       |

[a] Land elections are spread over the whole year and changes in the federal government also occur, of course, at different times during a year. The table is based on the data which were correct for most of the year.

[b] The votes in this category belong to Land governments which are made up of two or three parties of which at least one is a government party and one is an opposition party.

[c] The total number of Bundesrat seats changed after the merger of the Baden, Württemberg-Baden, and Württemberg-Hohenzollern Länder in 1952, after the Saarland joined the Federal Republic of Germany in 1957, and after German unification in 1990. In 1998 Hesse obtained an extra seat because of population growth. Until 1990 Berlin is ignored because legally it was not a part of the Federal Republic and its representatives had an efficient vote only on procedures.

[d] M = majority.

*Sources*: Author's calculations for the years 1949–90 based on Schüttemeyer (1990: 473–4).

opposition parties) was empty at that time. It was almost impossible to build alliances outside the two competing party-political camps. This has changed today. Länder in this category not only exist, but can also be won over by one side or the other when decisions on particular legislative projects are taken. In this way the absolute majorities necessary for Bundesrat decisions can be created. A good example to illustrate this strategic possibility is the 1999 decision on the German nationality law. This resulted from a negotiation process between the federal government (SPD/Green) and the government of Rhineland-Palatinate (SPD/FDP). The Bundesrat majority was secured with the votes from Rhineland-Palatinate. It is, by the way, as already mentioned, not impossible, albeit less likely, that Länder governments which belong to the opposition camp may decide to ignore party lines and vote with the government because they want to put the interest of their respective Land first. Another example is the Bundesrat majority for tax reform in July 2000. Rhineland-Palatinate (governed by an SPD–FDP coalition), Berlin, Bremen, Brandenburg (all SPD–CDU grand coalitions), and Mecklenburg-West Pommerania (an SPD–PDS coalition, the Party of Democratic Socialism (PDS) is the ex-communist party of East Germany) voted with the Länder governed by the SPD and the Greens, the parties in government at the federal level. In return for their support, the federal government conceded Rhineland-Palatinate's demand for a modification of the tax law which then gave more resources to small and medium-sized business. It also offered help to consolidate Bremen's budget, provided money for Berlin's cultural activities and the renovation of the city's Olympic stadium, and provided support for Brandenburg's traffic projects. Moreover, it also accepted the PDS as a future political negotiation partner to please the government in Mecklenburg-West Pommerania. This is one way in which gridlock can be overcome when there is divided government.

From 1949 to 1969 and in 1991 an important difference can be observed with regard to the relative weight of party-political and Länder interests in the voting behaviour of the Länder in the Bundesrat. In the post-war decades Länder interests had priority most of the time. Even though the CDU only had an absolute majority in the Bundesrat in 1955–7, they rarely had problems in passing legislation. In the 1990s the more pronounced degree of party-political polarization that started in the late 1960s is still important. Now, it is much more difficult for the government to overcome an opposition majority in the Bundesrat than it was in the first two decades of the Federal Republic. In addition, the political landscape has become less transparent (see Table 9.2). Land party systems are much less similar than they used to be and the number of Land coalitions which include both government and opposition parties has increased.

In contrast to the immediate post-war years, when the partners in this type of coalition would make informal decisions concerning the Land's voting behaviour in the Bundesrat, now such decisions need to be formalized before the coalitions are formed at all (Kropp and Sturm, 1998). Coalition partners agree on coalition treaties (between twenty and 140 pages in length) which not only set out their legislative programme in detail, but also contain a clause which determines their voting behaviour in the Bundesrat. Most of the time in the cases where party-political loyalties come into conflict representatives in the Bundesrat will abstain (the so-called Bundesrat clause). Parties in Rhineland-Palatinate, however, decided to draw a lot. Here, the idea was that

TABLE 9.2. *The diversity of Land governments (1998)*

| Länder with a CDU head of government | Länder with an SPD head of government |
| --- | --- |
| CDU/SPD grand coalition (Thüringia, Berlin) CDU one-party government (Saxony) CSU one-party government (Bavaria) CDU/FDP government (Baden-Württemberg) | SPD/CDU grand coalition government (Bremen) SPD one-party government (Lower Saxony, Brandenburg, Saarland) SPD/Alliance 90-Greens government (Hesse, Hamburg, North Rhine-Westphalia, Schleswig-Holstein) SPD/FDP government (Rhineland-Palatinate) SPD/PDS government (Mecklenburg-West Pommerania) SPD minority government (Saxony-Anhalt) |

*Key*: CSU, Christian Social Union (Bavarian party which co-operates with the CDU at the federal level).

the winning party would be allowed to decide how Land representatives should vote on the first occasion with the losing party deciding on the second occasion. This procedure has, however, not been used yet. To date, both coalition partners, the SPD and the FDP, have preferred to find a consensus rather than resort to a lottery.

In practice, and in contrast to the first two decades of the Federal Republic, the Bundesrat clause has meant that the federal government can no longer count on the help of Land governments classified here as 'others' to help them win an absolute majority in the Bundesrat. Divided government, therefore, is now also the rule when the opposition does not have an absolute majority in the Bundesrat. In most cases it is sufficient that the government cannot rely on an absolute majority of votes either.

### THE CAUSES OF DIVIDED GOVERNMENT IN GERMANY

There are two major reasons why divided government has become a feature of the German political system. The first concerns the role of parties in German politics. The second relates to the metamorphosis of federalism in Germany. As argued above, the founders of the German Constitution did not expect the Bundesrat to become an arena for party-political competition and it is still the case that Land elections are not seen by voters as Bundesrat elections. Once in government, however, Land politicians have found it difficult to ignore the line dictated by the national party organization. This has been true almost from start of the Federal Republic, but it is certainly true in the period since political confrontation between the CDU and the SPD increased from the late 1960s onwards.

After 1949 the party-political nature of co-ordination in the Bundesrat was soon established. Since the 1970s the Länder have met in separate groups to prepare Bundesrat decisions before the Bundesrat convenes: Länder with an SPD head of government assemble as the so-called A-Länder, and those with a CDU head of government meet as the B-Länder. This kind of co-ordination was fairly easy in the 1970s and 1980s. However, with the entry of new parties into German politics, above all the Alliance 90/Greens and the ex-communist party of the GDR, the PDS, Land party politics has become more diverse (Sturm, 1999*a*; Kropp and Sturm, 1999). As Table 9.1 illustrates, 'other' coalitions (that is, ones which cannot be classified as supporting either the government or the opposition) have now become a permanent feature of German federalism. Some have suggested that they should be classified as C-Länder. However, more important than the question of classification is the effect that the voting behaviour of this group of Länder has had on the system of divided government. Divided government has become much more unpredictable. More than ever before, whether or not divided government occurs is a function of political issues rather than the quasi-natural result of a political divide. This also means that to a certain degree Land interests can re-enter the political scene through the backdoor, because they are the lowest common denominator on which government and opposition parties can agree.

The arena for divided government is provided and its boundaries are defined by the special features of German federalism (Schultze, 1999; Sturm, 1999*b*, 2000). The Bundesrat is involved in legislation at the federal level (Articles 76 and 77 of the Basic Law). Every bill has to be sent to the Bundesrat for a decision. In this respect the Bundesrat acts like a second chamber of parliament. However, an important distinction is made between bills which need the consent of the Bundesrat (*Zustimmungsgesetze*), that is, bills that the Bundesrat can veto, and bills with which the Bundesrat may not agree to but where its decision can be overridden by the Bundestag (*Einspruchsgesetze*). If it is not clear to which category a bill belongs, and if Bundesrat and Bundestag disagree, the Federal Constitutional Court has the last word in this matter.

In political terms, divided government is only relevant in the cases where the Bundesrat has the right to veto legislation. It is remarkable that in the history of the Federal Republic the powers of the Bundesrat in this respect have expanded considerably. In 1949 there were thirteen categories of bills which needed the consent of the Bundesrat. Today the number has trebled. This increase was partly the responsibility of successive federal governments. They tried to bring about uniform living conditions across the whole of Germany by controlling more and more policies. In the late 1960s they also centralized their grip on economic policy-making in order to implement Keynesian demand management. The intervention of federal governments into areas which were also the responsibility of the Länder resulted in constitutional changes that had the effect of broadening the areas of legislation for which the consent of the Bundesrat was needed.

At the same time, though, this development was not possible without the support of the Länder themselves. For Land heads of government the federal arena is highly attractive. It has almost become a rule in German politics that the prime ministership of a Land government is a career step for anyone who wants to become Federal Chancellor. Moreover, Land governments are keen on their say in federal (and these days also European) politics. Where there is doubt, when for example from a strictly legal point of view only a certain section of a bill needs the consent of the Bundesrat, the Länder always argued along the lines of the doctrine of shared responsibilities (*Mitverantwortungstheorie*), which meant that the whole piece of legislation needed the consent of the Bundesrat.

In 1974 the Federal Constitutional Court ruled that legal reforms, which rewrite laws without changing the provisions concerning the relationship between the Länder and the federal government, did not need the consent of the Bundesrat a second time. Surprisingly, this stopped the trend towards a seemingly permanent increase of bills needing the consent of the Bundesrat for only a short period of time. The court ruling was of little practical relevance. The federal government rarely uses the possibility of either writing legislation so as to distinguish between the parts that need the consent of the Bundesrat and those that do not, or unbundling legislative packages in order to reduce the influence of the Bundesrat on federal legislation. Political routine and a lack of interest both by the federal government and the Länder seems to work in favour of divided government. Now, one-half to two-thirds of federal legislation provides the opposition with the opportunity to block legislation in the Bundesrat. But, as Table 9.3 shows, this is only a theoretical assumption. In practice a Bundesrat veto is a fairly rare occurrence, which may also explain why federal governments have not invested more time and energy into fine-tuning their legislative projects in order to avoid such a veto.

The relationship between the two causes of divided government, the characteristics of German federalism and party-political competition at the federal level, is such that the arrangements of federalism draw the boundary lines of the political arena in which conflict between different majorities in the Bundestag and Bundesrat can lead to gridlock. Gridlock is triggered by (*a*) the opposition majority in the Bundesrat in connection with (*b*) the decision of the opposition to use its majority to veto federal legislation. Table 9.3 illustrates that, in the 1970s and 1990s, when the opposition had a majority in the Bundesrat, the Bundesrat veto was used much more frequently. It is remarkable, however, that in the 1990s, when the opposition had an absolute majority in the Bundesrat for only two years, the Bundesrat vetoed federal legislation more frequently then in the 1970s. One explanation may be that, in addition to party-political reasons leading to a Bundesrat veto, vetoes based also at least in part on Länder interests are now more frequent. It seems that a new cause for divided government may be gaining importance, namely the confrontation between the federation and its constituent parts, which is a fairly traditional problem for federal systems.

## THE MANAGEMENT OF DIVIDED GOVERNMENT IN GERMANY

Five strategies have been developed, discussed, and to some extent also implemented to manage divided government in Germany.

### Ignore the Problem

The argument has been made that in Germany divided government is of little importance because only rarely does the Bundesrat's veto really obstruct

TABLE 9.3. *The veto of the Bundesrat*

| Bundestag | Bills needing the consent of the Bundesrat (as % of all bills) | Bundesrat veto as number of all cases (and %) | Veto overcome at conference committee stage |
|---|---|---|---|
| 1949–53 | 41.8 | 12 (3.6) | 4 |
| 1953–57 | 49.8 | 11 (2.5) | 5 |
| 1958–61 | 55.7 | 4 (1.2) | 4 |
| 1961–65 | 53.4 | 7 (2.0) | 4 |
| 1965–69 | 49.4 | 10 (3.0) | 8 |
| 1969–72 | 51.7 | 3 (1.0) | 2 |
| 1972–76 | 53.2 | 19 (5.3) | 11 |
| 1976–80 | 53.7 | 15 (5.7) | 6 |
| 1980–83 | 52.2 | 6 (4.7) | 4 |
| 1983–87 | 60.6 | 0 (0.0) | 0 |
| 1987–90 | 55.2 | 1 (0.2) | 0 |
| 1990–94 | 55.9 | 21 (4.4) | 13 |
| 1994–98 | 53.7 | 59 (n.d.) | 40 |
| 1949–98 | 52.8 | 168 (n.d.) | 101 |

*Sources*: Peter Schindler, *Datenhandbuch zur Geschichte des Deutschen Bundestag 1949 bis 1991* (Baden-Baden: Nomos 1999), ii. 2388–9 and 2450–1; iii. 4377–8.
n.d. = no data.

federal decision-making (Laufer and Münch, 1998: 196). Most of the time only 1–2 per cent of all bills are negatively affected by the Bundesrat's veto and the upper limit seems to be a modest 4 per cent. One could, of course, argue that the Bundesrat's veto is not a problem of quantity but quality. The Bundesrat would simply need to block the most important pieces of federal legislation to cripple the politics of the federal government. Empirically it can be shown that the relatively frequent vetoes of the Bundesrat in the early years of the Federal Republic stopped less important bills than was the case thereafter. In the 1950s and 1960s the Bundesrat tended to block legislation if it was not fulfilling the criteria for efficient implementation, in other words if Länder governments believed that their administration would have difficulty in implementing it. In the 1970s, however, the veto became 'politicized'. Examples include the veto of the CDU-led majority in the Bundesrat against the SPD/FDP's pension reform plans in 1972. This was the beginning of a series of Bundesrat vetoes that blocked Brandt's and Schmidt's initiatives in the field of social reform. More recently, during the latter part of Helmut Kohl's administration, the federal government suffered from a lack of support in the Bundesrat for its attempts to modernize Germany's social insurance and tax systems.

*Make the Bundesrat Politically Neutral*

The above examples show that ignoring the realities and consequences of divided government is not really an option. In this context, some scholars have argued that divided government is an abnormal development in the German political system. They believe that the Bundesrat should not be allowed to provide a forum for party-political conflict and argue that it should be neutral in this respect and should only represent the interests of the Länder. In order to achieve this aim and to remove party politics from the Bundesrat, Wilhelm Hennis (1998: 115) suggested that grand coalitions should be installed in all of the Länder. This would force the major competitors in the political system to co-operate and to redefine their priorities. Grand coalitions would eliminate the possibility of an opposition majority in the Bundesrat and would, therefore, make divided government impossible. This solution to the problem of divided government is, however, merely a theoretical one. No politician has responded to Hennis's suggestion, which he first made when the East German Länder joined the Federal Republic, and it is very unlikely that his ideas will ever be attractive for party politicians.

*Constitutional Reform*

Another reform which would be difficult to implement, but which enjoys greater political support, is the idea of a reduced role of the Bundesrat in federal politics through constitutional reform. The hurdle for such a fundamental reform is fairly high. A two-thirds majority in both the Bundestag and the Bundesrat is a precondition for constitutional change. Advocates of the idea of a radical reform of federalism want to do away with the vast areas of joint policy-making between the Länder and the federal government, because it implies a major role of the Länder in federal politics. Central to such a reform, which aims at a clear-cut separation of the tasks of the Länder and the federal government, would be an initiative to end:

- the joint federal–Länder tax policies which cover two-thirds of the tax income of all levels of government (Basic Law, Article 106(3))
- the so-called Common Tasks (Basic Law, Articles 91a, b), which comprise a complicated system of federal–Länder co-operation in a number of policy fields enumerated in the Constitution
- financial aid to the Länder and local governments by the federal government (Basic Law, Article 104*a*)—the areas in which aid is possible are so widely defined that federal legislation needing the consent of the Länder covers almost all kinds of subsidies
- framework legislation: this is legislation which allows the federal government to involve itself in policies reserved for the Länder; the federal

parliament legislates on a framework to which Länder parliaments must adhere when making laws; this kind of federal legislation needs the consent of the Bundesrat.

With a much smaller number of joint tasks between the federal government and the Länder there would be less need for joint legislation, which would mean, of course, that the number of cases in which the Bundesrat had a veto would be reduced dramatically. So, no matter what the party-political composition of the Bundesrat was, there would simply be much less opportunity for a majority in the Bundesrat to be used against the government of the day.

## The Conference Committee Procedures

Although hotly debated, the above suggestions for the management of divided government are of little practical importance. The major instrument for managing divided government remains the permanent conference committee of the Bundesrat and the Bundestag (*Vermittlungsausschuß*). This committee acts as a mediator between the two institutions. It has no right to make decisions. Its only task is to produce a suggestion for a compromise if divided government has led to gridlock. During the process of legislation it can meet three times to try to find a compromise formula. This is because three institutions have the right to set the mediation process in motion: the Bundesrat, the Bundestag, and the federal government. The conference committee consists of thirty-two members, one from each Land and sixteen sent by the Bundestag according to the strength of the parties there. Strictly speaking, negotiations take place not between the federal government and the Bundesrat, but between the two major institutions involved in legislation, the Bundesrat and the Bundestag. Needless to say, though, the government gives instructions to its own deputies. The conference committee elects one member from the Bundestag and one from the Bundesrat who rotate their functions as chairperson and vice-chairperson of the committee every three months.

The conference committee has three strategies to manage divided government. The first is to present what might be called a compromise, but which in practice does not really deserve such a title. If the opposition has a majority in both the Bundesrat and the conference committee, it may well be the case that the compromise produced by the committee is little more than a reworded statement of the views of the opposition majority in the Bundesrat. This means that the management of divided government is the same as attacking the government. No compromise is truly sought.

A second strategy, and the one most frequently chosen, is to try to find a middle way between the government's position and the position of the opposition.

This involves the usual bargaining processes, the give and take necessary to make a compromise acceptable to all sides. As this happens behind closed doors, there is no opportunity for special interests to interrupt or obstruct the process and politicians do not have to be afraid of damaging their public image when they agree to compromise their beliefs. As Table 9.3 shows, from 1949 to 1998 a compromise overcame the Bundesrat's veto in almost two-thirds of all cases. Even in the 1970s, in a period of heightened political conflict, it was possible to overcome divided government in this way. From 1972 to 1980, seventeen out of thirty-four Bundesrat vetoes were overcome with the help of the work of the conference committee.

It used to be the case that government majorities in conference committees were the rule. This facilitated negotiations because the opposition in the Bundesrat had to make the first move towards a political compromise if the conference committee was going to come up with any result at all. Recently, with an increase of the number of parties in the federal parliament, and by implication both a weaker representation of government supporters from the Bundestag in the conference committee and few Land governments which were ready to accept automatically the priority of party-political conflict, the negotiation process in the conference committee has become more complicated. In the 1990s the government rarely controlled the requisite seventeen-seat majority in the conference committee (see Table 9.4). As a consequence, the number of cases in which the Bundesrat's position was simply repeated by the conference committee has increased. Indeed, it is surprising that a political compromise in the case of fifty-three out of eighty Bundesrat vetoes in the time period from 1990 to 1998 could be found at all.

TABLE 9.4. *The strength of government and opposition support in the conference committee, 1990–1998*

| Period | Government votes | Opposition votes | Others[a] |
|---|---|---|---|
| Jan.–June 1990 | 11 | 11 | 0 |
| June–Oct. 1990 | 10 | 12 | 0 |
| end of 1990 | 18 | 13 | 1 |
| Jan. 1991 | 17 | 14 | 1 |
| Apr. 1991 | 16 | 14 | 2 |
| Apr. 1992 | 15 | 14 | 3 |
| June 1994 | 14 | 15 | 3 |
| Oct. 1994 | 11 | 15 | 6 |
| Sept. 1998 | 12 | 15 | 5 |

[a] 'Others' are members of the Bundesrat who represent Land governments made up of parties supporting both the federal government and the opposition. Their voting behaviour remains unpredictable as is their role in conference committee negotiations.
*Source*: Data based on the analysis by Dästner (1999).

## Informal Grand Coalitions

The great degree of consensus achieved even under very unfavourable circumstances might be taken as evidence that Germany is a consensus-based
democracy, or an informal grand coalition (Schmidt, 1996). In the German
case, as David Southern has argued, consensus means:

the recognition of the necessity not to push political differences beyond a certain point
and, when that point is reached, to agree on a common position. Thus the exercise of
political power, rather than articulating a government/opposition dichotomy, embod-
ies inter-party accord. This is fostered by the constitutional provisions which make the
government dependent upon support from the opposition and Land governments.
(Southern, 1994: 38)

One could argue that the most painless strategy for avoiding the negative
effects of divided government was to take on board the arguments of the
opposition at a very early stage in the legislative process in the Bundestag.
This kind of flexibility and the ongoing process of communication between
government and opposition may explain to some extent the relatively small
number of Bundesrat vetoes and the relatively high probability that they will
be overcome. Of course, this does not exclude tactical manœuvres. When they
have not liked pieces of federal legislation, Federal Chancellors have occasionally withdrawn them saying that there was no majority for the bill in
question in the Bundesrat. In this way, they have blamed the Bundesrat and
avoided criticism from their own supporters.

Informal grand coalitions are a solution in times of divided government, but
also a problem. They tend to produce incremental change and redistributive
policy coalitions. To be successful informal grand coalitions depend on a
booming economy and the ability and willingness of political élites to buy consent by avoiding zero-sum games. The empirical evidence we have for the
importance of informal grand coalitions for political decision-making in
Germany is based on the analysis of policy outputs or on references to studies
of political culture. The latter are particularly sceptical about the ability of
politicians to uphold a broad consensus in society in post-unification Germany.
It is still true that voters seem to prefer all-party agreements to inter- and intra-
party conflict, but with the changed economic climate in Germany in the 1990s
it is less likely that compromises with regard to the great number of controversial policies can now be found. For the Bundesrat this means that parties have
less of a choice. They may still see the advantages of all-party compromises
behind closed doors, but there is no longer enough substance to sustain such
compromises. All in all, it is now more difficult to convince competing political
interests of the advantages of an informal grand coalition strategy. It may well
be the case that muddling through at the conference committee level is no
longer as efficient and satisfactory as it used to be.

## CONCLUSION

In Germany divided government has attracted attention because it was seen as an obstacle to efficient government. Reformers who disliked the role of the Bundesrat and especially the need for compromising with the Bundesrat majority have praised the Westminster model of government. In Britain, it was argued, voters can clearly identify who is responsible for a decision, whereas in Germany informal grand coalitions made decisions behind closed doors with no particular level of government or institution wanting to take responsibility. In the worst case the result is gridlock. Modernizers have, therefore, attacked what they consider to be Germany's institutional sclerosis and have argued in favour of what they see as Anglo-Saxon efficiency.

These arguments tend to overlook an important difference between Britain and Germany, namely that in Germany the Länder constitute a level of government which is absent in Britain. The Bundesrat is indirectly elected. Majorities in the Bundesrat are not accidental. They reflect, as in the 1970s, the growth of new majorities in the country, or, as is the case today, the new diversity of German federalism. Divided government is an indicator of tensions not only in the legislative process, but also in German society. A reform of the federal system which reduced the role of the Bundesrat and, therefore, also the danger of gridlock is on the political agenda. However, if the Bundesrat's legislative role was diminished, it might well reduce the extent to which divided government was able to influence federal politics, but also to some extent insulate federal politics from social and political change.

# 10

# Divided Government in Ireland

## *Paul Mitchell*

To the extent that divided government exists in the Republic of Ireland it has nothing to do with the presidency. The familiar sight of a US president negotiating his legislative package and appointments with Congress, or of the president vetoing congressional initiatives has no analogue in Ireland, precisely because the Irish president has no executive power.[1] Similarly, although there is a bicameral legislature, different partisan control of the parliamentary chambers is not a likely as a potential source of divided government. First, an incoming Taoiseach's (prime minister's) constitutional power following an election to pick eleven of the sixty members of Seanad Éireann (Senate, the upper house) virtually guarantees a government majority in the upper house and thus a 'unified' relationship between executive and Senate.[2] Second, Dáil Éireann (the lower house) and the Seanad are in no sense equal, so that, from a prospective, government's perspective the balance of forces in the Dáil is

---

[1] 'Summing up this list of presidential roles and functions, it can be seen that they come nowhere near to giving the president any kind of executive power. The president may not veto or introduce legislation, has no power over the budget, and has no role in government formation. The president's only significant powers are not initiating but controlling ones, concerning the referral of bills to the judiciary and the ability, in certain circumstances, to deny a prime minister a dissolution of parliament' (Gallagher, 1999c: 109–10). Thus, Ireland is a parliamentary rather than semi-presidential democracy in which a directly elected president has a mostly ceremonial role.

[2] The only exception occurred during the 1992–7 parliament. In 1994, for the first time, the partisan composition of the government changed without an election so that the incoming Fine Gael-Labour-Democratic Left three-party coalition was stuck with the eleven 'Taoiseach's picks' made by the previous Fianna Fail incumbent in 1993. Thus during 1994–7 the government controlled only twenty-seven seats in the Senate to the combined opposition's thirty-three. This lack of control had distinct consequences: 'The result was a major change in the manner in which senate business was conducted . . . The government suffered two defeats on legislation and avoided defeat on other occasions by either conceding on issues or by postponing them altogether' (Coakley and Manning, 1999: 200). Hence if coalition reshuffles occur in the future without recourse to an election (and if the Senate is not reformed) a government's lack of control of the upper house of parliament could be a minor source of divided rule. However, the Senate's lack of effective powers means that this should not be exaggerated.

decisive.[3] Hence if anything analogous to divided government US-style exists in Ireland it must reside in the nature of the executive and its relationship with the lower house of parliament. In this chapter, the focus is on minority government in Ireland.

## THE INSTITUTIONAL AND POLITICAL CONTEXT IN IRELAND

### *Patterns of Government Formation: A Very Brief History*

Government formation can be divided into three periods according to the logic of party competition: before 1973, 1973–89, and after 1989. Before 1973 Ireland had a multi-party system in which the typical election produced a single-party (though quite often minority) government. Fianna Fáil (the largest party) governed for most of these decades, including two separate periods of continuous sixteen-year rule (1932–48, 1957–73). Indeed, after Fianna Fáil first came to power in 1932 it was displaced on only two occasions during the entire period (until 1973) and it required coalitions of almost the entire opposition to do this. On these occasions (1948–51, 1954–7) Fine Gael and Labour (the second and third largest parties in Ireland) combined with other parties to provide some alternation in government. More typically, Fine Gael and Labour pursued mutually exclusive strategies, each hoping to grow and overtake Fianna Fáil. In reality, however, Fianna Fáil's pivotal position was such that, if the opposition parties were unwilling or unable to unite, then no governing alternative existed. Fianna Fáil rule was the party system's default option (Mitchell, 2000: 130). During the second period (1973–89) the logic of competition remained Fianna Fáil versus 'the rest' (Mair, 1987), but 'the rest' consisted of just two parties (Fine Gael and Labour), rather than the five parties that had been required to replace Fianna Fáil in 1948. During these sixteen years Fianna Fáil single-party governments alternated with 'the coalition'. The third period began in 1989 when Fianna Fáil transformed the bargaining environment by entering its first executive coalition, ceding two cabinet seats to the Progressive Democrats. Since that time Ireland has been governed by successive coalitions, breaking the earlier pattern of alternating single-party

---

[3] While some powers are shared (e.g. the impeachment of a President), in law-making the Dáil is pre-eminent. In essence, the most that the Seanad can impose on an ordinary bill is a delay of ninety days. If the Seanad fails to pass a bill that has already passed through the Dáil or proposes amendments unacceptable to the lower house, the Dáil prevails. Following the delay the bill is 'deemed to have been passed by both Houses of the Oireachtas' (Article 23.1 of the Constitution). In the case of money bills (the chairman of the Dáil determines what constitutes a money bill) the Seanad's powers of delay are reduced to just twenty-one days (see Gallagher, 1999*a*, 1999*b*; Mitchell, 2001; for reviews of institutional arrangements).

and coalition governments. Indeed, no government since 1969 has been elected to a second successive term so that alternation and recently coalition reshuffles have become the norm. From 1948 to 1997 there have been eight single-party governments and eight coalitions, but the future of government formation is likely to be mostly coalitions.

## *Executive Power*

Before examining minority governments in greater detail we must briefly characterize the pattern of executive–legislative relations. Irish practice conforms fairly closely to the British style of an adversarial relationship between government and opposition. There is a strong (some might say virtually unquestioned) normative expectation that it is 'the job of the government to govern', free from too much 'interference' by parliament.

As in many other parliamentary democracies the formal position that the legislature makes laws and the government executes them elides the reality that the government (at least a majority government) largely controls the legislature. Virtually all bills are government bills and certainly only bills supported by the government have much prospect of being enacted. In Ireland the government's privileged position in the legislature has constitutional foundation through Article 17.2, which states that no provision involving revenue or spending can be passed by the Dáil unless it has been recommended by the government in a message signed by the Taoiseach. Parliament has a role in hiring, firing, and sustaining governments but very little role in actual policy-making.

But does parliament really make and break governments? The Irish parliament plays a direct role in inaugurating governments through a vote of investiture. Under the formal rule the president appoints a Taoiseach nominated by the Dáil. In reality the Dáil has little role in government formation in a majority of cases; either the voters directly decide by electing a majority single-party (or pre-electoral) coalition or the parties choose the government in post-election bargaining. 'We can say that parliament has in any real sense chosen the government only when the Dáil elects a government that does not control majority support' (Gallagher, 2000: 7; 1999*b*). However, minority governments are quite common (see below).

Similarly, the Dáil can play a significant role in terminating governments. On one level this may seem surprising, given that the Dáil has only directly terminated two governments by passing no-confidence motions. The first was in November 1982 when the Fianna Fáil minority government was defeated on its own confidence motion (proposed by the Taoiseach) after the Workers' party withdrew its external support (Mitchell, 1996: 123–4). In November 1992 another Fianna Fáil minority government lost a confidence motion the day after its coalition partners, the Progressive Democrats, resigned and joined the opposition (Mitchell, 1993: p. 113).[4] Nevertheless, the fact that the Dáil has only directly brought down two governments underestimates the confidence procedure as an institution framing parliamentary government. On at least eight other occasions (Aug. 1927, 1938, 1944, 1951, 1957, Jan. 1982, 1987, and 1994) governments opted for an election rather than face almost certain defeat on a confidence motion. Thus, 'one reason why governments have so rarely been dismissed by the Dáil is that, when they have seen defeat staring them in the face, they have usually jumped off the cliff rather than waiting to be pushed' (Gallagher, 1999*b*: 183).

It is worth stressing that both institutions—executive and legislature—are dominated by political parties; the parties and deputies view the institutions as largely complementary rather than as alternative power bases. The parties and their deputies are engaged in a partisan rather than interinstitutional battle for power. It is the job of backbench government deputies to support the government, and the whip's office helps ensure they do so. It is the job of opposition deputies to help their parties look like an alternative 'government in waiting'. Governments, for example, have typically preferred to avoid too active scrutiny from parliamentary committees, while the opposition that hopes soon to be the government has incentives to collude in this lack of oversight. Moreover, executive–legislative relations are the result of endogenous selection rather than external imposition. 'Focusing on the rules of parliament as a reason why parliamentary control is low misses the point . . . Rules that give the government effective control of the parliamentary agenda are not an externally imposed restraint against which MPs chafe but, rather, a rule made by MPs, a symptom of apparently widespread support for the notion of strong government' (Gallagher, 2000: 26). Ambitious opposition deputies want to be cabinet ministers not committee chairs (Gallagher, 1999*b*). In short, governance in Ireland is characterized by clear executive dominance. Of course this applies more to majority than minority administrations; minority governments may have to amend their behaviour somewhat, given that the acquiescence of other forces in parliament cannot so readily be taken for granted.

## THE FREQUENCY OF DIVIDED GOVERNMENT IN IRELAND

Ireland has a tradition of minority executives that spans the entire history of the independent state, from the first cabinets in the 1920s right up through

---

[4] On a third occasion (in Jan. 1982) a minority coalition government resigned because it lost the first division on its budget, which incidentally was the vote on raising beer prices (see Mitchell, 1996: 106–16). While not officially a confidence motion, it is a strong convention in Ireland that a government defeated on any division on its budget is deemed to have lost the confidence of the Dáil and thus the Taoiseach immediately offers the government's resignation to the President.

the cabinet that closed out the twentieth century. Moreover, minority governments have been frequent in both comparative and absolute terms. For example, in a recently compiled data set of seventeen European countries in the post-war period, Ireland ranked fourth (at 50 per cent) in a frequency table of minority governments (behind only Denmark, Sweden, and Norway; see Strøm *et al.*, 2001). In this chapter, I include all of the thirty-two cabinets covering the period from 1922 until the Ahern I cabinet which formed in 1997 (and was still in power at the end of 2000).[5] Table 10.1 shows that 69 per cent of cabinets have been composed of single parties and 31 per cent have been coalition governments. In total, 44 per cent of cabinets have been minority governments (and 56 per cent majoritarian).[6] There have been minority governments in every decade (except the 1970s), though they were somewhat more common in the earlier decades.[7] While minority administrations still occur they are likely to be somewhat less frequent in the future, assuming that the pattern since 1989 of one coalition replacing another continues, since whenever possible coalitions tend to build towards minimum

TABLE 10.1. *Divided and unified governments in Ireland, 1922–1997 (%)*

| Executive | Legislative support | | |
|---|---|---|---|
| | Majority | Minority | Total |
| Single-party | Unified (34.5) | Single-party (34.5) | 69 |
| Coalition | Multi-party (21.8) | Multi-party (9.4) | 31 |
| Total | 56 | 44 | 100 |

*Source*: adapted from Laver and Shepsle (1991: 254).
*Note*: Thirty-two cabinets beginning with the Dec. 1922–1923 government. Three earlier provisional cabinets (during 1922) are excluded (see list of minority cabinets in Table 10.2).

[5] Three earlier short-lived cabinets (all during 1922) which were really 'provisional' governments in revolutionary circumstances are excluded.

[6] On three occasions (1937, 1989, 1992*a*) governing parties controlled exactly 50% of the parliamentary seats. These are treated as majority cabinets since the incumbents could not be defeated without a defection from within their own ranks. There is also a convention that the speaker of the Dáil (Ceann Comhairle) votes with the government in the event of tied votes. This convention dates back at least until 1927 when the then Ceann Comhairle (Michael Hayes) declared: 'The vote of the Chair should, I think, always be given in such a way as to provide, if possible, that the House would have an opportunity for reviewing the decision arrived at. Secondly, the status quo should, if possible, be preserved' (*Dáil Debates*, xx, cols. 1749–50, quoted in Farrell, 1987*a*: 30).

[7] The thirty-two cabinets can be conveniently divided into two periods: 1922–59 and 1961–97 (each period containing sixteen cabinets). In the first period the cabinets formed were 56% minority and 44% majority; in the second period 31% minority and 69% majority.

winning size in Ireland. However, the parliamentary arithmetic is usually very tight. Governments very rarely enjoy sizeable majorities; their average parliamentary support is about 51 per cent.

In just over one-third of cases government can be said to be unequivocally 'unified'— single-party cabinets enjoyed a majority in parliament and could be expected to implement their agenda without legislative impediment. However, Table 10.1 demonstrates that just as many single-party cabinets were minority governments and, thus, lacked this certainty that their policies would prevail in the Dáil. At least arithmetically, these are the closest approximation to what we might classify as 'divided government'. The executive needs the active support or at least the acquiescence of legislative members beyond itself in order to be able to win votes in parliament. In addition to the single-party variant there are also coalition governments in which the executive branch is divided or shared. While there have been three minority coalitions, most are majority governments.

The fourteen[8] minority governments in the period 1922–97 are listed in Table 10.2.[9] Strøm (1990: 60) reports that minority governments in Europe are often much smaller than 'nearly-winning' theories predict: 60 per cent of all minority governments enjoyed less than 45 per cent support in parliament, and a substantial number were much smaller than 35 per cent. The average parliamentary basis of minority governments in Ireland is exactly 45 per cent. However, while some governments in the early years of the new state were quite small, the post-1945 average size of minority governments is 48 per cent. Thus, in Ireland it is fair to say that most minority administrations are 'nearly-winning' governments: in most recent cases the government is only a

[8] There have also been some cases of majority governments becoming minorities through legislative atrophy: in something of an anomaly Ireland fills vacancies using by-elections (see Gallagher, 1996). Two examples illustrate some of these dynamics. First, in 1954 a three-party coalition of Fine Gael, Labour, and Clann na Talmhan was formed with the barest of majorities (seventy-four out of 147 Dáil seats). However, the government's security was enhanced for a time by a pledge of external support from Clann na Poblachta (providing three extra seats). Economic problems, new IRA violence in the north, and six by-elections during 1956 weakened the government's position, which became a minority in Jan. 1957 when Clann na Poblachta withdrew its support and joined the opposition. This left five independents holding the balance of power. The government could probably have survived but 'the truth seems to be that the government had more or less lost confidence in itself, and was relieved at the prospect of leaving office' (Gallagher, 1982: 31). A new election was called for Mar. 1957. Second, a Fine Gael-Labour majority government (formed in 1982) was undermined by internal defections and became a minority administration in June 1986 with the resignation from Labour of Joe Bermingham (reducing the coalition to eighty-two votes, excluding the Ceann Comhairle); two months earlier Fine Gael TD Michael Keating had defected to the Progressive Democrats. The Fine Gael–Labour minority government then became an even smaller Fine Gael minority government in January 1987 when Labour resigned. An election was held in Feb. 1987.

[9] The rules for counting a new government are: an election, change of party composition, change of prime minister, or formal resignation requiring a new investiture vote.

few votes short of a bare majority (see column 6 of Table 10.2). Moreover, the few extra votes needed have often been available, or at least potentially so. Ireland is the only country in Western Europe in which independent legislators are regularly elected (see column 7). The legislative management strategies of minority governments are examined shortly. An early clue to the viability of these governments lies in the election of independents: there have often been more independents elected than votes needed by minority governments (see Table 10.2, columns 6 and 7). Minority governments have often attempted to improve their prospects by attracting a few of the non-committed independents, as an essentially low-cost method of enhancing their viability.

## THE CAUSES OF DIVIDED GOVERNMENT IN IRELAND

For early coalition theories, driven as they were by office-seeking assumptions, minority governments were at best unwelcome anomalies (see Taylor and Herman, 1971; Herman and Pope, 1973; Taylor and Laver, 1973). Viewing the prize solely as a fixed set of offices made it virtually impossible to explain why legislative majorities would allow executive minorities to govern.[10] Explanations of minority government became more convincing only once policy pursuit was taken seriously as a motivating factor. Office, vote, and policy-seeking motivations have been assembled in various combinations (for reviews see Budge and Laver, 1986; Laver and Schofield, 1990; Müller and Strøm, 2000), but the key point for present purposes is that, since policy payoffs can be enjoyed by all, it is no longer essential to be in government to receive some rewards. Irish minority governments have employed a wide range of legislative management strategies, ranging from explicitly offering opposition TDs 'policy, patronage and pork', to just plain daring the opposition to defeat the government and face a possibly unwelcome immediate election. However, before examining what such governments have actually done in response to their minority status, we should first consider why there are so many minority governments in the first place. The existing literature suggests a number of explanations that are listed here in ascending order of their probable relevance to Ireland.

---

[10] Alternative explanations within the office-seeking tradition depend on longer time horizons: namely, a party chooses to remain in opposition for a short time hoping for a more auspicious environment to enter government. Given that governing in Europe usually costs incumbents votes at next election, 'abstaining' from governing is a potentially credible explanation of the viability of some minority cabinets (see Strøm, 1990; Narud and Valen, forthcoming).

## Corporatism and Minority Governments

Put crudely, this is the idea that opposition parties are less desperate to enter government because they and their ancillary organizations can have policy influence by other than strictly parliamentary means through networks of corporatist intermediation (Luebbert, 1986). While corporatist (or at least tripartite) arrangements among trade unions, employers, and the government have some relevance in Ireland (Hardiman, 1988; Murphy, 1999), the executive branch is clearly the dominant actor in policy-making. Certainly, Ireland's main parties do not turn down opportunities to be in government because of any parallel channels of extra-parliamentary influence.

## Traditional Approaches

Minority governments are presented as 'temporary, caretaker or defective' and occur in times of 'crisis, fractionalisation and intense cleavage conflict'. Majority governments are the norm and minority cabinets are deviants. (For a review and refutation of most of these propositions see Strøm, 1990.) With the possible exception of the first few governments in the 1920s (when the main opposition party refused to take its seats in parliament) they are of little relevance in explaining Irish minority governments, which have generally been neither temporary nor born of crisis in an ideologically polarized party system. By any comparative standards, Ireland has centrist parties and low ideological range.

## Electoral Decisiveness and Oppositional Influence

This approach (Strøm, 1990) predicts that minority governments are more likely when the electoral costs of governing are high and the policy benefits are relatively low. Faced with these conditions the incentive to enter government at every opportunity is not all pervasive.

1. Electoral decisiveness has been quite high in Ireland[11] and governing has certainly been electorally costly (more below). On occasions some Irish parties have preferred a period in opposition to recuperate their electoral strength (Marsh and Mitchell, 1999). However, while electoral decisiveness is relevant, it seems to be a contributory contextual factor rather than a primary explanation of the incidence of minority governments. The main Irish parties have generally been office-seekers willing to incur incumbency costs (ibid).

---

[11] Strøm (1990: 72–7) operationalized electoral decisiveness as a composite measure of the identifiability of governing alternatives, the proximity of elections, electoral responsiveness (electoral success and government participation positively co-vary) and volatility. Comparatively, Ireland was scored highly on the first three of these measures and low to moderately on volatility (but has been rising since Strøm completed his data set). Clearly, elections matter a great deal in the government formation game.

TABLE 10.2. *Minority governments in Ireland, 1922–99*

| 1. PM | 2. Years | 3. Effective no. of Dáil parties[a] | 4. Govt. composition | 5. Dáil support (%) | 6. Dáil votes needed[b] | 7. Independents[c] | 8. Formation | 9. Maintenance | 10. Termination |
|---|---|---|---|---|---|---|---|---|---|
| W. Cosgrave I | 1922–3 | 3.33 | Pro-treaty SF | 45.3 | 6 | 10 | | Effectively a majority given abstention from Dáil of main opposition (anti-system) party | Dissolution to allow first post-civil-war election |
| W. Cosgrave II | 1923–7 | 3.73 | CG | 41.2 | 14 | 17 | | Effectively a majority given abstention from Dáil of main opposition (anti-system) party | Dissolution near end of term |
| W. Cosgrave III | 1927 | 4.81 | CG | 30.7 | 30 | 16 | Began same as above; also Farmers' party mostly supported govt. | Became a substantive minority after FF took its seats in Aug. 1927 | Resigns to avoid probable defeat in Dáil |
| W. Cosgrave IV | 1927–30 | 3.19 | CG | 40.5 | 15 | 12 | CG minority govt; a 'quasi-coalition' with Farmers' party leader a junior minister (giving 44.4%) | | Resigns after a Dáil defeat; then reappoints same govt. |
| W. Cosgrave V | 1930–2 | 3.19 | CG | 40.5 | 15 | 12 | Same govt. reappointed | | Dissolution near end of term |
| de Valera I | 1932–3 | 2.77 | FF | 47.1 | 5 | 14 | FF minority with external support from Labour | Labour support gives effective majority (51.6%); loose | Tactical dissolution in search of majority: succeeded |

| | | | | | | | | alliance in which Labour gets some policy influence/ consultation | |
|---|---|---|---|---|---|---|---|---|---|
| de Valera I | 1943–4 | 3.15 | FF | 48.5 | 2 | 9 | Inauguration via abstention of Labour and CnT | | Tactical dissolution in search of majority: succeeded |
| Costello I | 1948–51 | 3.62 | FG–Lab–NL–CnT–CnP | 45.6 | 7 | 12 | Five-party coalition plus three independents (effectively 47.6%) | | Tactical dissolution; legislative atrophy, intra-party conflict especially in CnP |
| de Valera I | 1951–4 | 3.26 | FF | 46.9 | 5 | 14 | FF minority, five short of majority | *Ad hoc*, lots of independents | Tactical dissolution; weakened by two by-election defeats |
| Lemass II | 1961–5 | 2.16 | FF | 48.6 | 3 | 6 | FF minority, only three short of majority | *Ad hoc*; govt by-election gains; divisions amongst opposition | Dissolution near end of term |

TABLE 10.2. *cont.*

| 1. PM | 2. Years | 3. Effective no. of Dáil parties[a] | 4. Govt. composition | 5. Dáil support (%) | 6. Dáil votes needed[b] | 7. Independents[c] | 8. Formation | 9. Maintenance | 10. Termination |
|---|---|---|---|---|---|---|---|---|---|
| FitzGerald I | 1981–2 | 2.56 | FG–Lab | 48.2 | 3 | 5 | Minority coalition won investiture with support of one independent and abstention of three others | No arrangements with the independents; merely appeals on the basis of policy | Warnings by key independents ignored, who then defected and voted against govt. on its budget |
| Haughey II | 1982 | 2.56 | FF | 48.8 | 2 | 4 | FF minority won investiture with external support of three SFWP and independents (including a large 'pork' deal negotiated by one independent, 'the Gregory deal') | Ad hoc—no pledge of ongoing support. Virtual civil war within FF | Legislative atrophy (one govt. TD died and another incapacitated); then SFWP withdrew support and govt. lost a confidence vote |

| | | a | | | | | | |
|---|---|---|---|---|---|---|---|---|
| Haughey III | 1987–9 | 2.9 | FF | 48.8 | 3 | 4 | FF minority won investiture via abstention of key independents | Fragmented opposition and main opposition party offered external support on policy grounds | Tactical dissolution in hope of majority: failed |
| Ahern I | 1997– | 2.94 | FF–PD | 48.8 | 2 | 8 | External support arrangements with three independents in return for policy and 'pork' | Assiduous cultivation of the three independents who receive policy, patronage and 'pork' | Pending |

*Key*:

SF: Sinn Féin; CG: Cumann na nGaedhael (to FG); FF: Fianna Fáil; FG: Fine Gael (from CG); Lab: Labour; NL: National Labour; CnT: Clann na Talmhan; CnP: Clann na Poblachta; SFWP: Sinn Féin The Workers Party.

a Laakso–Taagepera index.

b That is additional votes needed to be a majority government. In this chapter governments that controlled at least 50% of legislative votes are treated as majority governments. Thus, this column shows how many extra legislative votes each minority government needed to reach exactly 50% (in Dála with an even number of members; an overall majority in Dála with an odd number of members).

c In this table (and chapter) the figures for 'independent' include individuals elected on their own and individuals elected under the label of a very small party (defined as only one member elected). This is necessary to avoid underestimating the number of independents, since some candidates that are really individual independents use a party label (e.g. the Blaney family seat in Donegal North East using the party label 'Independent Fianna Fáil'; there are many other examples). This means that the single Green Party TD elected at the 1989 and 1992 elections is treated as an independent, whereas in 1997 having elected two TDs it is categorized as a parliamentary party. Some such decision rule is required: the resulting classification may not be perfect but it is consistent.

2. Oppositional influence refers to the idea that in some countries (especially in Scandinavia) parties not in government can still influence policy by parliamentary means, usually through powerful committee systems. Ireland has never had powerful committees.[12] Government membership is virtually a prerequisite of significant policy influence, so that opposition parties, whatever else they do, have little policy input. They are truly 'out in the cold'.

## Divided Oppositions

This is also a policy-seeking account of bargaining whose central premise is that 'certain governments which control much less than a majority of seats may be effectively unbeatable' (Laver and Schofield, 1990: 79; see also Budge and Laver, 1986; Laver and Shepsle, 1996), once the policy preferences of the government and opposition are taken into account. Most obviously a centrally located minority government faced with a bipolar opposition might be quite secure since very few (or no) policy packages can unite the opposition in preference to the government's policy position. Several of Ireland's minority governments have been single-party Fianna Fáil cabinets faced with divided oppositions.

## External Support

Minority cabinets can do more than merely dare a divided opposition to try and beat them. In addition to such dares (which have really amounted to threatening the opposition with a snap election), minority cabinets might prefer to buy some security by attracting other legislative votes either on an ad hoc or an ongoing basis. Given that the main opposition parties (in an

---

[12] Traditionally committees in Ireland have had 'no great significance' (Gallagher, 1999b) as is usually the case in Westminster parliamentary systems. There have been intermittent but increasing attempts to enhance the role and functions of committees, especially in the 1980s and 1990s, but most without great success. The latest reform came in 1997 and since then committees do seem to have become somewhat more active, even influential. Of the nineteen (joint and standing) committees in 1999 (excluding two procedure committees chaired by the speaker) thirteen (68%) were chaired by TDs of the governing coalition, five by opposition TDs, and one by an independent (supporting the government). Thus, committee chairs were shared but not proportionally. In Strøm's original rankings Irish committees were scored as having one out of five of the indicators of oppositional influence. A renewed scoring should probably be two out of five (chairs shared and 'correspondence') since the committees now mostly shadow government departments. Nevertheless, Irish committees are hardly a deep reservoir of oppositional influence. For example, most of the 1999 committees have fourteen TDs including seven from the government side. Since the relevant minister is an *ex officio* member with voting rights the government side, barring defections always has a majority. Finally, committee assignments have become a source of patronage now that there are now four paid positions on each committee (chair, vice-chair, government whip, and opposition whip). (Gallagher, 1999b; *Irish Political Studies*, 2000: 258).

adversarial parliament like Ireland's) will rarely support the government, the opportunity for minority governments to secure their position depends on the existence of other legislative actors, such as small parties and independents.

In sum, the first two explanations of minority government appear to be of little relevance in Ireland.[13] 'Opposition influence' and 'electoral decisiveness' have mixed relevance: no party has ever preferred to stay in opposition because it expected to enjoy policy influence from that locale, but some, with good cause, have preferred a time in opposition to recover from electoral losses. At least for the Irish case the more promising explanations of the viability of minority cabinets are the existence of divided opposition and available 'others'. Of course these are not mutually exclusive: some minority cabinets have sought to exploit the opposition's policy differences and to secure external support. Before discussing legislative management techniques I will take a closer look at the causes of divided opposition and plentiful 'others'.

## Minority Governments and Divided Oppositions

Divided opposition means that the effective winning post might be considerably less than a majority of seats in parliament. It was noted earlier that the configuration of the Irish party system has often been such that Fianna Fáil rule was the default outcome of the government formation game. If after an election Fianna Fáil obtained a majority it would automatically form a government. If it missed a majority it would still form a government unless the opposition could agree to combine against it. Given that the two main parties in any oppositional alliance, Fine Gael and Labour, were often sharply divided, after many elections there was no credible alternative government to the Fianna Fáil status quo. From 1932, when Fianna Fáil first entered government, to 1973, it was displaced (and this took the effort of almost the entire opposition) on only two occasions, and governed for all but six of these forty-one years. While Fianna Fáil won some overall majorities (of seats) in this period (1933, 1938, 1944, 1957, 1969), there were also occasions when it did not but governed anyway (1932, 1943, 1951, 1961).

This leads to the obvious question: what divided the opposition enough to allow them to let a party they did not much care for govern for such long periods? This is particularly puzzling since, although the 'correct' ranking of

---

[13] Farrell (1987c: 142) offers a less theoretical account: 'Frequently, it was division, incompetence and lack of leadership on the opposition benches that allowed the formation and maintenance of minority administrations.' However, individual-level characteristics cannot really explain 'the failings' of all the opposition leaders. At times they were motivated for electoral and policy reasons to remain in opposition, their 'choice' of course being heavily influenced by Fianna Fáil's strategic dominance. Farrell also emphasizes Fianna Fáil's role in creating a divided opposition.

Irish parties in one or multidimensional policy spaces is a matter of some debate (varying by time period, research technique, and substantive dimension), all agree that policy distance is low. As Mair (1987: 191) put it, 'the overall space of competition is limited, the mean positions of the parties are reasonably close to one another and to the centre, and competition itself appears essentially centripetal'. Part of the answer is that sharp party competition does not require large policy distances.[14] The mutual avoidance of Fine Gael and Labour has multiple sources, including some real policy differences and the related electoral desire of each to grow enough seriously to challenge Fianna Fáil. However, the non-co-operation of Fine Gael and Labour in the government formation arena has been at least as much about electoral considerations as about insurmountable policy differences. At various times (for example, after 1957) each has eschewed coalition in the hope that emphasizing a distinct identity would bring electoral rewards. Thus the 1961–5 Fianna Fáil minority government (three short of a majority) was fairly secure: Fine Gael remained conservative, and Labour ruled out coalition, labelling the big two 'the twin reactionary parties' (Gallagher, 1982: 163). At other times Fine Gael and Labour preferred to go into opposition in an attempt to recover from a devastating election. Here, 1987 (see below) is a good example.

However, while opposition policy divisions and electoral considerations were undoubtedly important in explaining minority rule by means of divided oppositions, the catalyst promoting this outcome was really the tough bargaining posture of Ireland's dominant party (at least before 1989). Fianna Fáil's large size, central location, and mental toughness led to a bargaining position (some said an article of faith) that denounced all coalitions as 'shoddy little arrangements'.[15] Fianna Fáil's traditional coalition avoidance was based on a rational strategy of facing down a divided opposition, thus keeping them marginalized and mostly apart.

---

[14] Indeed, in an opportunistic largely office-seeking thesis, policy differences may play only a modest part in party competition, and not enough to prevent coalescence (Cohan, 1982). 'Fianna Fáil drove them [the other parties] to opposite ends of an ill-defined and barely ideological spectrum. Their fragmentation offered Fianna Fáil a monopoly on government' (Farrell, 1987c: 142). But this still leaves the big question to which office-seeking accounts have no adequate answer: if policy differences have little or nothing to do with it and office is the prime or only motivation, why did opposition leaders not combine on every occasion (every all-minority parliament) to defeat Fianna Fáil?

[15] Laver has argued that the logic was that 'it could be better for Fianna Fáil to go into opposition for a limited period, maintaining the credibility of its bargaining posture and in this way increasing its long-term chances of returning to power as a single party government rather than to give in to demands for coalition' (Laver and Arkins, 1990: 193). After 1989 Fianna Fáil changed strategy and entered coalition (see also Mair, 1990, 1993; Laver, 1999; Mitchell, 2000a).

## STV and the Election of Independent TDs

The viability of minority governments is clearly linked to the flexibility introduced into legislative arithmetic by the consistent election of independent members and small parties. Although the size of the parliamentary party system has generally been moderate rather than large (the effective number of Dáil parties for 1922–97 is 2.95),[16] there have always been small parties or independents (and usually both) beyond Fianna Fáil, Fine Gael, and the Labour party, to which the latter three might appeal. Small parties are hardly unique to Ireland but what is different is that it is the only country in Western Europe in which independent legislators are always elected. Indeed, there has been only one occasion (1969) when the three main parties came within only one seat of totally monopolizing the Dáil (only one independent was elected and the three parties shared all the other seats among them). The number of independents is shown in Table 10.3. The mean is 7.8 but with considerable variation from election to election.[17]

The Irish electoral system of the single transferable vote (STV) in multimember constituencies facilitates the election of independent candidates and thus may indirectly increase the likelihood of potentially viable minority governments.[18] In most systems of proportional representation each voter's

TABLE 10.3. *Independent deputies in Ireland, 1923–1997*

| Election | Independents/others | Election | Independents/others |
|---|---|---|---|
| 1922 | 10 | 1957 | 9 |
| 1923 | 17 | 1961 | 6 |
| 1927/1 | 16 | 1965 | 2 |
| 1927/2 | 12 | 1969 | 1 |
| 1932 | 14 | 1973 | 2 |
| 1933 | 9 | 1977 | 4 |
| 1937 | 8 | 1981 | 5 |
| 1938 | 7 | 1982/1 | 5 |
| 1943 | 9 | 1982/2 | 3 |
| 1944 | 9 | 1987 | 4 |
| 1948 | 12 | 1989 | 6 |
| 1951 | 14 | 1992 | 6 |
| 1954 | 5 | 1997 | 8 |

[16] The Laakso-Taagepera index calculated for parliamentary parties 1922–97 (mean 2.95, SD .55, range 2.16–4.81). Thus, independents are excluded from this measure.

[17] The standard deviation is 4.38, and range 1 to 17. With regard to who is counted as 'an independent' see n. *c* to Table 10.2.

[18] General statements about the causal effects of STV cannot be tested with any real confidence for the practical reason that it is only regularly used to elect the national parliaments of two countries, Ireland and Malta. Thus, the point is that it is easier to elect independents under STV than most other leading electoral systems, not that STV inevitably

principal decision is to choose between rival party lists. Although many countries' list systems have some intra-party preference voting, electors nevertheless usually vote first for the party; their preference vote may or may not make a difference in the selection between party candidates and their vote may even help elect an individual whom they oppose (Mitchell, 2000*b*). The central feature of Ireland's electoral system is that the electorate votes directly for individual candidates by listing them in rank order in multi-member constituencies.[19] Under STV preference voting is not limited to an intra-party choice: voters can (and do) cross party lines. 'STV is unique among PR systems in that a vote cannot help a candidate unless it explicitly contains a preference for her or him' (Gallagher, 1988: 128). Thus, candidates need to secure direct personal endorsement and cannot rely exclusively on the power of the party label.

Voters have the opportunity to rank individual candidates in constituencies with a small district magnitude (since 1947 between three and five seats). This typically means that only two or three of a major party's candidates have much chance of being elected and that the voters alone decide which of the party's candidates are successful. A frequent result is intense intra-party competition at all levels of electoral campaigning and candidate selection. From the perspective of individual candidates the electoral threat from intra-party competition is tangible and severe. Between 1923 and 1997, 34 per cent of all seat turnovers at general elections were intra-party, with incumbents losing to party colleagues.[20] An astonishing 56 per cent of Fianna Fáil's defeated TDs lost to candidates from their own party (Gallagher and Komito, 1999: 219). This provides incentives towards constituency service since three or four candidates of one party (with limited ideological differentiation feasible) compete for the two or three seats that the party can realistically hope to win. The electoral incentive towards candidate differentiation does not of course necessitate that constituency service be the method of competition. Candidates could compete as effective legislators, ministers, or take up distinctive ideological positions if these were

leads to lots of independents. Indeed, since its independence in 1964 no independents have ever been elected to the Maltese parliament (Gallagher *et al.*, 2001: 321). Independents have been elected to parliaments and assemblies in Northern Ireland using STV.

[19] In addition, while STV does not as such permit 'split-ticket' voting, because votes are transferable it may encourage—and certainly does not penalize—'sincere voting'. The rationality of voting for a favoured independent or micro-party candidate is enhanced without fear of wasting one's vote.

[20] For example, taking only three recent elections (1987, 1989, 1992) Gallagher (1996*b*: 510) reported that, of the thirty-three Fianna Fáil incumbents that were defeated, twenty were displaced by party colleagues. In Fine Gael ten of the thirty-three defeated TDs lost to running mates. Thus, the risk of being ousted by a party colleague (if you belong to Fianna Fáil or Fine Gael) is real. This very rarely applies to other parties since they typically run single candidates in each constituency. In the same elections no incumbents of other parties were defeated by a running mate.

thought highly valued by voters. Strong localism, while certainly not caused by the STV electoral system, flourishes within it as candidates endeavour to stress their individual qualities as constituency servants (see Gallagher and Komito, 1999; Sinnott, 1999; for reviews).

These candidate-centred electoral contests emphasizing local provision in small multi-seat constituencies (thereby lowering the effective threshold of representation) facilitate the election of independents. By their very nature 'independents' hail from a diverse range of backgrounds. While a few have had no known prior party backgrounds (for example, Tom Gildea in the twenty-eighth Dáil) and some have presented themselves as independent left candidates (for example, Noel Browne and Tony Gregory), most have probably been rebels from the major parties.[21] The importance of local campaigning might suggest that deputies are free to do as they please as long as they look after local interests. However, Irish voters are primarily party voters, and loyalty to a party usually outweighs local orientations (as evidenced by transfer patterns, see Carty, 1983; Gallagher, 1977; Marsh, 1981; Sinnott, 1995). Even a local TD who has built up an elaborate personal election machine will often find that voter loyalty is contingent on their remaining within the party (Gallagher, 1988: 133). Having surveyed the electoral fortunes of candidates who leave established parties to stand as independents, Mair (1987: 67) concluded, 'there is not much life outside party'. But while most rebels do lose there are notable exceptions (the most recent examples are Neil Blaney, John O'Connell, Sean Treacy, Michael Lowry). In addition, cases exist of the successful election of ex-party candidates who are not outgoing deputies, but stood as independents precisely because their party denied them the opportunity to stand for the party (recent examples are Johnny Fox in 1992, and Jackie Healy-Rae in 1997).

Whatever their source, the existence of independents and micro-parties has increased the likelihood and prospects of minority governments, who have often sought support from non-party sources. And certainly minority governments seem to be more likely during parliaments with a larger number of independents. In situations when minority governments formed immediately following an election (thirteen cases, ignoring inter-electoral cabinet changes because for example of a retiring Taoiseach), the average number of independent TDs elected was 10.1, almost double the number (5.5) present when majority governments formed (thirteen cases).[22] In short, the election of independent deputies has often made minority governments viable.

---

[21] As far as I know there has been no comprehensive study of independent members, though see Sinnott (1995) for some consideration.

[22] As Table 10.2 and Figure 10.1 demonstrate, there were an especially large number of independents in the 1920s. Taking only the post-war figures (1948–97), when minority governments formed there were on average 7.6 independents present in the Dáil and 4.2 when majority governments formed.

### THE MANAGEMENT OF DIVIDED GOVERNMENT IN IRELAND

By definition minority governments do not have the numbers to pass periodic legislative tests. They need the help of others via abstentions or active support. First, any prospective government must win a vote of investiture. The president on the nomination of the Dáil (that is, after a vote) appoints a Taoiseach. It is important to note that the 'content' of the investiture vote is solely the nomination of a Taoiseach, not a vote on any specific legislative policy programme, as is the case in some other countries.[23] Given that the programme need not be specified in advance, the cabinet may engage in continuous ad hoc legislative coalition-building throughout its term.[24] Thus, the institutional rules favour or at least allow flexible support arrangements. Following an election, some independents are usually willing to support a candidate for Taoiseach, not least because they do not relish having to defend their hard-won seats in the event of another election being called.[25] Even if not enthused about the incoming government, independents can offer initial support at investiture without having to sign up for the duration and without having to support the government's entire policy package. Equally, of course, nothing prevents minority cabinets from working to reduce uncertainty by building legislative majorities by means of more explicit support arrangements.

Irish minority governments have adopted a wide variety of legislative strategies and any particular government may use a range of techniques during its life, so that the 'options' outlined below are not mutually exclusive.[26] Nevertheless, it is useful to identify some of the main responses to minority status and provide an illustrative example of each. Essentially, the options available boil down to the answers to a few simple questions. The minority cabinet must decide whether it explicitly negotiate support arrangements or not. If not, the government may ignore its minority status and hope that its (unamended) policy package will be attractive enough to sustain it. Similarly, it may count on a divided opposition and (without negotiation), craft its policy package to try to ensure that the opposition remains so. Alternatively, if a prospective government chooses to negotiate with 'others' in the legislature

---

[23] e.g. in Italy both chambers of parliament vote on the government programme.

[24] While it has become common (in the last decade or so) for governments, especially coalitions, to issue detailed government policy programmes, they are not required to do so by institutional rules (see Mitchell, 2000*a*).

[25] As noted, the Taoiseach's dissolution powers have been an important weapon in the armoury of minority governments, especially in the hands of Eamon de Valera. Also, government formation usually follows an election. A change of government in 1994 (with one coalition replacing another) was the first time that the partisan composition changed without an election.

[26] Because the 'cells' would not be mutually exclusive the options are presented as an à la carte menu of legislative management techniques rather than a typology.

it may seek *ad hoc* or consistent support. Finally, if deals are available, what precisely is offered? In general, potential supporters may seek policy input and consultation, non-cabinet offices and patronage and/or pork (generally, privileged access to ministers to secure constituency benefits). Thus, at least the four following strategies are possible (on a rough continuum from 'passive' to 'active' management, with examples).

## Legislative Management: Four Cases

### Behave 'as if' a majority government (Fine Gael–Labour 1981–1982)

This minority cabinet governed without making any explicit deals over policy, offices, or anything else. It behaved 'as if' it were a majority government, hoping that its policy package would appeal to enough deputies. In a sense it was a minority government 'in denial'.[27] While such a cavalier approach is quite rare, the 1981–2 Fine Gael–Labour minority coalition is a striking example of the minimalist approach. In 1981 the *de facto* size of the Dáil was 164, so that a prospective government would have a bare majority with eighty-two votes.[28] After the election the outgoing Fianna Fáil government had seventy-eight deputies, four short of the effective majority figure. The prospective Fine Gael–Labour coalition had eighty, leaving six 'others'. One of these, ex-Labour independent John O'Connell, was persuaded to become Ceann Comhairle, and another, Neil Blaney, although independent, mostly voted with his political *alma mater* Fianna Fáil. Amongst the four remaining deputies, at least three were left-leaning (Joe Sherlock, Noel Browne, and Jim Kemmy) and were therefore not especially predisposed to voting with Fianna Fáil. Given careful legislative management, the prospects for a viable minority coalition with support from key independents appeared good. The coalition was elected (81–78) with Kemmy supporting the coalition and the other independents abstaining.

Although Kemmy had unilaterally indicated his willingness to vote with the government for a time (partly because he was opposed to the Haughey-led Fianna Fáil alternative), the coalition made almost no effort to solicit the support of independents—indeed they were barely even consulted. Facing an economic and fiscal crisis the coalition sought to cut spending and raise taxes on several occasions. Although recognizing that tough decisions were necessary, Kemmy in particular made it very clear that he would oppose further shifts from direct to indirect taxation and said so on radio (*The Irish Times*, 16 January 1982: 6). However, the minority coalition consistently miscalculated

---

[27] For a detailed account see Mitchell, 1996: 66–116.

[28] Since 1981 the Dáil has comprised 166 seats. However, in 1981 two Irish Republican prisoners (H-Block candidates) won seats on an abstentionist platform, since they did not recognize the legitimacy of the Dáil. Clearly neither deputy would be casting votes in the Dáil.

the intentions of key independents.[29] The coalition introduced a particularly grim budget in January 1982 and became the first ever to be defeated on its budget. Independents Loftus, Kemmy, and Sherlock later confirmed that FitzGerald had offered no deals immediately prior to the vote, but had merely asked them to do what they thought was 'right for the nation' (*Irish Independent*, 28 January 1982: 4). Given no indications of a change in policy direction, they proceeded to do exactly that and promptly walked into the opposition lobby. The result was a new election and a clear example of how not to handle the legislative fate of a minority government.

*Divided opposition (Fianna Fáil 1987–1989)*

After a period in government together, the 1987 election was a long anticipated but still devastating blow for Fine Gael and Labour (between them they lost twenty-three seats, 27 per cent of their 1982 totals). Labour in particular interpreted the outcome as an electoral instruction to go into opposition, so that a Fianna Fáil government three votes short of an overall majority formed.[30] The size of the party system increased with the arrival of a new party, the Progressive Democrats (PDs), who debuted with 12 per cent of the votes and fourteen seats. The PDs' injection of a new neo-liberal tax- and deficit-cutting agenda increased the policy range among the opposition parties and virtually guaranteed that there would be no governing alternative to Fianna Fáil during this parliament. Any 'winning' alternative would require Fine Gael, Labour, the PDs, the Workers' Party, plus at least two of the four independents, an impossible coalition in 1987. Thus, the bottom line was that Fianna Fáil could rely on opposition divisions (plus the desire of Fine Gael and Labour to forestall a new election) and had no need to strike a deal with other forces in the Dáil (see Laver *et al.*, 1987). The minority government did lose a few votes but its stability was not seriously impaired. As Laver and Arkins (1990: 195) have commented:

---

[29] Indeed, the then Taoiseach still sounds perplexed in his own memoirs: 'We knew of course that both the cuts in food subsidies and the increases in some indirect taxes would be sensitive areas for the two socialist independents who supported us, Noel Browne and Jim Kemmy. We might, I suppose, have minimised or even perhaps eliminated the risk of losing their support by proposing a somewhat less ambitious reform programme, either on the tax or social welfare side, but, rightly or wrongly, I was reluctant to compromise our reform programme for what seemed such a perverse reason: a fear of losing *left-wing* support. Logically, I felt, these two socialist independents must when the crunch came support such a redistributive budget, and this view was shared by most of my colleagues in Government, including the Labour Party members' (FitzGerald, 1991: 395; emphasis in original).

[30] After the vote was tied 82–82 (with a key independent, Tony Gregory, abstaining) the Fianna Fáil leader became Taoiseach on the casting vote of the Ceann Comhairle (Farrell and Farrell, 1987: 241).

When push came to shove, despite all the posturing, [the opposition parties] voted in such a way as to allow a Fianna Fáil minority government to take office. Once the government had formed, the story was much the same. There were a few skirmishes and the odd government defeat on particular issues but, on anything big enough to bring down the government, the gauntlet was thrown down and the opposition backed off.

In addition, in an unprecedented move, Fine Gael unilaterally offered to support the Fianna Fáil government as long as it continued to follow a sound economic programme (Marsh and Mitchell, 1999: 50–4). The government only ended when the Fianna Fáil leader gambled on an early election to capitalize on popularity gains. The risk proved unwise and Fianna Fáil lost four seats (see Gallagher and Sinnott, 1990). Divided opposition rendered the government viable.

### Negotiate ad hoc support (1982)

After the February 1982 election the outgoing Fine Gael–Labour coalition held seventy-eight seats and Fianna Fáil eighty-one. A small party, Sinn Féin the Workers' party (SFWP) and four independents held the balance of power, and each side canvassed their support. When the Dáil met on 8 March to elect a Taoiseach the outcome was uncertain, although it was later revealed that SFWP had secretly decided to vote for Haughey, the Fianna Fáil leader, but without negotiating a deal of any kind. Others were not so reticent. Uncertainty about how SFWP would vote enhanced the bargaining power of the independents. In particular, a left-wing independent deputy representing a deprived inner-city area of Dublin, Tony Gregory, negotiated what is now known in Irish political folklore as simply 'the Gregory deal'.

All three major party leaders held discussions with Gregory and his associates . . . After further negotiations, Gregory undertook to vote for Haughey as Taoiseach in return for wide-ranging, specific concessions designed to meet the needs of the inner city. The full details were cobbled into a thirty-page document signed by both men and 'witnessed' by the general secretary of the Irish Transport and General Workers' Union . . . The minimum cost to the Exchequer was variously estimated between £80 million and £175 million. The deal was unprecedented testimony to the influence of a single deputy and an incentive for voters to demand that their representatives, irrespective of party, exercise similar muscle. (Farrell, 1987a: 17)

Haughey was elected Taoiseach by eighty-six to seventy-nine votes (with the support of Gregory, the three SFWP deputies, and another independent, Neil Blaney). This short-lived government was surely the most bizarre ever in modern Ireland and it has been chronicled extensively elsewhere (see, for example, Joyce and Murtagh, 1983). For present purposes, the important point is that it was quite unstable. In particular while Gregory and SFWP had helped Haughey become Taoiseach they had not promised ongoing support for the government. Dáil divisions would have to be won on the basis of ad hoc legislative coalitions. Scandals, near civil war inside Fianna Fáil, and other calamities led the government's popularity quickly to spiral downwards. It had lost one motion in the Dáil on a factory closure in Kilkenny (but won the subsequent confidence vote with the support of the Workers' party) and had only survived on two other divisions on the casting vote of the Ceann Comhairle. The situation became virtually untenable when on 18 October government backbencher Bill Loughnane died, to be followed the next day by TD Jim Gibbons suffering a severe heart attack. This reduced the government's strength to seventy-nine. The government was finally defeated two weeks later on a confidence motion proposed by the Taoiseach after the Workers' party withdrew their support (*The Irish Times*, 5 Nov. 1982).

## Negotiate consistent support (1997–)

While governments have occasionally been supported externally by other parties (for example, Labour supporting Fianna Fáil from 1932 to 1936 and Clann na Poblachta supporting the 1954–7 coalition),[31] they have more commonly sought support amongst the micro-parties and independents. While external support has often been ad hoc and somewhat unreliable, this method of securing a minority government was raised to a new level of consistency by the coalition that formed after the 1997 election.[32] The 1997 contest was a straight fight between two pre-electoral coalitions with transfer pacts: the outgoing 'rainbow' three-party government and the opposition coalition of Fianna Fáil and the Progressive Democrats. The opposition combination achieved an advantage over the government (securing eighty-one seats to the incumbents' seventy-five), but was still two votes short of the bare minimum needed in the Dáil (eighty-three out of 166). Ten other deputies were elected who were independents or belonged to very small parties. While, as we have seen, some Irish minority governments have relied on shifting ad hoc legislative coalitions, the party leaders on this occasion were willing to negotiate with the independents, who suddenly found themselves very much in demand.

Fianna Fáil leader, Bertie Ahern, let it be known that he would talk to independents about 'smaller issues' than, by implication, the legendary 'Gregory deal' (see above). The political lineage and policy preferences of the independents (where known) quickly suggested that the deputies to pursue were those who might be thought of as belonging to the Fianna Fáil extended family (Jackie Healy-Rae, Mildred Fox, and Harry Blaney). Blaney essentially wanted 'reassurance' in two policy areas: a hard-line anti-abortion policy and no concessions to unionists concerning Northern Ireland. Such reassurance from Ahern was forthcoming, though in very general and vague terms. Healy-Rae

---

[31] At inauguration the three-party 1954–7 coalition was actually a bare majority government (seventy-four seats out of 147). Clann na Poblachta's (three seats) pledge of external support provided much-needed security.

[32] This section is mostly drawn from Mitchell (1999).

and Fox, on the other hand, wanted what most deputies want—spending com-mitments in their constituencies that would help their re-election bids. Fox in particular was quite explicit about this demand. Having secured various demands in direct negotiations with Ahern (for example, new roads, schools, and hospital equipment) she pledged to support the government for the full duration of the parliament as long as her commitments were implemented. As she put it: 'just like any other deputy, I will be facing the electorate in five years and I have issues which have to be addressed' (*The Irish Times*, 27 June 1997: 9). Healy-Rae secured a similar package of specific proposals. He also hinted that his ongoing support would come at an ongoing price: referring to road improvements that he was promised in his negotiations with Bertie Ahern he said, 'we'll get a hell of a lot more as well as that' (*The Irish Times*, 27 June 1997: 7). In addition to pork, every effort was made to keep the 'non-party three' sweet. In addition to delivering on specific commitments, it was understood that the three were to be 'facilitated' by the governments' ministers and staff (*The Irish Times*, 18 January 1998: 7), and Healy-Rae even received an office benefit on his appointment as chair of the Dáil's Environment Committee, to the envy of many government backbenchers.[33]

## THE PERFORMANCE OF MINORITY GOVERNMENT IN IRELAND

While much is now known about the circumstances surrounding the making and breaking of governments, much less is known about how—and how well—they govern. Substantive judgement concerning the policy effectiveness of different government types is an analytically difficult task, given current data constraints and value judgements. Certainly, we have no readily avail-able information on whether Irish minority governments perform 'better or worse' than majority governments. Nevertheless, we can consider data on two matters that can readily be quantified: the relative stability and electoral performances of different cabinet types.

### Duration

One of the traditional objections to minority cabinets is that they are alleged to be inherently unstable and temporary. Consistent with the comparative data, the evidence from Ireland refutes this claim. Certainly, as in other countries,

---

[33] The independents supporting the government may have even evolved into a bargain-ing unit. On 24 Oct. 2000, *The Irish Times* reported that: 'The TDs are still negotiating with the government on packages for their constituencies in return for their vote. They have met a senior advisor and will meet the Taoiseach, Mr Ahern, next month. Ms Fox said they met the senior advisor as a group for the first time.'

minority governments tend to dissolve more quickly than their majority sib-
lings but they have not been merely caretakers or 'temporary'. In the post-war
period (1948–97) minority cabinets account for 38 per cent of total government
duration in Ireland (not including the as yet uncompleted minority coalition
formed in June 1997, currently in its fourth year). On average (1948–97) minority cabinets have lasted for 800 days (2.2 years) compared to 1260 days (3.5
years) for majority governments. Of course, in evaluating the 'performance' of
minority governments in terms of duration we should also note that differential tenure is most likely at least partly a function of the earlier use of voluntary
dissolution powers by minority cabinets (rather than proof of debilitating
instability). Indeed, this was the favourite tactic of the first Fianna Fáil leader:
on three occasions (1933, 1938, and 1944) de Valera voluntarily ended his
minority governments (each of which had been in office for less than one year)
in search of a majority. Each time his gamble paid off. A later Fianna Fáil
leader, Charles Haughey, was much less successful with the same tactic
(1987–9), not only missing the increasingly elusive majority, but also actually
losing his party four seats (on the same first preference vote). However, the
Irish evidence is that while minority governments have certainly been shorter
on average than majorities, they have not generally been characterized by tur-
moil and cabinet instability.

## *Electoral Costs*

The electoral consequences of governing should affect parties' decisions
about the types of governments in which they are willing to take part. The
tendency in Europe for governments, especially coalitions, to lose votes at the
next election is an important element of Strøm's explanation of minority governments. Basically, if the projected electoral losses are high, a party may
decide not to govern. Similarly, if a vote-seeking party decides to govern it
should prefer to form or join cabinets with lower projected losses. Minority
governments have clear electoral advantages:

Majority coalitions should be preferred only by parties that are strongly office motivated. Policy-seeking and especially vote-seeking parties might well find minority governments to be a more attractive option. The more government stability a potential
governing party is willing to trade off for policy effectiveness and electoral advantage,
the more inclined it will be to opt for a minority cabinet. (Strøm, 1990: 130)

For parties solely concerned about their electoral futures, joining a government in Ireland is one of the worst things they can do. On average all government parties lose votes at the next election: the net loss for the governing
parties during the entire period (1923–97) is 2.7 per cent. The losses appear to
be increasing over time, no doubt reflecting higher levels of volatility.[34]

---

[34] The net government loss for 1923–57 was 1.81%, whereas for 1961–97 it was almost
exactly double (3.58%).

Moreover, and for whatever reasons, electoral prospects vary quite substantially by cabinet type (along broadly the same lines that Strøm found).

Table 10.4 clearly shows that majority coalitions are the most electorally disastrous, on average costing the governing parties a net loss of 8.5 per cent. However, in the present context especially interesting is the wide discrepancy in the electoral fortunes of minority and majority governments. On average, all majority governments lose heavily (minus 5.3 per cent), whereas minority governments do much better, managing to break even.[35] Thus, for parties who wish to govern, but are also concerned about their electoral futures, minority governments are a good place to be.

TABLE 10.4. *Subsequent electoral loss of government parties in Ireland by cabinet type 1923–1997 (% votes)*

| Cabinet type | Mean (%) | SD | *N* |
|---|---|---|---|
| Majority | | | |
| single-party | −3.26 | 5.09 | 8 |
| coalition | −8.50 | 3.93 | 5 |
| Minority | | | |
| single-party | 0.79 | 6.39 | 10 |
| coalition | −2.85 | 4.03 | 2 |
| All majority | −5.28 | 5.23 | 13 |
| All minority | 0.18 | 6.07 | 12 |

## CONCLUSION

Coalition majority governments involve a partisan rather than an inter-institutional division of power. The best case for an equivalent to US-style 'divided government' in parliamentary democracies is provided by the minority governments that are very common in a number of European countries, including Ireland. Strictly speaking, they are not a direct analogue. In the US the interinstitutional division involves one party controlling the executive branch and the other party controlling at least one house of the legislature. In the European multi-party case, the minority executive does not itself control the legislature, but nor does anybody else. Since 'the opposition' in the legislature is not a unified bargaining actor, what is left is an 'all minority situation'.[36] Nevertheless, a partial analogy is possible since in both cases the

---

[35] Of course in absolute terms majority governments obviously have more votes to lose. Nevertheless, there is a substantial differential even when only relative vote shares are considered.

[36] This is akin to what Shugart (1995) described as 'no-majority governments' in presidential systems.

executive needs the co-operation of forces in the legislature, beyond its own members, to be viable.

Minority governments in Ireland have been common, relatively stable, and reasonably effective. While a number of contributory factors help explain the frequency of minority outcomes to the government formation process, it seems clear that a divided opposition and/or the availability of independents are the biggest factors. 'Nearly-winning' minority governments often have been able to attract the support of a few independent deputies, mostly in exchange for policy or constituency spending commitments. At other times, the opposition parties have been divided in such a way that minority Fianna Fáil governments have been much more secure than the parliamentary arithmetic alone would suggest.

Since minority governments in Ireland and elsewhere are much more likely to be composed of single parties than coalitions, Ireland's apparent transformation into a fully fledged coalition system suggests that minority governments may be less common in the future. However, the anticipation of electoral futures represents a possible countervailing pressure: 'Minority governments form in circumstances in which anticipation of elections weighs heavily on party leaders' (Strøm, 1990: 244). If Irish party leaders wish to govern, but are also concerned about their electoral health, minority governments are the safest place to be. This may help explain why minority governments continue to form.

# 11

# Divided Government in Comparative Perspective

## *Robert Elgie*

The aim of this book is to analyse the politics of divided government from a cross-national perspective. The rationale for this aim is that most of the work on divided government has focused on the US. True, in this context there is a voluminous literature on the subject. As a result, there are different interpretations of the term, as well as competing and mutually exclusive explanations as to what causes divided government and how it can be managed. However, while a limited amount of comparative work explicitly on this theme has been undertaken, to date the concept of divided government has remained doggedly US-centric. Thus, the main task of this volume is to examine the experience of divided government, understood in an arithmetic sense, in a variety of institutional and country-specific contexts, so as to identify similarities and differences regarding its causes and the ways in which it is managed.

By its very nature, an exercise of this sort is bound to produce an eclectic set of results. So, for example, while the focus was on the experience of divided government in the arithmetic sense of the term, clear evidence was also provided of divided government in the behavioural sense of the term. In this respect, findings in the Mexico chapter indicated that from 1988 to 1997, once the PRI had lost its super-majority status, the country experienced divided government in a behavioural sense, meaning that there was an ongoing need for cross-party coalition-building. It was also shown that a similar situation occurred on occasions in Finland prior to the 1990s, when a one-third minority in parliament could effectively block government legislation. In a slightly different context, evidence also suggested that in Ecuador divided government was affected by the fluid nature of party competition, which led to continuing problems in coalition-building. All told, to the extent that work on divided government in the behavioural sense has already pointed to links between US-style gridlock and parliamentary-style coalition politics (see Ch. 1), then the evidence from the case-study chapters provided at least some evidence to confirm such links and reaffirmed the potential for a highly fruitful research agenda.

In addition, the case-study chapters also outlined, quite unsurprisingly, a host of country-specific factors that shaped the analysis of divided government in individual countries. For example, it was shown that in Denmark divided government has now become part of the established political culture of the country. Both voters and politicians expect minority governments to occur and they also expect non-governmental parties in parliament to be able to influence the policy-making process. Arguably, this set of attitudes makes divided government easier to manage in Denmark than in countries that exhibit a more conflictual political culture. A somewhat different example can be found in the case of Finland. Here, in the post-war period, as a result of the country's history and its geographical position, the president came to dominate foreign-policy matters. The concentration of power in this domain meant that during periods of divided government the problems of managing policy-making were eased in at least one significant policy area. By contrast, in France the long-standing tradition of presidential government meant that, during periods of 'cohabitation', there was perhaps a greater likelihood of confrontation between the president and prime minister than might otherwise be the case as the president tried to maintain an influence over the political system.

It is apparent, therefore, that the case-studies provided a wide-ranging set of results. At the same time, though, they addressed some of the most basic questions concerning the politics of divided government that were outlined at the beginning of this study. The remainder of this chapter provides an overview of the findings in four sections. The first reviews the various forms of divided government that were observed and reflects briefly on the frequency with which they occurred. The second section reconsiders some of the proposed causes of divided government that were outlined in Chapter 1. Here, it will be shown that there was only limited support for theories of rational split-ticket voting or policy balancing. The third section focuses on the management of divided government. Here, a distinction is drawn between the cases where divided government is associated with interim governments, crisis situations, and cases where it is seen as a 'normal' part of the political process. The final section concludes.


THE FORMS AND FREQUENCY OF DIVIDED GOVERNMENT

In the opening chapter divided government was defined in an arithmetic sense as the situation where the executive fails to enjoy majority support in at least one working house of the legislature. On the basis of this definition, the case-study chapters revealed several different forms of divided government (see

Figure 11.1). At the same time, these chapters also showed that in general terms divided government was a relatively long-standing and common phenomenon, even if they failed to indicate any across-the-board trend in the general frequency with which it has occurred over time.[1]

---

### Executive vs Legislature

| | |
|---|---|
| Presidential | US, Ecuador, Mexico |
| Parliamentary | Denmark, Germany, Ireland |
| Semi-presidential | Finland, France, Poland |

### Executive vs Executive

| | |
|---|---|
| Presidential | no examples |
| Parliamentary | no examples |
| Semi-presidential | Finland, France, Poland |

---

FIGURE 11.1.  Forms of divided government in nine selected countries

The first form of divided government to be identified was the situation where the executive was pitted against at least one house of the legislature. This is the typical situation in the US and is the one with which students of divided government are already most familiar. As might be expected, this situation was also shown to apply to the two other presidential regimes under consideration, Ecuador and Mexico. It should be noted, though, that, in contrast to the situation in both the US and Mexico, in Ecuador the president was often faced with the situation where there was no coherent opposition majority in the legislature. In this case, the basic line of conflict was still found to lie between the executive and the legislature, but the party-political situation was still somewhat different to the one experienced in Mexico from 1997 to 2000 and in the two-party US system more generally.

In addition to these cases, the executive was also in opposition to the legislature in both parliamentary and semi-presidential regimes as well. In terms

---

[1] As noted in the preface, it is not claimed that the case-studies constituted a representative cross-section of all countries. Thus, even if a trend had emerged, statistical significance could not have been read into the results.

of the former, in both Denmark and Ireland[2] the division was between the government and the main (or sole) working house of the legislature. By contrast, in Germany the division was between the government and the upper house only. In terms of the latter, Finland, France, and Poland all experienced the situation where the president and prime minister were drawn from the same party or coalition background, whereas the government still failed to enjoy a majority in the sole (or sole working) house of the legislature. In short, all the parliamentary and semi-presidential countries under examination experienced periods of minority government.

The main lesson to be drawn from these observations is that the executive failed to enjoy majority support in the legislature across the full range of constitutional systems under consideration. Thus, the basic situation that has manifested itself so frequently in the US was also found in a wide variety of other countries as well.[3] This only strengthens the case for trying to understand divided government as a cross-national phenomenon.

The second form of divided government to be identified was the situation where the executive was in opposition to itself. This situation was experienced in the three semi-presidential case-studies, Finland, France, and Poland. The fact that this situation was not witnessed in any of the presidential or parliamentary examples might seem to bear out Pierce's (1991) argument that French-style 'cohabitation', or semi-presidential split-executive government, is not really the same as US-style divided government. Such a conclusion, though, would be misleading. Leaving aside the behavioural similarities or differences between the two, French-style 'cohabitation' was still brought about because one part of the executive failed to enjoy majority support in the legislature. In other words, it was brought about for what amounts to the same reason as US-style divided government. It was simply that on these occasions divided government in semi-presidential systems then manifested itself in a somewhat different way to divided government in presidential systems because of the different constitutional framework in the two cases.

Thus, the main observation to be made is that the basic situation that characterizes the presidential form of divided government, as well as minority government in parliamentary systems, is also the equivalent of split-executive

[2] Elsewhere, the author has defined Ireland as semi-presidential (Elgie, 1999). However, to the extent that political practice in Ireland is unequivocally parliamentary-like, then for the purposes of this chapter Ireland is considered alongside Denmark and Germany.

[3] Due to the problem of selection bias, the claim is not that all countries experience this situation, but merely that all the countries chosen for study experienced it. However, to the extent that the countries chosen represent examples of three different regime types, then it is also true that there is at least the potential for all presidential, semi-presidential, and parliamentary countries to be contronted with this situation.

government in semi-presidential countries. Again, therefore, it follows that the potential for the cross-national comparison of divided government is great.

Turning to the frequency of divided government, there was no across-the-board trend. In the first place, there were some countries where the frequency of minority government has increased over time. This was true for Mexico, with the first instance of divided government occurring as late as 1997. It was also true for the US if we compare the period 1896–1948 with the period 1948–2000. Equally, in France split-executive government has only occurred since 1986. Finally, in Denmark, whereas there was undoubtedly a tradition of minority government in the period 1945–71, since this time minority government has become very much the norm. Moreover, it might also be noted that since 1982 coalition minority governments have replaced single-party minority governments as standard practice.

At the same time, there were two examples where the incidence of divided government has decreased over time. This was the case for Ireland, where until 1965 single-party minority governments were relatively frequent, even though single-party and, more recently, coalition minority governments have still occurred after this time. This was also the case for Finland, where there has not been a single instance of minority government since 1982. In this case, though, it might be noted that, following the reform of the presidential election system in 1994, there is now a greater potential than before for split-executive government to occur, even if the powers of the president have also been considerably reduced with the introduction of the new constitution in 2000.

Finally, there were a number of examples where the experience of divided government has remained relatively stable over time, albeit at a comparatively high level. This point certainly applies to Ecuador, where divided government has been a constant feature of the political landscape since the return to civilian rule in 1979. The same is also true for Poland since the democratization process began properly in 1991. Equally, but in a slightly different context, the incidence of divided government has remained pretty stable in Germany since 1949, with only three periods (totalling fourteen years) of unified government since this time. Similarly, while in the US there has been an increase in divided government in the period 1948–2000 (62 per cent) compared with the period 1896–1948 (15 per cent), the frequency of divided government in the contemporary period is only slightly higher than the figure in the period 1836–96 (50 per cent), pointing to a certain degree of constancy over time.

We can conclude that divided government takes a number of different forms and that it occurs in presidential, parliamentary, and semi-presidential regimes. Moreover, while it is not claimed that the set of case-studies in this book constitutes a statistically representative sample of countries, we can nevertheless also conclude with a reasonable degree of conviction that divided government has long been and certainly remains a relatively common phenomenon.

## THE CAUSES OF DIVIDED GOVERNMENT

In the opening chapter, it was shown that existing work had identified both behavioural and institutional explanations for divided government. The evidence from the case-study chapters confirmed the salience of both sets of factors. However, in contrast to the received wisdom, there was more evidence to support the importance of fragmented partisan preferences as an important behavioural cause of divided government. At the same time, while in individual cases the electoral system was regularly identified as the main institutional reason for divided government, there was no evidence to suggest that any particular type of electoral system was generally responsible for divided government cross-nationally.

### *Behavioural Explanations of Divided Government*

The case-study chapters showed that the existence of fragmented partisan preferences was an important reason for the presence of divided government. In other words, voters were 'institution-blind'. For the most part, they voted for a particular political party, given the institutional context in which the party was operating. They did not vote strategically for a particular institutional arrangement, given the party system with which they were faced. That is to say, voters chose a certain party—perhaps because they enjoyed a long-standing identification with that party, or because they preferred the policies that the party was putting forward at the election in question. Moreover, voters undoubtedly chose that party on the basis of at least some understanding of how the electoral system would translate their preferences into votes. In this case, though, divided government was simply the by-product of a certain aggregation of preferences in a particular institutional context. By contrast, most voters did not vote for a given party because of a preference for divided government per se, although it is certainly true that in some cases voters voted for parties knowing that divided government may be the result of their preferred choice.

### *The fragmentation of party preferences*

The fragmentation of partisan preferences appeared to be linked to divided government. In terms of parliamentary systems, this point was made very forcefully in the case of Denmark. There have never been large parties in the Danish system and since the so-called 'earthquake' election of 1973 the fragmentation of the party system within the basic left- and right-wing blocs has only increased. Thus, there is no sense in which Danes have deliberately structured their vote so as to bring about minority government. They have been aware that, by maintaining the fragmented structure of the party system minority governments are likely to occur, but they need not be seriously concerned precisely because in the Danish system they can rely on the expectation that all or most parties will in any event exercise policy influence. A similar point applies to Germany. Here, it must be remembered that the Bundesrat is not directly elected. Instead, representation in the upper house simply reflects the partisan composition of Land governments. Moreover, it must also be remembered that in the last decade or so Land party systems have become more complex as a result of the unification of the country and the arrival of new parties into the electoral arena. Thus, again, there is no question of divided government being the consequence of a strategic calculation. On the contrary, the presence of divided government in the German system is simply the result of an increasingly volatile set of voter allegiances at the Land level manifesting themselves in the specific set institutional arrangements that can be found at the Bund level.

The same picture emerged from the study of the semi-presidential systems under consideration. Like Denmark, in Finland and Poland the party system has been highly fragmented. In Finland party preferences have long been divided, volatile, and polarized. As a result, stable governmental coalitions have been difficult to form. In addition, there has been great potential for opposing presidential and parliamentary majorities. In Poland, the party system is much younger, but no less unstable. As a consequence, the electorate has been disoriented, resulting at one time in twenty-nine parties and eighteen parliamentary groups being represented in the legislature. Thus, while in the Polish case there is at least some support for the policy-balancing thesis (see below), there is no doubt that the high volatility of political preferences is the main cause of unstable parliamentary politics as well as opposing presidential/parliamentary majorities. Finally, a similar point applies to France. Here, the long-term stability of the electorate in the 1960s and 1970s was one of the main causes of unified government. However, the decline of class and religion as determining factors in voting behaviour produced a much more volatile electorate. As a result, there was greater likelihood that presidential and parliamentary majorities would fail to coincide. This happened for the first time in 1986 and again in both 1993 and 1997.

The same story can also be told with regard to the presidential countries under consideration. The cases of Ecuador and Mexico are exemplary. In Ecuador political parties have consistently failed to act as effective channels of representation. They have failed to aggregate preferences in a coherent manner. Instead, they have served as little more than short-term vehicles for aspiring leaders. The result is a party system that frequently leads to a no-majority situation in the legislature and the constant presence of divided government. By contrast, in Mexico the situation used to be very different. The PRI was the dominant party in the system from its formation in 1929 to the late 1980s. Since this time, though, the PRI's position has weakened. The party's corporatist support structure has declined and it has been unable to rely on the benefits of political patronage in the same way as before. As the demographic and socio-economic bases of the PRI's support have weakened, opposition parties have come to the fore, leading to the first period of divided government in 1997. Again, therefore, in Mexico as in Ecuador, divided government occurred as the unintended consequence of electoral volatility rather than intentional voting.

Finally, the situation in the US requires special attention. Here, as Alan Ware clearly showed, strong partisan preferences were the main cause of divided government in the period 1836–96. At this time, most voters were strong party identifiers and support for the two main parties was relatively even. Only a small percentage of floating voters was willing to shift their vote from one party to another. This situation meant that there was little split-ticket voting and that the support of the floating voters was crucial for victory. As a result, when presidential and congressional elections were held together, unified governments tended to occur. When there were mid-term elections the floating voters often shifted their support away from the presidential majority. Thus, divided government occurred frequently, but usually following mid-term elections. By contrast, weak partisan preferences were the main cause of divided government in the period 1948–2000. During this period levels of party identification fell. In addition, there has been a rise of candidate-centred contests. The result is that presidential and congressional majorities have been uncoupled. There has been a rise in split-ticket voting and, in stark contrast to the earlier period, divided government has frequently occurred in years when presidential and congressional elections have been held simultaneously. All told, while the cause may have changed over time, the main reason for the increasing incidence of divided government in the US, namely changing party preferences, is very similar to the one proposed in most of the other case-study chapters in this book.

*Strategic voting*

In the opening chapter two US-focused strategic explanations of divided government were cited. The first suggested that the public have contradictory preferences (lower taxes and higher spending) and that they vote rationally (for a Republican president and a Democrat Congress respectively) so as to bring them about (Jacobson, 1990). The second argued that the public vote deliberately to bring about divided government because it results in policy outcomes closer to their own preferences (Fiorina, 1996). While it was shown in Chapter 1 that neither argument was necessarily applicable outside the US

(Jones, 1995), one of the aims of the book was to see whether either or both of these explanations had any explanatory power in a comparative context.

As it happened, neither explanation found very much favour in any of the case-study chapters. This was particularly true for the rational split-ticket voting hypothesis. Admittedly, this argument was not applicable to the parliamentary countries under examination. However, none of the other contributors proposed it as a serious explanation either. Indeed, this was perhaps most notably the case in the chapter on the US where other factors were deemed to be more important (see above). By the same token, the policy-balancing thesis was only slightly more popular. For example, in Poland there was some support for the basic elements of the argument. Here, if voters find that a particular government has proved to be too extreme in its policies, then there is some evidence to indicate that they will vote for a more centrist, less confrontational candidate at the next election. This Polish variant of the argument is some way removed from Fiorina's original thesis, but it does at least suggest that there is some potential for further exploration. The same point might appear to apply to the French case. Here, it was noted that 'cohabitation' has been very popular among the public. This finding has led some commentators to suggest that the French (or at least a proportion of them) may vote strategically so as to force a president and prime minister from opposing parties to co-operate. However, this argument was shown to be flawed. The public do not like 'cohabitation' per se. Instead, the prime minister's supporters like 'cohabitation' because the former opposition now has a chance to govern. At the same time, the president's supporters also like 'cohabitation' because the former majority still maintains a certain degree of influence. So, while voters know that they will have to put up with a period of 'cohabitation' if they want to see a different set of policy outcomes, their vote is still a party vote rather than a strategic policy-balancing vote. All told, therefore, most of the contributors were prepared to agree with Alan Ware's contention that there was absolutely no evidence to support the policy-balancing thesis.

## *Institutional Explanations of Divided Government*

As noted above, the behavioural evidence suggested that for the most part voters were 'institution-blind'. This means that divided government occurred simply as an unintended consequence of exogenous voter preferences. The public did not vote for divided government as an end in itself. This is not to say, however, that institutions were not important in helping to create the context in which divided government could occur. On the contrary, most writers pointed to the salience of institutional factors in causeing divided government. In this respect, a number of country-specific reasons were highlighted and the importance of a mid-term electoral cycle was also identified.

At the same time, the factor that was regularly singled out as the key institutional variable was the electoral system.

A number of country-specific reasons were put forward to explain the experience of divided government. For example, in the US the incumbency effect was highlighted. Over the years, members of Congress have served for longer terms. This has meant that senior figures have increasingly been able to use their powers to provide material benefits for their constituents ('pork'). In this way, as Ware points out, incumbency has started to have an independent effect on the outcome of elections.

In more general terms, though, the presence of mid-term elections was noted as an important cause of divided government in a number of countries. In the US, the presence of mid-term congressional elections has already been highlighted as a major factor that brought about divided government in the period 1836–96. In addition, a similar factor also played a role in Poland. Here, the presidential term is five years, while the parliamentary term is only four years. Thus, synchronous presidential and parliamentary elections are held only once every twenty years. In this context, and given the fragmentation of the Polish electorate (see above), there is a greater potential than might otherwise be the case for the president and the prime minister to be in opposition. The same point applied to France at least prior to the constitutional reform of 2000. Before this time, the president was elected for seven years and the legislature for five years. Thus, prior to the reform, even though the president had the right to dissolve the National Assembly immediately following the presidential election, at some stage during the presidency a set of 'mid-term' elections has to be held. In 1986 and 1993 this requirement provided the opportunity for the president's party to be defeated and, thus, can be treated as one of the main institutional causes of 'cohabitation'.

Overall, though, there is no doubt that the electoral system was the most frequently cited institutional reason for divided government. Indeed, this was identified as an important factor in parliamentary, presidential, and semi-presidential regimes alike. It should be noted, however, that proportional and majoritarian electoral systems were variously identified as potential culprits. Moreover, different varieties of proportional and majoritarian systems were singled out for attention. Thus, while electoral systems were clearly important in bringing about divided government, there was no evidence to suggest that any particular type of system was generally responsible for bringing about divided government.

In terms of proportional electoral systems, list systems were clearly important in Denmark and Poland. Here, the system allowed the fragmentation of partisan preferences to be represented proportionally in the legislature. In the former, the low 2 per cent threshold meant that the resulting choice was usually between minority and coalition governments and, for the reasons highlighted by Strøm (1990), the former often prevailed. In Ireland, however, the situation was slightly different. Here, the presence of the single transferable vote (STV) electoral system in multi-member constituencies was shown to be important. The STV system encourages candidate-based contests. Indeed, this system encourages competition between candidates of the same party However, this system also helps the election of non-party single-issue candidates, disaffected major party candidates, and/or simply popular well-known local figures. As Paul Mitchell notes, in the case where a single party or a coalition is returned only just short of a parliamentary majority, the presence of independents makes minority governments more viable than they would otherwise be.

In terms of majoritarian systems, the importance of the two-ballot majority system, or the majority run-off system, was highlighted in both Ecuador and Poland for presidential elections and in France for parliamentary elections. In Ecuador, the problem with the majority run-off system was that it provided few incentives for parties to co-operate in support of a single presidential candidate. Instead, it encouraged small parties to stand candidates at the first ballot so as to increase their electoral visibility. Moreover, it also encouraged outsiders to stand for election. The result was that there was less likelihood that the successful presidential candidate would be supported by a coherent majority. The same was true in Poland. In France, the situation was slightly different. Here, while the effect of the two-ballot majority system for presidential elections was similar to the situation in Ecuador and Poland in that it provided incentives for candidates to stand (Elgie, 1996), the use of a similar system for parliamentary elections had a very different effect. The system 'manufactured' parliamentary majorities when they may not otherwise have occurred. Thus, rather than encouraging minority government, the two-ballot system facilitated 'cohabitation'.

Finally, the effect of the presidential electoral system in Finland also needs to be mentioned. Here, until only recently, the president was elected on the basis of a de facto system of direct election via an electoral college. In short, the president had to build a majority coalition in order to be elected. In this context, and in direct contrast to the situation in Ecuador, the presidential majority was often then reflected in governmental coalition-building. So, although minority governments and 'cohabitation' were both present in the Finnish system, the effect of the presidential electoral system was to reduce the likelihood of divided government somewhat.

## THE MANAGEMENT OF DIVIDED GOVERNMENT

As might be expected, the experience of managing divided government varied considerably from one country to another. While it is tempting simply to catalogue the various country-specific experiences, it is more rewarding to

distinguish between three overarching types of behaviour. Thus, divided
government was managed in three general ways: occasionally it was treated
as an interim measure; in a very limited number of cases it provoked a political crisis; more usually it constituted a routine part of the political process,
sometimes resulting in gridlock and sometimes leading to compromise.

### *Divided Government as an Interim Measure*

As Strøm (1990) has already noted, there is a tendency for minority governments to be considered as caretaker or temporary governments. In fact,
though, such an observation is misplaced. Minority governments can and do
stay in office for a considerable period of time. This book showed that what
is true for minority governments specifically is also true for divided government more generally. For the most part, divided government was seen as a
normal, although sometimes unloved, part of the political process. That said,
there were occasions when divided government was seen as merely an interim
measure. Indeed, specific attention was drawn to this fact in the chapters on
Ireland, Finland, and France. In these cases, on a very limited number of
occasions, divided government was seen as merely a stop-gap solution to a
wider political problem.

In Ireland and Finland there were clear examples of minority governments
being treated as caretaker governments. In Ireland, however, this attitude was
confined to the early 1920s during the early days of state-building when the
pattern of party competition was very different from the one that was established subsequently. By contrast, in Finland caretaker governments have
been slightly more prevalent. So, in the 1920s during the First Republic two
caretaker governments were formed because of disagreements over foreign
policy issues and attitudes towards the Communist party. Thereafter, during
the Second Republic, seven caretaker governments were formed because of
conflict over economic issues. All the same, these examples are exceptions
rather than the rule. In both Ireland and Finland, divided government is not
unusual and generally it has been treated as a normal part of the political
scenery.

In France, the situation was slightly more complex. Here, at least two of the
three periods of 'cohabitation' (1986–8 and 1993–5) were viewed by many
people as periods of temporary political expediency. On these occasions, such
people were simply waiting for normal service, presidential government, to be
resumed.[4] This is not to say that, during these periods, governments simply
marked time. On the contrary, the 1986–8 administration in particular introduced a series of controversial institutional, social, and economic reforms. It

---

[4] Indeed, there are some observers who feel that the period after 1997 should also be
viewed in this way.

is simply to say that for many people, key political actors included, 'cohabitation' was deemed to be somehow abnormal. Thus, even though these governments were stable for two years and were only brought to an end as a result of the subsequent presidential contest, they were still treated as caretaker-like governments. That said, the basic point still stands. The case-studies showed that divided government was not generally associated with short-term, purely interim administrations.

### Divided Government as a Crisis Situation

The case-studies showed that, on a limited number of occasions, divided government was associated with crisis situations. As might be expected, though, these situations manifested themselves in various ways. In some countries, there was evidence of physical violence, intimidation, and skulduggery. For example, in Mexico, the onset of divided government after so many years of unified PRI rule was met by heckling, fisticuffs, and broken chairs. In Poland, tempers were less enflamed, but politicians were still willing to engage in dirty political tricks. So, in 1992 the interior minister produced files which allegedly showed that President Walesa had secretly collaborated with the security services during the communist regime. However, in this category the experience of Ecuador is undoubtedly the most exceptional. Here, for example, the early period of President Febres's term was marked by fights on the floor of the Chamber of Deputies and tear-gas bombs. Indeed, paratroopers even kidnapped the president for a day and the air force attempted two ultimately unsuccessful uprisings. All told, the fact that democracy survived in such circumstances is remarkable.

In other cases, crises manifested themselves in a purely party-political form. On occasions, presidents took the initiative. For example, in Finland, conflict between the president and government has sometimes resulted in the dissolution of parliament. This was particularly noteworthy in 1962 when President Kekkonen dismissed the incumbent minority government and dissolved parliament at the height of the so-called 'note affair'. Similarly, in France, as mentioned above, the first period of 'cohabitation' was brought to an end in 1988 when President Mitterrand dissolved parliament so as to overturn the incumbent right-wing majority. On other occasions, though, the legislature was active. In the US, it is likely that President Nixon would have been impeached over the Watergate affair even if he had not been faced with an opposition Congress. However, as Alan Ware notes, in the case of President Clinton the impeachment proceedings can be seen as the culmination of a long-term trend towards partisan warfare during periods of divided government. As before, though, the situation in Ecuador represents the most extreme case. Here, it is not particularly unusual for individual ministers to be threatened with impeachment by a hostile legislature. However, in 1997 the legislature declared the presidency vacant and did so by declaring the highly unpopular incumbent, Bucaram, to be mentally incompetent, so forcing him out of office and into exile in Panama.

The final examples concern situations where divided government has created a momentum for political reform. These examples are very different from the ones examined immediately above in that they are not characterized by moments of acute political tension. Instead, they are the result of a more ongoing dissatisfaction with certain elements of the political system, including the experience of divided government. In this respect, the recent decision to reform the Constitution in France is a case in point. The fact that 'cohabitation' was seen as an annoying and somewhat dysfunctional political interlude eventually provided the motivation to reduce the president's term in office to just five years. The passage of the new constitution in Finland is another example in this regard. Here, the reform was undoubtedly motivated by factors other than just the relatively common incidence of both minority governments and 'cohabitation'. However, there is no doubt that the reforms were designed to address these issues and make the political system work more smoothly. Finally, in Germany the position of the Bundesrat in the system has been a regular topic for debate. To date, major reforms have not been introduced. However, as Roland Sturm showed, various reforms have been proposed to try to overcome this supposed obstacle to efficient governmental decision-making.

### Divided Government as a Routine Matter

The case-studies showed that, in the main, divided government has been treated as a normal part of the political process. This is not to say that divided government was always easy to manage on these occasions. Quite the opposite, as Paul Mitchell pointed out, even when divided government is not seen as either an interim situation or a crisis moment, political actors still have to decide whether or not to negotiate with each other. In this context, while there were plenty of examples of negotiations leading to routine decision-making, there were also occasions when gridlock occurred, often resulting in the recourse to exceptional constitutional and political powers. However, these examples were mainly confined to presidential and semi-presidential countries.

In the opening chapter, three strategies for routinizing the activity of minority governments were identified: ongoing support, policy-specific support, and issue-by-issue support (Strøm, 1990). In the case-study chapters, examples of each strategy were identified. In terms of ongoing support the Irish case was perhaps most noteworthy. Here, for example, in the early 1930s the Fianna Fáil government was supported by the Labour party. This created a de facto majority situation. Most notably, though, in 1997 the head of government negotiated a deal with sundry independents. As a result, in return for certain more-or-less vague policy promises and/or for guaranteeing particular constituency benefits, again the government could operate as if it was in a majority situation.

In terms of policy-specific support there were a number of cases. For example, in Denmark two alternative policy-related majorities were sometimes present in the Folketing. There was an economic policy majority usually comprising the Conservatives, Venstre, the Centre Democrats, the Christian People's party, and Radikale Venstre. There was also an 'alternative' majority composed of the Left Socialists, the Socialist People's party, the Social Democrats, and Radikale Venstre. The former was concerned primarily with economic issues. The latter was active in the field of foreign and security policy as well as green issues, energy policy, law reform, housing policy, and social policy. In Mexico a similar situation occurred from 1997 to 2000. Here, the president negotiated on a case-by-case basis. However, as Table 4.4 showed, the result was in fact a fairly consistent set of policy-specific coalitions. The PAN tended to vote with the PRI on economic and politico-constitutional issues, while the PRI, the PAN, the PVEM, and the PT tended to vote together on public security issues. Finally, mention should also be made of the semi-presidential countries in this respect. In Finland, France, and Poland, the president was influential in foreign affairs. This meant that, even during times of both 'cohabitation' and minority government, the president maintained a certain degree of independent decision-making power.

In addition, there were also plenty of occasions when governments negotiated support on an issue-by-issue basis. In the context of presidential systems, this type of support was identified in the US. Here, while inter-branch conflict was the general experience of divided government, on three occasions (the Eisenhower presidency, the Ford presidency, and the first six years of the Reagan administration) the executive and the legislature worked together relatively well. In the context of parliamentary systems, issue-by-issue support was associated most clearly with both Denmark and Germany. In Germany, there was a regular process of give and take behind close doors. As a result, a compromise position was usually found that was acceptable to all parties. In Denmark, the situation was similar but it was not unusual for government policy to be defeated. In such cases, however, the government made it clear in advance, as an accepted part of the rules of the game, that it would only resign if defeated on a key matter relating to its economic policy. In these circumstances, some governments set out to win support on an issue-by-issue basis in the knowledge that, while they would most likely lose some votes, they would still be able to pass a proportion of their programme.

Even though governments adopted various strategies to routinize decision-making during divided government, there were also times when negotiations broke down and gridlock was the main result. As might be expected, the US provided one of the main examples in this regard. Here, the relationship between the president and Congress was particularly difficult in the period 1990–2000, leading to partial shutdowns of the federal government in both 1990 and 1995. In Poland too the relations between the president and prime minister were very strained at times. In 1995, for example, President Walesa adopted a 'go-it-alone' strategy, ratcheting up the level of political confrontation in an attempt to force the government to concede. Finally, in Ecuador, as Monica Barczak pointed out, legislative paralysis was common. This was particularly true of the Febres presidency when the legislative majority was explicitly opposed to the head of state.

In these countries and others, gridlock (or at least the threat of it) was often accompanied by the recourse to exceptional political measures in the attempt to block opposition proposals or to break through the impasse. So, as Alan Ware notes, in the US President Nixon stretched the constitutional interpretation of his powers beyond their usual limits in relation to the secret bombing of Cambodia and the impoundment of congressional funds. In Poland President Walesa tried to veto legislation, only to see the veto overturned. In Ecuador, presidents resorted to the use of emergency decrees in the attempt to circumvent the legislature. In a slightly wider context, the use of exceptional powers was also noted in France with the 1986–8 government repeatedly using a variety of exceptional constitutional measures in order to pass legislation during the first period of 'cohabitation'. In Finland too, on rare occasions, presidents refused to present bills to parliament. On equally rare occasions they refused to ratify legislation passed by parliament.

As all of these examples suggest, gridlock was mainly confined to presidential and semi-presidential countries. The reason for this situation lies in the fixed terms of office for either or both the president and the legislature. In this context, political opponents were condemned to coexist for better or worse. In parliamentary systems, however, irreconcilable conflict usually leads to the dismissal of the government or the dissolution of parliament rather than the ongoing stalemate. In the case-study chapters this point was demonstrated in the Irish case. Here, the failure to construct a majority on an issue-by-issue basis resulted in the premature fall of the Fianna Fáil minority government in 1982. Only in Denmark, where the acceptance of power-sharing is so culturally ingrained, was this sort of behaviour effectively absent.

## CONCLUSION

This book constitutes the first attempt to study the politics of divided government from a comparative perspective. From this perspective, two final observations can be made. The first is that the experience of divided government was clearly shown to vary greatly from one country to the next. So, for example, the situation in Ecuador was very different from the situation in Finland; the situation in France was very different from the situation in US; the situation in Denmark was very different from the situation in Mexico; and so on. This observation will comfort those who still believe that divided government is an essentially US problem, or that it is at least confined to presidential regimes alone. After all, there is no doubt that the basic form of divided government was clearly identifiable in the three presidential case-studies examined in this book and that there were certain similarities between the causes of divided government and the ways in which it was managed in each case. The second observation, however, is that, despite the variety of experiences, there were also great similarities between many aspects of divided government across the various types of regimes under consideration. So, for example, the main behavioural cause of divided government in Ecuador (the fragmentation of the party system) was actually quite similar to the equivalent cause in Finland. The presence of gridlock and the use of extraordinary powers in the US was reminiscent of equivalent behaviour in France. The construction of policy-specific majorities in Mexico was like the construction of equivalent majorities in Denmark. And so on. In other words, governments in very different systems face a very similar sort of problem. This problem is caused by similar sorts of reasons. Moreover, it is managed in similar sorts of ways. This is not to deny the peculiarities of individual countries. It is simply to emphasize that there is plenty to be gained from the cross-national study of divided government. This study has provided a start in this respect. It is hoped that it will encourage similar studies in the future.

# Bibliography

Aldrich, John (1995), *Why Parties? The Origins and Transformation of Party Politics in America* (Chicago: University of Chicago Press).

Anckar, Dag (1984), *Folket ock presidenten* (Helsingfors: Finska Vetenskaps-Societeten).

——(1990), 'Democracy in Finland: The Constitutional Framework', in Jan Sundberg and Sten Berglund (eds.), *Finnish Democracy* (Jyväskylä, Finnish Political Science Association), 26–50.

——(1999), 'Jäähyväiset semipresidentialismille', unpublished paper.

Andolina, Robert (1999), 'Colonial Legacies and Plurinational Imaginaries: Indigenous Movement Politics in Ecuador and Bolivia', Ph.D. dissertation, University of Minnesota, Twin Cities.

Arter, David (1981), 'Kekkonen's Finland: Enlightened Despotism or Consensual Democracy?', *West European Politics*, 4/3: 219–34.

——(1987), *Politics and Policy-Making in Finland* (Brighton: Wheatsheaf).

Balladur, Édouard (1995), *Deux ans à Matignon* (Paris: Plon).

Bigaut, Christian (1995), 'Les Cohabitations institutionnelles de 1986–1988 et de 1993–1995', *Regards sur l'actualité*, 211:3–30.

Bingham Powell, Jr., G. (1991), ' "Divided Government" as a Pattern of Governance', *Governance*, 4/3: 231–5.

Brady, David W., and Craig Volden (1998), *Revolving Gridlock: Politics and Policy from Carter to Clinton* (Boulder, Colo.: Westview Press).

Brandenburg, Frank (1964), *The Making of Modern Mexico* (Englewood Cliffs, NJ: Prentice-Hall).

Budge, Ian, and Hans Keman (1990), *Parties and Democracy: Coalition Formation and Government in Twenty States* (Oxford: Oxford University Press).

——and Michael Laver (1986), 'Office Seeking and Policy Pursuit', *Legislative Studies Quarterly*, 11/4: 485–506.

Camacho Guzman, Oscar, and Ciro Pérez Silva (1997), 'En San Lazaro, confesiones y euforia del nuevo bloque tricoazul', *La jornada* (15 Dec.).

Camp, Roderic A. (1995), 'Mexico's Legislature: Missing the Democratic Lockstep?', in David Close (ed.), *Legislatures and the New Democracies in Latin America* (Boulder, Colo.: Lynne Rienner), 17–36.

——(1999), *Politics in Mexico* (3rd edn. New York, Oxford University Press).

Capdevielle, Jacques, Elisabeth Dupoirier, Gerard Grunberg, Etienne Schweisguth, and Colette Ysmal (1981), *France de gauche vote à droite* (Paris: Presses de la FNSP).

Carrillo, Ulises, and Alonso Lujambio (1998), 'La incertidumbre constitucional: Gobierno dividido y aprobación presupuestal en la LVII Legislatura del congreso mexicano, 1997–2000', *Revista Mexicana de Sociología*, 60/2: 239–63.

Carty, R. K. (1983) *Party and Parish Pump: Electoral Politics in Ireland* (Brandon: Mercier Press).

Casar, María Amparo (1996), 'Las bases político-institucionales del poder presidencial en México', *Política y Gobierno*, 3/1: 61–93.

——(2000), 'Legislatura sin mayoria: Como va el score', *Nexos*, 265: 39–46.

——(forthcoming), 'Executive-Legislative Relations: The Case of Mexico', in Scott Morgenstern and Benito Nacif (eds.), *Legislative Politics in Latin America* (New York: Cambridge University Press).

Coakley, John, and Maurice Manning (1999), 'The Senate Elections', in Michael Marsh and Paul Mitchell (eds.), *How Ireland Voted 1997* (Boulder, Colo.: Westview Press), 195–214.

Cohan, A. S. (1982) 'Ireland: Coalitions Making a Virtue of Necessity', in Eric Browne and John Dreijmanis (eds.), *Government Coalitions in Western Democracies* (London, Longman), 260–82.

Cohendet, Marie-Anne (1993), *La Cohabitation: Leçons d'une expérience* (Paris: Presses Universitaires de France).

Coleman, John J. (1996), *Party Decline in America: Policy, Politics and the Fiscal State* (Princeton: Princeton University Press).

Colombani, Jean-Marie, and Jean-Yves Lhomeau (1986), *Le Mariage blanc* (Paris: Grasset).

Conaghan, Catherine M. (1994), 'Loose Parties, "Floating" Politicians, and Institutional Stress: Presidentialism in Ecuador, 1979–1988', in Juan J. Linz and Arturo Valenzuela (eds.), *The Failure of Presidential Democracy: The Case of Latin America* (Baltimore, The Johns Hopkins University Press), 254–85.

——(1995), 'Politicians Against Parties: Discord and Disconnection in Ecuador's Party System', in Scott Mainwaring and Timothy R. Scully (eds.), *Building Democratic Institutions: Party Systems in Latin America* (Stanford, Calif.: Stanford University Press), 434–58.

Cox, Gary W., and Samuel Kernell (1991), 'Conclusion', in Gary W. Cox and Samuel Kernell (eds.), *The Politics of Divided Government* (Boulder, Colo.: Westview Press), 239–48.

Damgaard, Erik (1990), 'Parlementarismens Danske Tilstand', in Erik Damgaard (ed.), *Parlementarisk Forandring I Norden* (Oslo: Universitetsforlag), 15–44.

Dästner, Christian (1999), 'Der "unechte Einigungsvorschlag" im Vermittlungsverfahren. Oder: Hat der Vermittlungsausschuß versagt?', *Zeitschrift für Parlamentsfragen*, 30/1: 26–40.

de la Garza, Paul (1997), 'Opposition's Takeover of Major Committees Dilutes Power of Mexico's Ruling Party', *Chicago Tribune* (2 October).

de la Garza, Rudolph O. (1972), *The Mexican Chamber of Deputies as a Legitimizing Agent of the Mexican Political System* (Research Series, 12; Tucson, Ariz.: Institute of Government Research, University of Arizona).

Dillon, Sam (1997a), 'Opposition Parties Unite in Bid to Elect Congressional Leader', *New York Times* (13 Aug.).

——(1997b), 'Mexico Leader Gets his Budget Past Opposition', *New York Times* (15 Dec.).

——(1999), 'In Outpouring of Venom, Mexico Lawmakers Battle Over Budget', *New York Times* (25 December).

Downie, Andrew (1999), 'Last-Minute Compromises Behind Mexican Budget Deal', *Financial Times* (2 Jan.).

Duhamel, Olivier (1993), 'La Cohabitation pacifique', in Philippe Habert, Pascal Perrineau, and Colette Ysmal (eds.), *Le Vote sanction: Les Élections législatives des 21 et 28 mars 1993* (Paris: Presses de la FNSP), 283–95.

——(1998), 'Dissolution ratée dans une démocratie déréglée', in Pascal Perrineau and Colette Ysmal (eds.), *Le Vote surprise: Les Élections législatives des 25 mai et 1er juin 1997* (Paris: Presses de la FNSP), 17–25.

Duverger, Maurice (1980), 'A New Political System Model: Semi-Presidential Government', *European Journal of Political Research*, 8: 165–87.

——(1986), *Bréviaire de la cohabitation* (Paris: Presses Universitaires de France).

——(1987), *La Cohabitation des Français* (Paris: Presses Universitaires de France).

——(1990), *Le Système politique français* (Paris: Presses Universitaires de France).

Elgie, Robert (1993), *The Role of the Prime Minister in France, 1981–91* (London: Macmillan).

——(1996), 'The Institutional Logics of Presidential Elections', in Robert Elgie (ed.), *Electing the French President: The 1995 Presidential Election* (London: Macmillan), 51–72.

——(ed.) (1999), *Semi-Presidentialism in Europe* (Oxford, Oxford University Press).

——and Steven Griggs (2000), *French Politics: Debates and Controversies* (London: Routledge).

——and Moshe Maor (1992), 'Accounting for the Survival of Minority Governments: An Examination of the French Case (1988–1991)', *West European Politics*, 15/3: 57–74.

——and Vincent Wright (1996), 'The French Presidency: The Changing Public Policy Environment', in Robert Elgie (ed.), *Electing the French President, The 1995 Presidential Election* (London: Macmillan), 172–94.

Estévez, Federico, and Beatriz Magaloni (1998), 'Hostages: Parties and their Constituencies in the Budget Battle of 1997', paper delivered at the XXI International Congress of the Latin American Studies Association, Chicago, 24–6 Sept.

EVA (1999), *Mielipiteiden sateenkaari: Raportti suomalaisten asenteista 1999* (Helsinki: Centre for Finnish Business and Policy Studies).

Farrell, Brian (1987*a*), 'The Context of Three Elections', in H. Penniman and Brian Farrell (eds.), *Ireland at the Polls: 1981, 1982, and 1987* (Washington, DC: American Enterprise Institute), 1–30.

——(1987*b*), 'Government Formation and Ministerial Selection', in H. Penniman and Brian Farrell (eds.), *Ireland at the Polls: 1981, 1982, and 1987* (Washington, DC: American Enterprise Institute), 131–55.

——(1987*c*), 'The Road from 1987: Government Formation and Institutional Inertia', in Michael Laver, Peter Mair and Richard Sinnott (eds.), *How Ireland Voted: The Irish General Election of 1987* (Dublin: Poolbeg and PSAI Press), 141–52.

——and David Farrell (1987), 'The General Election of 1987', in H. Penniman and Brian Farrell (eds.), *Ireland at the Polls: 1981, 1982, and 1987* (Washington, DC: American Enterprise Institute), 232–43.

Favier, Pierre, and Michel Martin-Roland (1991), *La Décennie Mitterrand*, ii *Les Épreuves* (Paris: Seuil).

Fich, Ove (1993), 'Markedsudvalget: Dets Styrke og Svagheder', *Udenrigs*, 4: 59–67.

Fiorina, Morris P. (1991), 'Coalition Governments, Divided Governments, and Electoral Theory', *Governance*, 4/3: 236–49.

——(1996), *Divided Government* (2nd edn. Needham Heights, Mass.: Simon and Schuster).

FitzGerald, Garret (1991), *All in a Life: Garret FitzGerald, An Autobiography* (London: Macmillan).

Fitzmaurice, John (1981), *Politics in Denmark* (London: Hurst).

——(1987), *Security and Politics in the Nordic Area* (Aldershot: Avebury).

Foley, Michael, and John E. Owens (1996), *Congress and the Presidency: Institutional Politics in a Separated System* (Manchester: Manchester University Press).

Fournier, Jacques (1987), 'Politique gouvernementale: Les Trois Leviers du président', *Pouvoirs*, 41: 63–74.

Galderisi, Peter F. (1996), 'Introduction: Divided Government Past and Present', in Peter F. Galderisi, Roberta Q. Herzberg, and Peter McNamara (eds.), *Divided Government: Change, Uncertainty, and the Constitutional Order* (Lanham, Md: Rowman & Littlefield), 1–7.

Gallagher, Michael (1977), 'Party Solidarity, Exclusivity and Inter-Party Relationships in Ireland, 1922–77: The Evidence of Transfers', *Economic and Social Review*, 10: 1–22.

——(1982), *The Irish Labour Party in Transition, 1957–82* (Manchester: Manchester University Press).

——(1988), 'Ireland: The Increasing Role of the Centre', in Michael Gallagher and Michael Marsh (eds.), *Candidate Selection in Comparative Perspective: The Secret Garden of Politics* (London: Sage), 119–44.

——(1996), 'By-Elections to Dáil Eireann: The Anomaly that Conforms', *Irish Political Studies*, 11: 33–60.

——(1999*a*), 'The Changing Constitution', in John Coakley and Michael Gallagher (eds.), *Politics in the Republic of Ireland* (3rd edn. London: Routledge), 71–98.

——(1999*b*), 'Parliament', in John Coakley and Michael Gallagher (eds.), *Politics in the Republic of Ireland* (3rd edn. London: Routledge), 177–205.

——(1999*c*), 'Republic of Ireland', in Robert Elgie (ed.), *Semi-Presidentialism in Europe* (Oxford: Oxford University Press), 104–23.

——(2000), *Parliamentary Control of the Executive in Ireland: Non-Party, Inter-Party, Cross-Party and Intra-Party* (Copenhagen: Joint Sessions of the European Consortium for Political Research).

——and Lee Komito (1999), 'The Constituency Role of TDs', in John Coakley and Michael Gallagher (eds.), *Politics in the Republic of Ireland* (3rd edn. London: Routledge), 206–31.

——and Richard Sinnott (eds.) (1990), *How Ireland Voted 1989* (Galway: Centre for the Study of Irish Elections and PSAI Press).

——Michael Laver, and Peter Mair (2001), *Representative Government in Modern Europe: Institutions, Parties and Governments* (New York: McGraw-Hill).

Garrido, Luis Javier (1982), *El partido de la revolución institucionalizada: La formación del nuevo estado en Mèxico (1928–1945)* (Mexico City: Siglo XXI).

Garrido, Luis Javier (1989), 'The Crisis of Presidencialismo', in Wayne A. Cornelius, Judith Gentleman, and Peter H. Smith (eds.), *Mexico's Alternative Political Futures* (La Jolla, Calif.: Center for US–Mexican Studies, University of California at San Diego), 417–34.

Geddes, Barbara (1994) *The Politician's Dilemma* (Berkeley, Calif.: University of California Press).

Germer, Peter (1995), *Statsforfatningsret* (Copenhagen: Jurist og Okonomiforbundetets Forlag).

González Casanova, Pablo (1970), *Democracy in Mexico* (New York: Oxford University Press).

Goul Andersen, Jørgen (1995), *Politik og Samfund I Forandring* (Copenhagen: Colombus).

Greilsammer, Ilan (1989), 'Cohabitation à la française, cohabitation à l'israélienne', *Revue française de science politique*, 39/1: 5–20.

Habert, Philippe (1990), 'Les Élections européennes de 1989: Le Temps des mutations', *Commentaire*, 13/49: 17–30.

Hague, Rod, Martin Harrop, and Shaun Breslin (1998), *Comparative Government and Politics: An Introduction* (4th edn. London: Macmillan).

Hardiman, Niamh (1988), *Pay, Politics, and Economic Performance in Ireland 1970–1987* (Oxford: Clarendon Press).

Hennis, Wilhelm (1998), *Auf dem Weg in den Parteienstaat* (Stuttgart: Reklam).

Herman, Valentine, and John Pope (1973), 'Minority Governments in Western Democracies', *British Journal of Political Science*, 3: 191–212.

Hernández, Luis Guillermo, Jorge Arturo Hidalgo, and Marcela Ojeda (1999), 'Repite PRI Golpe a Oposición', *Reforma* (29 Dec.).

Hernández Chávez, Alicia (1994), 'Mexican Presidentialism: A Historical and Institutional Overview', *Mexican Studies/Estudios Mexicanos*, 10/1: 217–25.

Holt, Michael F. (1999), *The Rise and Fall of the American Whig Party* (Oxford: Oxford University Press).

Howorth, Jolyon (1993), 'The President's Special Role in Foreign and Defence Policy', in Jack Hayward, (ed.), *De Gaulle to Mitterrand: Presidential Power in France* (London: Hurst), 150–89.

*Irish Political Studies* (2000), 'Irish Political Data, 1999', 15: 249–335.

Jacobson, Gary C. (1990), *The Electoral Origins of Divided Government: Competition in US House Elections, 1946–1988* (Boulder, Colo.: Westview Press).

——(1996), 'Divided Government and the 1994 Elections', in Peter F. Galderisi, Roberta Q. Herzberg, and Peter McNamara (eds.), *Divided Government: Change, Uncertainty, and the Constitutional Order* (Lanham, Md.: Rowman & Littlefield), 61–83.

Jansson, Jan-Magnus (1993), *Hajaannuksesta yhteistoimintaan: Suomalaisen parlamentarismin vaiheita* (Tampere: Gaudeamus).

Jasiewicz, Krzysztof (1996), 'Poland', *European Journal of Political Research*, 30: 435–46.

Jewell, Malcolm E., and Morehouse, Sarah M. (2000), *Political Parties and Elections in American States* (4th edn. Washington, DC: Congressional Quarterly Press).

Jones, Charles O. (1997), 'The American Presidency: A Separationist Perspective', in Kurt von Mettenheim (ed.), *Presidential Institutions and Democratic Politics: Comparing Regional and National Contexts* (Baltimore: The Johns Hopkins University Press), 19–44.

Jones, Mark P. (1995), *Electoral Laws and the Survival of Presidential Democracies* (Notre Dame, Ind.: University of Notre Dame Press).

Joyce, Joe, and Peter Murtagh (1983), *The Boss: Charles J. Haughey in Government* (Dublin: Poolbeg Press).

Juárez, María Victoria, and Xiomara Navas (1993), 'Ecuador', in Dieter Nohlen (ed.), *Enciclopedia Electoral Latinoamericana y del Caribe* (San José, Costa Rica: Instituto Interamericano de Derechos Humanos).

Jyränki, Antero (1981), *Presidentti* (Juva: WSOY).

Kalela, Jaakko (1993), 'Mauno Koivisto and the Framework of Foreign Policy in the Nineties', in Keijo Immonen (ed.), *The Long Perspective: Mauno Koivisto, Statesman* (Helsinki: Kirjayhtymä).

Keeler, John T. S. (1993), 'Executive Power and Policy-Making Patterns in France: Gauging the Impact of the Fifth Republic Institutions', *West European Politics*, 16/4: 518–44.

Key, V. O. (1956), *American State Politics* (New York: Knopf).

Klesner, Joseph L. (1993), 'Modernization, Economic Crisis, and Electoral Alignment in Mexico', *Mexican Studies/Estudios Mexicanos*, 9/2: 187–224.

——(1997), 'Electoral Reform in Mexico's Hegemonic Party System: Perpetuation of Privilege or Democratic Advance?', Paper presented at the Annual Meeting of the American Political Science Association, Washington, DC, 28–31 Aug.

——(1999), *The 1998 Mexican State Elections: Post-Election Report* (Western Hemisphere Election Study Series, 17/1; (Washington, DC: Center for Strategic and International Studies).

Krehbiel, Keith (1996), 'Institutional and Partisan Sources of Gridlock: A Theory of Divided and Unified Government', *Jounral of theoretical Politics*, 8/1: 7–40.

Kropp, Sabine, and Roland Sturm (1998), *Koalitionen und Koalitionsvereinbarungen* (Opladen: Leske & Budrich).

——and ——(1999), 'Politische Willensbildung im Föderalismus', *Aus Politik und Zeitgeschichte*, 13: 37–46.

Lancelot, Alain (1986), 'France: où en est la sociologie électorale?', *1986 Universalia* (Paris: Encyclopedia Universalis), 257–60.

*Latin American Regional Reports* (*LARR*), Andean Group Report, 1986–99, various weekly issues.

Laufer, Heinz, and Münch, Ursula (1998), *Das föderative System der Bundesrepublik Deutschland* (Opladen: Leske & Budrich).

Laver, Michael (1999), 'Divided Parties, Divided Government', *Legislative Studies Quarterly*, 24/1: 5–29.

——and Audrey Arkins (1990), 'Coalition and Fianna Fáil', in Michael Gallagher and Richard Sinnott (eds.), *How Ireland Voted 1989* (Galway: Centre for the Study of Irish Elections and PSAI Press), 192–207.

Laver, Michael, and Norman Schofield (1990), *Multiparty Government: The Politics of Coalition in Europe* (Oxford: Oxford University Press).

——and Kenneth A. Shepsle (1991), 'Divided Government: America is not "Exceptional"', *Governance*, 4/3: 250–69.

——and Kenneth Shepsle (1996), *Making and Breaking Governments: Cabinets and Legislatures in Parliamentary Democracies* (New York: Cambridge University Press).

Laver, Michael, Peter Mair, and Richard Sinnott (eds.) (1987), *How Ireland Voted: The Irish General Election of 1987* (Dublin: Poolbeg and PSAI Press).

Lehmbruch, Gerhard (1998), *Parteienwettbewerb im Bundesstaat* (2nd edn. Opladen: Westdeutscher Verlag).

Lijphart, Arend (1990) 'The Political Consequences of Electoral Laws, 1945–85', *American Political Science Review*, 80: 481–96.

——(1994) *Electoral Systems and Party Systems* (Oxford: Oxford University Press).

Loaeza, Soledad (1999), *El Partido Acción National: La Larga Marcha, 1939–1994: Oposición Leal y Partido de Protesta* (Mexico City: Fondo de Cultura Económica).

Luebbert, Gregory (1986), *Comparative Democracy: Policy Making and Coalitions in Europe and Israel* (New York: Columbia University Press).

Lujambio, Alonso (2000), *El poder compartido: Un ensayo sobre la democratización mexicana* (Mexico City: Oceano).

Mabry, Donald J. (1974), 'Mexico's Party Deputy System: The First Decade', *Journal of Interamerican Studies and World Affairs*, 16/2: 221–33.

McGerr, Michael E. (1986), *The Decline of Popular Politics: The American North, 1865–1928* (New York: Oxford University Press).

Machin, Howard (1993), 'Representation and Distortion in the 1993 French Election', *Parliamentary Affairs*, 46/4: 628–36.

Mainwaring, Scott and Matthew S. Shugart (1997*a*), 'Juan Linz, Presidentialism, and Democracy: A Critical Appraisal', *Comparative Politics*, 29/4: 449–71.

——and ——(eds.) (1997*b*), *Presidentialism and Democracy in Latin America* (New York: Cambridge University Press).

Mair, Peter (1987), *The Changing Irish Party System: Organisation, Ideology and Electoral Competition* (London: Frances Pinter).

——(1990), 'The Irish Party System into the 1990s', in Michael Gallagher and Richard Sinnott (eds.), *How Ireland Voted 1989* (Galway: Centre for the Study of Irish Elections and PSAI Press), 208–20.

——(1993), 'Fianna Fáil, Labour and the Irish Party System', in Michael Gallagher and Michael Laver (eds.), *How Ireland Voted 1992* (Dublin: PSAI Press and Folens), 162–73.

Majcherek, Janusz A. (1997), 'Realne, pozorne i zastepcze konflikty', *Rzeczpospolita* (23 May), 5.

Markowski, Radowslaw (1997), 'Political Parties and Ideological Spaces in East Central Europe', *Communist and Post-Communist Studies*, 30/3: 221–54.

Marsh, Michael (1981), 'Electoral Preferences in Irish Recruitment: The 1977 Election', *European Journal of Political Research*, 9: 61–74.

——and Paul Mitchell (1999), 'Office, Votes and then Policy: Hard Choices for Political Parties in the Republic of Ireland, 1981–1992', in Wolfgang Müller and Kaare Strøm (eds), *Policy, Office or Votes? How Political Parties in Western Europe Make Hard Decisions* (New York: Cambridge University Press), 36–62.

Massot, Jean (1993), *Chef de l'État et chef du gouvernement: Dyarchie et hiérarchie* (Paris: La documentation française).

——(1997), *Alternance et cohabitation sous la Ve République* (Paris: La documentation française).

Mayhew, David R. (1991), *Divided we Govern: Party Control, Lawmaking, and Investigations, 1946–1990* (New Haven: Yale University Press).

Milkis, Sidney (1993), *The President and the Parties: The Transformation of the American Party System since the New Deal* (New York: Oxford University Press).

Millard, Frances (1994). *The Anatomy of the New Poland: Post-Communist Politics in its First Phase* (Aldershot: Edward Elgar).

Mitchell, Paul (1993), 'The 1992 General Election in the Republic of Ireland', *Irish Political Studies*, 8: 111–17.

——(1996), 'The Life and Times of Coalition Governments: Coalition Maintenance by Event Management', Ph.D. dissertation, Florence, European University Institute).

——(1999), 'Government Formation: A Tale of Two Coalitions', in Michael Marsh and Paul Mitchell (eds.), *How Ireland Voted 1997* (Boulder, Colo.: Westview Press and PSAI Press), 243–63.

——(2000*a*), 'Ireland: From Single-Party to Coalition Rule', in Wolfgang Müller and Kaare Strøm (eds.), *Coalition Governments in Western Europe* (Oxford: Oxford University Press), 126–57.

——(2000*b*), 'Voters and their Representatives: Electoral Institutions and Delegation in Parliamentary Democracies', *European Journal of Political Research*, 38/3: 335–51.

——(2001), 'Ireland: "O What a Tangled Web . . ." Delegation, Accountability and Executive Power', in Torbjorn Bergman, Wolfgang Müller, and Kaare Strøm (eds.), *Delegation and Accountability in Parliamentary Democracies* (Oxford: Oxford University Press).

Molinar Horcasitas, Juan (1991), *El Tiempo de la Legitimidad: Elecciones, Autoritarismo y Democracia en México* (Mexico City: Cal y Arena).

Müller, Wolfgang, and Kaare Strøm (eds.) (2000), *Coalition Governments in Western Europe* (Oxford: Oxford University Press).

Murphy, Gary (1999), 'The Role of Interest Groups in the Policy Making Process', in John Coakley and Michael Gallagher (eds.), *Politics in the Republic of Ireland* (3rd edn. London: Routledge), 271–93.

Mylly, Juhani (1993), *Murrosten ja kasvun vuodet 1931–1940. Tasavallan presidentit: Svinhufvud, Kallio* (Porvoo: Weilin & Göös).

Nacif, Benito (1997), *La No Reelección Consecutiva y la Persistencia del Partido Hegemónico el la Camara de Diputados de Meexico* (Working Paper, 63; Mexico City: Centro de Investigación y Docencia Económicas).

——(forthcoming), 'Legislative Parties in the Mexican Chamber of Deputies', in Scott Morgenstern and Benito Nacif (eds.), *Legislative Politics in Latin America* (New York: Cambridge University Press).

Narud, Hanne Marthe, and Henry Valen (forthcoming), 'Coalition Membership and Electoral Performance in Western Europe', in Wolfgang Müller, Kaare Strøm, and Torbjorn Bergman (eds.), *Coalition Governance in Parliamentary Democracies* (Oxford: Oxford University Press).

Nousiainen, Jaakko (1985), *Suomen presidentit valtiollisina johtajina K. J. Ståhlbergista Mauno Koivistoon* (Porvoo, Helsinki, and Juva: WSOY).

——(1997), 'Finnland: Die Konsolidierung des parlamentarischen Regierungsweise', in. Wolfgang C. Müller and Kaare Strøm (eds.), *Koalitionsregierungen in Westeuropa* (Vienna: Signum Verlag).

Nousiainen, Jaakko (1998), *Suomen poliittinen järjestelmä: Kymmenes, uudistettu laitos* (Porvoo, Helsinki, and Juva: WSOY).

Nyholm, Pekka (1982), 'Finland: A Probabilistic View of Coalition Formation', in Eric Browne and John Dreijmanis (eds.), *Government Coalitions in Western Democracies* (London: Longman).

Paloheimo, Heikki (1984), *Governments in Democratic Capitalist States 1950–1983: A Data Handbook* (University of Turku, Department of Sociology and Political Science), 8.

——(1994), *Kohti yhdentyvää maailmaa 1982–2000: Tasavallan presidentit: Koivisto* (Porvoo: Weilin & Göös).

Parodi, Jean-Luc (1981), 'Sur quelques enseignements institutionnels de l'alternance à la française', *Revue politique et parlementaire*, 892: 42–9.

——(1988), 'La France de la cohabitation: Profil de l'année politique (1986–1987)', *Pouvoirs*, 44: 167–78.

——(1997), 'Proportionnalisation périodique, cohabitation, atomisation partisane: un triple défi pour le régime semi-présidentiel de la Cinquième République', *Revue française de science politique*, 47/3–4: 297–312.

Pedersen, Mogens (1988), 'The Defeat of All Parties: The Danish Folketing Election of 1973', in Kay Lawson and Peter A. Merkl (eds.), *When Parties Fail* (Princeton: Princeton University Press), 257–81.

Perrineau, Pascal, and Colette Ysmal (1993), 'Introduction', in Philippe Habert, Pascal Perrineau, and Colette Ysmal (eds.), *Le Vote sanction: Les Élections législatives des 21 et 28 mars 1993* (Paris: Presses de la FNSP), 13–19.

Peters, B. Guy (1997), 'The Separation of Powers in Parliamentary Systems', in Kurt von Mettenheim (ed.), *Presidential Institutions and Democratic Politics: Comparing Regional and National Contexts* (Baltimore: The Johns Hopkins University Press), 67–83.

Peterson, Paul E., and Jay P. Greene (1993), 'Why Executive–Legislative Conflict in the United States is Dwindling', *British Journal of Political Science*, 24: 33–55.

Petrocik, John R., and Joseph Doherty (1996), 'The Road to Divided Government: Paved without Intention', in Peter F. Galderisi, Roberta Q. Herzberg, and Peter McNamara (eds.), *Divided Government: Change, Uncertainty, and the Constitutional Order* (Lanham, Md.: Rowman & Littlefield), 85–107.

Pfiffner, James P. (1992), 'The President and the Postreform Congress', in Roger H. Davidson (ed.), *The Postreform Congress* (New York: St Martin's Press), 211–32.

——(1994), *The Modern Presidency* (New York: St. Martin's Press).

Phillips, Kevin (1969), *The Emerging Republican Majority* (New Rochelle, NY: Arlington House).

Pierce, Roy (1991), 'The Executive Divided against Itself: Cohabitation in France, 1986–1988', *Governance*, 4/3: 270–94.

Pietiäinen, Jukka (1992), *Tasavalta perustetaan 1919–1931. Tasavallan presidentit: Ståhlberg, Relander* (Jyvbäskylä: Weilin & Göös).

Polsby, Nelson W. (1968), 'The Institutionalization of the US House of Representatives', *American Political Science Review*, 62: 144–68.

Portes, Alejandro (1977), 'Legislatures under Authoritarian Regimes: The Case of Mexico', *Journal of Political and Military Sociology*, 5/2: 185–201.

Powers, Denise M., and James H. Cox (1997), 'Echoes from the Past: The Relationship between Satisfaction with Economic Reforms and Voting Behaviour in Poland', *American Political Science Review*, 91/3: 617–33.

Preston, Julia (1997), 'Democratic Civility Prevails in Mexican Budget Approval', *New York Times* (16 Dec.).

——(1998), 'Political Costs Widen in Mexico Bank Bailout', *New York Times* (12 Dec.).

Quintero, Rafael (1980) *El Mito del Populismo en el Ecuador: Análisis de los Fundamentos Socio-Económicos del Surgimiento del 'Velasquismo'* (Quito: FLACSO).

Quirk, Paul J. (1991), 'Domestic Policy: Divided Government and Cooperative Presidential Leadership', in Colin Campbell and Bert A. Rockman (eds.), *The Bush Presidency: First Appraisals* (Chatham, NJ: Chatham House), 69–91.

Rasmussen, Erik (1985), 'Finanslovens Forkastelse in Dansk Parlementarismen: Normer og Konsekvenser. En historisk-politologisk debatanalyse 1894–1984', *Historie, Jyske Sammelinger*, NS 16/1: 56–118.

Reynolds, John F., and Richard L. McCormick (1986), 'Outlawing "Treachery": Split Tickets and Ballot Laws in New York and New Jersey, 1880–1910', *Journal of American History*, 72/4: 835–58.

Richardson, James (1996), *Willie Brown: A Biography* (Berkeley, Calif.: University of California Press).

Rossell, Mauricio, and Blanca Fernanda Gutiérrez (1999), 'Reelección legislativa para un Congreso fuerte', *Nexos*, 254: 13–15.

Sarmiento, Sergio (1997), 'Lucha de poder', *Reforma* (15 Dec.).

Sartori, Giovanni (1976), *Parties and Party Systems: A Framework for Analysis* (New York: Cambridge University Press).

Schindler, Peter (1995), 'Deutscher Bundestag 1976–1994: Parlaments- und Wahlstatistik', *Zeitschrift für Parlamentsfragen*, 26/4: 551–66.

Schmidt, Gregory D. (1996), 'Fujimori's 1990 Upset Victory in Peru: Electoral Rules, Contingencies, and Adaptive Strategies', *Comparative Politics*, 28/3: 321–54.

Schmidt, Manfred G. (1996), 'The Grand Coalition State', in Josep M. Colomer (ed.), *Political Institutions in Europe* (London: Routledge), 62–98.

Schultze, Rainer-Olaf (1999), 'Föderalismusreform in Deutschland: Widerspruuche–Ansätze–Hoffnungen', *Zeitschrift für Politik*, 46/2: 173–94.

Schüttemeyer, Suzanne S. (1990), 'Die Stimmenverteilung im Bundesrat 1949–1990', *Zeitschrift für Parlamentsfragen*, 21/3: 473–4.

Shugart, Matthew Soberg (1995), 'The Electoral Cycle and Institutional Sources of Divided Presidential Government', *American Political Science Review*, 89/2: 327–43.

——and John M. Carey (1992) *Presidents and Assemblies: Constitutional Design and Electoral Dynamics* (Cambridge: Cambridge University Press).

Sinclair, Barbara (1991), 'Governing Unheroically (and Sometimes Unappetizingly): Bush and the 101st Congress', in Colin Campbell and Bert A. Rockman (eds.), *The Bush Presidency: First Appraisals* (Chatham, NJ: Chatham House), 155–84.

Sinnott, Richard (1995), *Irish Voters Decide: Voting Behaviour in Elections and Referendums since 1918* (Manchester: Manchester University Press).

——(1999), 'The Electoral System', in John Coakley and Michael Gallagher (eds.), *Politics in the Republic of Ireland* (3rd edn. London: Routledge), 99–126.

Slodkowska, Inka (1997), 'Partie i ugrupowania polityczne polskiej transformacji', in Jacek Wasilewski (ed.), *Zbiorowi aktorzy polskiej polityki* (Warsaw: PAN ISP), 9–87.

Smith, Peter H. (1979), *Labyrinths of Power: Political Recruitment in Twentieth-Century Mexico* (Princeton: Princeton University Press).

Southern, David (1994), 'The Chancellor and the Constitution', in Stephen Padgett (ed.), *Adenauer to Kohl: The Development of the German Chancellorship* (London: Hurst), 20–43.

Strøm, Kaare (1990), *Minority Government and Majority Rule* (Cambridge: Cambridge University Press).

——Wolfgang Müller, and Torbjorn Bergman (eds.) (2001), *Coalition Governance in Western Europe* (Oxford: Oxford University Press).

Sturm, Roland (1999a), 'Party Competition and the Federal System: The Lehmbruch Hypothesis Revisited', in Charlie Jeffery (ed.), *Recasting German Federalism* (London: Pinter), 197–216.

——(1999b), 'Der Föderalismus im Wandel: Kontinuitätslinien und Reformbedarf', in Eckhard Jesse and Konrad Löw (eds.), *50 Jahre Bundesrepublik Deutschland* (Berlin, Duncker & Humblot), 81–99.

——(2000), 'The Federal System: Breaking through the Barriers of Interlocking Federalism?', in Ludger Helms (ed.), *Institutions and Institutional Change in the Federal Republic of Germany* (London: Macmillan), 105–23.

Sundquist, James L. (1988), 'Needed: A Political Theory for the New Era of Coalition Government', *Political Science Quarterly*, 103: 613–35.

——(1992), *Constitutional Reform and Effective Government* (rev. edn. Washington, DC: Brookings Institution).

Tangeman, Michael (1999), 'The Limits of Austerity', *Latin Finance* (Jan./Feb.).

Taylor, Michael, and V. Herman (1971), 'Party Systems and Government Stability', *American Political Science Review*, 65: 28–37.

——and Michael Laver (1973), 'Government Coalitions in Western Europe', *European Journal of Political Research*, 1: 205–48.

Toka, Gábor (1997), 'Political Parties in East Central Europe', in Larry Diamond, Marc F. Plattner, Yun-han Chu, and Hung-Mao Tien (eds.), *Consolidating the Third Wave Democracies: Themes and Perspectives* (Baltimore: The Johns Hopkins University Press), 93–134.

Törnudd, Klaus (1968), *The Electoral System of Finland* (London: Evelyn).

Tribunal Supremo Electoral (TSE) (1989), *El Proceso Electoral Ecuatoriano* (Quito: Corporación Editora Nacional).

Tsebelis, George (1995), 'Decision Making in Political Systems: Veto Players in Presidentialism, Parliamentarism, Multicameralism and Multipartyism', *British Journal of Political Science*, 25/3: 289–325.

Turtola, Martti (1993), *Sodan ja rauhan miehet 1940–1956. Tasavallan presidentit: Ryti, Mannerheim, Paasikivi* (Porvoo, Weilin & Göös).

Ugalde, Luis Carlos (2000), *Vigilando al Ejecutivo: El Papel del Congreso en la Supervisión del Gasto Público, 1979–1999* (Mexico City: Miguel Angel Porrúa).

Uslaner, Eric M. (1993), *The Decline of Comity in Congress* (Ann Arbor, Mich.: University of Michigan Press).

Van der Meer Krok-Paszkowska, Ania (1999), 'Poland', in Robert Elgie (ed.), *Semi-Presidentialism in Europe* (Oxford: Oxford University Press), 170–92.

Väyrynen, Raimo (1994), *Tasavalta kasvaa ja kansainvälistyy 1956–1981. Tasavallan presidentit: Kekkonen* (Porvoo: Weilin & Göös).

Verdesoto, Luis (1991), 'El Sistema de Partidos Políticos y la Sociedad Civil en Ecuador', in Luis Verdesoto (ed.), *Gobierno y Política en el Ecuador Contemporáneo* (Quito: Instituto Latinoamericano de Investigaciones Sociales).

Verdier, Marie-France (1998), 'La III<sup>e</sup> cohabitation ou le retour aux sources du Sénat?', *Revue politique et parlementaire*, 997: 74–88.

von Mettenheim, Kurt (1997), 'Presidential Institutions and Democratic Politics', in Kurt von Mettenheim (ed.), *Presidential Institutions and Democratic Politics: Comparing Regional and National Contexts* (Baltimore: The John Hopkins University Press), 1–15.

Ware, Alan (1985), *The Breakdown of Democratic Party Organization, 1940–1980* (Oxford: Clarendon Press).

——(2000), 'Anti-Partism and Party Control of Political Reform in the US: The Case of the Australian Ballot', *British Journal of Political Science*, 30/1: 1–29.

Wasilewski, Jacek (1994), 'Scena polityczna w postkomunistycznej i postsolidarnosciowej Polsce', in Jacek Wasilewski (ed.), *Konsolidacja elit politycznych 1991–1993* (Warsaw: PAN ISP), 9–50.

Wattenberg, Martin P. (1991), 'The Republican Presidential Advantage in the Age of Party Disunity', in Gary W. Cox and Samuel Kernell (eds.), *The Politics of Divided Government* (Boulder, Colo.: Westview Press), 39–55.

Weldon, Jeffrey A. (1998), 'Committee Power in the Mexican Chamber of Deputies', paper delivered at the XXI International Congress of the Latin American Studies Association, Chicago, 24–6 Sept.

——(2000), 'Voting in Mexico's Chamber of Deputies, 1998–1999', paper delivered at the XXII International Congress of the Latin American Studies Association, Miami, 16–18 March.

——(forthcoming), 'The Legal and Partisan Framework of the Legislative Delegation of the Budget in Mexico,' in Scott Morgenstern and Benito Nacif (eds.), *Legislative Politics in Latin America* (New York: Cambridge University Press).

Wesolowski, Wlodzimierz (1996), 'The Formation of Political Parties in Post-Communist Poland', in Geoffrey Pridham and Paul G. Lewis (eds.), *Stabilising Fragile Democracies* (London: Routledge), 229–253.

Wilkie, James W. (1970), *The Mexican Revolution: Federal Expenditure and Social Change since 1910* (Berkeley, Calif.: University of California Press).

Williams, Philip M. (1972), *Conflict and Compromise: Politics in the Fourth Republic* (London: Longman).

Zahle, Henrik (1997), *Institutioner og Regulering: Dansk Forfatningsret* (Copenhagen: Christian Ejlersforlag).

Zarka, Jean-Claude (1992), *Fonction présidentielle et problématique majorité présidentielle/majorité parlementaire sous la Cinquième République (1986–1992)* (Paris: Librairie Générale de Droit et de Jurisprudence).

# Index